Florida Crime Writers

Florida Crime Writers

24 Interviews

Edited by
STEVE GLASSMAN

McFarland & Company, Inc., Publishers
Jefferson, North Carolina, and London

LIBRARY OF CONGRESS CATALOGUING-IN-PUBLICATION DATA

Florida crime writers : 24 interviews / edited by Steve Glassman.
    p.   cm.
Includes bibliographical references and index.

ISBN-13: 978-0-7864-3083-3
softcover : 50# alkaline paper ∞

1. Novelists, American—20th century—Interviews. 2. Novelists, American—Florida—Interviews. 3. Detective and mystery stories—Authorship. 4. Florida—In literature. 5. Crime in literature.
I. Glassman, Steve.
PS374.D4F63   2008
813'.08720905—dc22   2007035873

British Library cataloguing data are available

©2008 Steve Glassman. All rights reserved

No part of this book may be reproduced or transmitted in any form or by any means, electronic or mechanical, including photocopying or recording, or by any information storage and retrieval system, without permission in writing from the publisher.

Cover images © 2007 PhotoSpin

Manufactured in the United States of America

McFarland & Company, Inc., Publishers
  Box 611, Jefferson, North Carolina 28640
    www.mcfarlandpub.com

To Marguerite Glassman,
my mother and role model,
and Enrique Badillo,
matador and great guy

Table of Contents

Preface 1

Nancy Bartholomew, Panhandle Mystery Writer
    APRIL VAN CAMP 7

James O. Born, Crime Novelist and Career Cop
    STEVE GLASSMAN 16

Nancy J. Cohen, Writer of Soft-Boiled Mysteries
    STEVE GLASSMAN 24

Tom Corcoran, Key West Crime Writer
    MARY BETH ELLIS 32

Tim Dorsey, Satirical Crime Writer Extraordinaire
    RICHARD MCKEE 40

Carolina Garcia-Aguilera, Award-Winning Hispanic
Mystery Novelist
    CYNTHIA DAVIS 50

James W. Hall, Maverick Master of the Keys and South Florida
    RICK HOFER 58

Vicki Hendricks, South Florida Noir Specialist
    ELLEN SMITH 64

Stuart Kaminsky, Midwestern-Florida Crime Master
    CAL BRANCHE 74

Jonathon King, Edgar-Winning Mystery Novelist
    CAL BRANCHE 88

Christine Kling, Writer of South Florida Nautical Crime
    DAN MCGAVIN 102

Paul Levine, Attorney, Novelist, and Television Mystery Writer
CAL BRANCHE 113

Michael Lister, Prison Chaplain and Novelist
MATTHEW MCLENDON. 119

John Lutz, Sometime Florida Crime Writer
ANNA LILLIOS 128

Bob Morris, Central Florida Journalist and Mystery Novelist
HANK RAULERSON 137

Barbara Parker, Mistress of Crime Writing
CLAUDIA SLATE 150

Nancy Pickard, Socially Conscious Crime Writer
NANCY M. SHELTON 161

Aileen Schumacher, Author of Historical Crime Fiction
AMY GOTTFRIED 170

Les Standiford, Florida Crime Novelist and Nonfiction Writer
STEVE GLASSMAN. 181

James Swain, Magical Mystery Writer
CAL BRANCHE 192

Elaine Viets, Classy Crime Writer
MELANIE BROWN. 195

M. Diane Vogt, Author of Florida Legal Mysteries
ELLEN SMITH 203

Randy Wayne White, Naturalist and Crime Writer
BILL OTT 212

Dirk Wyle, Author of Scientific Crime Novels
ELLEN SMITH 222

About the Contributors 235
Index 239

Preface

The purpose of a preface is to give the prospective reader an idea what is in the book. So let me tell you. This book contains two dozen interviews with Florida crime writers.

But why read (or purchase) a book of interviews of Florida crime writers? If these people were writing real literature, perhaps, you may retort. But about mystery stories? And why limit those chosen to be interviewed only to the writers in one state, Florida? And if you are interested in learning about a certain author or authors, why this book? Why not simply go to the Internet and find an interview there?

Let me begin with that last point. All of the authors interviewed in this book are currently publishing and almost all actively promote their books. They are frequently interviewed by journalists and fans. The people who interviewed them for this volume, though, are not journalists or adoring fans. They are literary critics. And that makes a telling difference. The purpose of this book was not to simply replicate another of those interviews that are so generic that the answers could be swapped from one to another. Each interviewer, all of whom have extensive critical credentials, was charged to familiarize him/herself with the work of the writer interviewed, dipping not only into one or two novels but reading the entire canon. She or he was then tasked to produce, by the use of skillfully designed questions, a critical essay in the guise of an interview. Therefore, the reader of this book can expect considerably more heft in the answers than in journalistic or other kinds of interviews.

Regarding the other two points, that is, why be interested in mystery writers and, if so, why limit yourself merely to those writing about Florida, let's digress a bit. Let's go back to 1964. In many ways, 1964, the year the Beatles came to our shores and the Viet Nam War was heating up, can be regarded as the birth of a distinct social epoch. It's entirely possible that a case could be made that World War II and the postwar era finished in that year, and that the last part of the 20th century which we may or may not still be in, began. Florida literature before this date could probably be summed up in three words—Ernest, Marjorie and Zora (with a few flourishes here and there, such as Stephen Crane's "The Open Boat"). The first of those Big Three figures, Ernest Hemingway, though frequently identified with Florida, really just happened to live in the Keys for a relatively short time, and incidentally wrote a few stories about the place, few or none of which are considered central to his work. During the lifetime of Marjorie Kinnan Rawlins and Zora Neale Hurston, the former was considered by far the greater writer. She garnered a Pulitzer prize and a movie made from her trademark novel, *The Yearling*, won the Academy Award. Not surprisingly, her editor, Maxwell Perkins, was the most renowned in the country. Hurston, unlike Rawlins, was born poor and black and in Florida. These two women shared, however, a concentration on Florida places and characters. Had neither of them paid attention to our state, it's quite possible we would not now know who they are today.

All three of those authors had ceased writing (and living) before 1964, but it was in that year that the first of John D. MacDonald's Travis McGee color-coded novels appeared. To a wide circle of American readers, MacDonald put Florida, if not on the literary, at least on the reading map. Can John D. MacDonald really be considered a literary writer? Had John D. been asked that question himself, he probably would have laughed. He came out of the pulp magazines and the paperback novels. He knew the formula. He could produce sympathetic characters and he could weave them into compelling plots. And his writing was not without certain powerful motifs, foremost among them being an abiding love for his adopted state and its environment. But he was not "literary" in any of the ways the word was used at that time.

Long before MacDonald died in the mid 1980s and the twenty-plus novels in the McGee series came to an end, academicians started doing a very unusual thing. Instead of paying attention only to the elite exemplars of society, they began studying all aspects of it. As usual in terms of intellectual movements, the germ of this idea started in France with historians like Fernand Braudel, who took as their subject matter the peasants and other little people (and broader social and economic movements) of earlier times. In America, the prime mover was something called the Popular Culture Society. Suddenly, all aspects of American popular culture became fair game for critical scrutiny. Advanced critical methods were applied to such things as television series and B-movies. Entities which had formerly been considered escapist junk began to be seen as holding hidden clues to the cultural and other values of American society.

In the meantime, John D. MacDonald passed from the scene, and Florida became spotlighted by an enormously successful television series called *Miami Vice*. And following along the path blazed by MacDonald and *Miami Vice* came writers who, though clearly writing whodunits, concocted their tales with dazzling style. It was at this point that the current age of Florida literature began. Chief among these authors was Charles Willeford, whose *Miami Blues* became a successful movie as well as a novel. By the early 1990s, the trickle of Florida crime writers became a wave, with the advent of James W. Hall, Randy Wayne White, and Barbara Parker among others, and by the mid 90s, it developed into a storm surge. True, a few literary folk were writing about the state—Connie Mae Fowler and Joy Williams—come to mind, but most of the of authors who set their work in the state were writing what could be termed crime fiction, and even Joy Williams dabbled occasionally in crime writing.

Why should the vast majority of serious writers about Florida be drawn to the crime genre? Facetiously, some have answered that the peninsula with the panhandle attached resembles a handgun; ergo, crime writing and Florida are a natural fit. More seriously, a historical perspective may help answer this perplexing question. From the very first Florida has been a land made noteworthy by crime. The Father of Spanish Florida murdered the putative Father of French Huguenot Florida, thus sealing the doom of the neighboring Gallic colony. Naturally, the Spanish had raided and plundered the French Fort Caroline. The Spanish then made war on the natives of the state by way of Christianizing them. Later, British proxies waged campaign after campaign on the now so-called Spanish Indians, as a means of weakening their Iberian overlords. After the Americans took control, the first significant event was the Second Seminole War. It droned on for seven years, the longest, costliest of the wars against the American aborigines. After that, the next notable chapter in the state's history was the Civil War and then came the multitudinous postwar lawlessness occasioned by any number of conscription dodgers, carpetbaggers, and outlaws cast out from the lost Confederate cause. During the rest of the 19th century and much of the early 20th century, the institutional terror of Jim Crow pitted one of the state's races against the other. Florida in those days frequently had the lamentable status of being the state with the most lynchings. The 1923 Rosewood massacre, in which an entire community was wiped out by white racists, was arguably the worst such incident in American history. Nevertheless, it was completely hushed up until about fifteen years ago.

The Florida peninsula, projecting as it does from the continental United States into the Caribbean, was readymade for smuggling. Contraband runners from the Civil War through Prohibition, and beyond have taken advantage of the state's proximity to the Bahamas and Cuba. Perhaps the most notable wave of smuggling occurred during the 1980s when floating bales of marijuana (euphemistically called square groupers), cast loose by drug runners, were a common phenomenon in the Florida surf. Following marijuana came cocaine, and with cocaine came the so-called cocaine cowboys. Suddenly gangsters with names like Monkey Morales were commonly mentioned in the papers and on tabloid television. Their exploits, in terms of public shootouts and the like, brought Chicago in the 1920s to mind. Also, occurring about this time was the Mariel Boatlift. For a brief window, Fidel Castro allowed anyone to float into Mariel harbor and remove family members and loved ones to Florida. Waiting for the boats, along with the family members and loved ones, was the flower of Cuba's criminal justice system. The jails were emptied of violent criminals, who with the criminally insane, established footholds on street corners throughout Miami and, to a lesser extent, South Florida. Almost unthinkably bold street crimes, such as the kidnapping of a victim off the sidewalk, stripping him of all valuables, and, after a few gratuitous blows to the body, tossing him out on the next block, became commonplace.

It was against this historical backdrop that John D. MacDonald lay down his mantle and Charles Willeford tried it on. Willeford himself claimed to write crime fiction only because it was a hot literary item at the time. Willeford was an extremely droll individual. He loved putting you on. But even if we take him at his word, how can we explain the fact that, in the two decades or so that have passed, dozens of other Florida writers have adopted the crime-fiction form? Clearly, it is the literary mode best able to investigate the social fabric of this state, which today still reflects its volatile past. That Florida, as the fourth most populous and one of the most dynamic states of the Union, is a suitable candidate for intellectual inspection, I shall not argue. If you have read this far, you already agree that it is. The output of any state or geographical region that is somehow distinct and possesses an identifiable literary trend is worthy of critical scrutiny, and Florida as one of the most populous and fast-growing states, one that has a diverse ethnic make up, that has a distinct climate (sociological as well as geophysical) and dozens of writers pursuing career in a single genre clearly meets these criteria. The same can be said of crime fiction as worthy of critical endeavor. Crime writers delve into every aspect of social customs. Naturally, not all writers of the genre are equally adept as social critics or commentators, and probably none are entirely free of the drawbacks of the genre. On the basis of the sheer weight of numbers and their performance, clearly it is the case that the form provides the best vehicle to examine the political, cultural and economic fabric of the state that is the crossroads of the Americas. For that reason, I am pleased to offer the special insight into American culture, Florida style, that the interview-essays contained herein provide.

Finally, let me say a word about those who are interviewed and who conducted the interviews. In short, we invited everyone who writes crime fiction about Florida to participate. You will find herein nationally and, in some cases, internationally famous writers, as well as those who are best known only within the state. I include both sorts, side by side, unblushingly; crime fiction may well be the only genre in which paperback originals are routinely, if infrequently, reissued as hardcover books. Two Florida authors, John D. MacDonald and Charles Willeford, are exemplars of this publishing rarity; ergo, there is no telling which writers will be seen by future generations as the best spokesperson for Floridian or American fiction or crime fiction. You will notice a few missing names. A couple of Florida crime writers are notorious recluses, and declined our offer to discuss their work. Several others were not able to meet our own production schedule. But by and large, we have a broad and representative cross section of those who write crime fiction about Florida.

Most of the interviewers are working academics at a variety of private and public two- and four-year colleges and universities, generally in the state of Florida, although one hails from as far away as Maryland. There are a couple of exceptions, and they are both notable. One of the most knowledgeable critics of the crime genre is Bill Ott, publisher of *Booklist,* an official organ of the American Library Association. On average, Bill devotes one issue of *Booklist* a year to crime fiction, and we were thrilled when he agreed to conduct an interview with Randy Wayne White. Another who comes from ranks other than higher education is Cal Branche, and Cal is indeed an exception. He accounts for four of the interviews in this book. Cal is one of the most perceptive thinkers about crime fiction in the state, to which I believe he is a fairly recent immigrant. His first career was as a high school teacher in Massachusetts, where he used crime fiction in the classroom. Ellen Smith, professor emerita, Stetson University, must also receive special notice for a slightly different reason. She is responsible for three of the interviews contained in this book. She and her husband Bob, also professor emeritus at Stetson, traverse the state going from one crime fiction (or book) event to another. She and Bob (along with Bill Ott and Cal Branche) are among the best read devotees of Florida crime fiction I know. Their great knowledge shows in the perceptiveness of their questions.

Thanks go to Bryan White, my assistant at ERAU, who handled much of the formatting and related chores.

Read the following interviews. Learn from them. It is my profound hope that you will also enjoy them.

Steve Glassman
Embry-Riddle University
October 2007

Nancy Bartholomew, Panhandle Mystery Writer

by April Van Camp

Nancy Bartholomew is the author of numerous mysteries, including a Florida panhandle–based series which chronicles the dangerous and zany life of exotic dancer/sleuth Sierra Lavotini. The series includes four books: *The Miracle Strip, Film Strip, Drag Strip,* and *Strip Poker*. Nancy Bartholomew holds a B.A. in psychology and creative writing and an M.S.W. in social work, and the very believable character Sierra Lavotini is clearly a product of Bartholomew's academic expertise.

Although Bartholomew's written work extends beyond the Florida peninsula, her Panama City sleuth's exploits represent her best effort. Bartholomew captures the exotic Florida landscape and the erotic panhandle night life in Sierra Lavotini's near-death experiences. The books are simply fun to read.

At her home in Greensboro, North Carolina, Bartholomew's personal life is nearly as eventful as her character's. Each day, she manages to accomplish the nearly impossible: raise children, manage a menagerie of pets, direct her own psychotherapy practice, and write mysteries. Ms. Bartholomew's real life is full and colorful, and the wit and humor she integrates into her home life is revisited, revived, and reinvented in Sierra Lavotini's dialogue.

APRIL VAN CAMP: *Why did you choose to set Sierra Lavotini's world in Florida?*

NANCY BARTHOLOMEW: Initially, the Sierra Lavotini series started with a short story I entered in a contest sponsored by the south Florida chapter of Mystery Writers of America. The only requirement was that the story be set in Florida. That was no problem for me as I'd spent lots of time on the panhandle and in Tallahassee and really loved not only the beach but the lush green of northern Florida with its Spanish moss–covered trees, old motels, rich springs and unbelievable characters.

Did you win the contest? I only wonder because it would be just too neat for Sierra to have launched your career, or even cooler, rescued it or something rather romantic, daring, and dangerous.

Well, yes, actually Sierra did rescue me! You see, I was taking a lot of heat from my then (operative word) husband to quit this "foolish obsession" and focus on my private psychotherapy practice. "I don't understand why you are so obsessed with writing when it doesn't pay nearly as much as your practice does!" Anyway, I made a deal with the devil. I told him that we should go to Sleuthfest, which was held in Ft. Lauderdale (one of the Devil's favorite childhood vacation spots). I said it would be a romantic vacation for us and that I would enter the short story contest. I said, "If I don't place in the top ten, I'll quit writing (yes, my fingers were crossed behind my back!), and I'll be the best little psychotherapist ever."

Needless to say, I was a nervous wreck! The *romantic* honeymoon lost out to all-out panic as I waited for the big night. Stuart Kaminsky was the judge. I'd entered two stories, a *safe* but boring one and the tale of my heart, "Sierra Reveals All." When Stuart called out 8th place and my name, I never asked which story had placed. Instead, I walked up, accepted my award and went back to my seat. Honorable Mention.

Stuart called out more names, but as he did, I watched my husband's face. I knew he didn't think 8th place was good enough for a writing *obsession*.

And then the miracle happened. Stuart Kaminsky was getting ready to announce first place. He said, "Something has happened that has never happened before in the history of this contest. A writer who entered two stories has placed twice in the top ten. As you know, these are blind submissions, so we really had no way of knowing ... blah ... blah ... blah ... Nancy Bartholomew is our first-place winner!"

I am sad to say, I showed Miss America how to really make a fool of herself.

I jumped up, I screamed, I thanked my mother, I fanned my face with my fingers as I tried not to cry. I was a total idiot! Worse, I forgot to ask which story won! For about five minutes I was too shocked to even think. But when I did muster up the courage to ask, Stuart said, "Why, 'Sierra Reveals All!' I thought you knew that!" And he went on to say she'd make a great protagonist in a novel, "But then, a stripper might be a hard sell."

And that is how Sierra saved my creative life—ruined my marriage, but saved my life!

Sierra definitely has the means to ruin a marriage, but she doesn't have the conscience for that kind of thing. Can you imagine setting Sierra Lavotini's world outside of Florida?

Nope! Where else could she do the things she does with the people who wander in and out of her life but in Florida?!

Is there anything about Florida's history, particularly in the panhandle, that influenced your decision to set the Sierra Lavotini series there?

No, unfortunately, it's more my history with Florida that makes me set the Sierra series in Florida. I spent many a happy young adult/teenaged vacation/summer there. In fact, I returned every year to the panhandle, mostly to Mexico Beach, to take time out to review my life and work on my 20-year plan. It became the place I went to sort things out for myself and so Sierra came there to find herself as well. I even lived for a brief time in the trailer Sierra moved into.

If you could live anywhere in Florida, where would it be? Why?

Grayton Beach, only Grayton Beach as it was in the late '80s to mid–90s. It was undeveloped, with shack-y beach houses dripping character and a funky, semi–Caribbean/Key West–meets–Nantucket flavor to it. When the kids were little and I was at my wits' end, I'd always say I wanted to run away to Panama City and work in a Waffle House. (Don't know why that particular option seemed to hold more appeal than cranky toddlers and a dirty house, but hey, it was my fantasy and I'm sticking to it!) Later, when I discovered the sweet children's book *The Napping House*, I settled on Defuniak Springs as my fantasy retirement home. I'd live in a lovely old white house near the center of town, raise roses in the back yard and dry my clothes on a line strung across the backyard. I even did realtor.com and found the house for a ridiculous $49K! Then, of course, THEY discovered it and property skyrocketed. Nowadays, I have a new fantasy: my girlfriends and I will buy an old Mom and Pop motel, inland but still in North Florida, like Wewahitchka maybe (only because I also choose towns for their funky, cool-sounding names). We'll each have a room and we'll hire the handsome "Guido" and lovely "Ursula" to tend to us in our old age.

There is something else that struck me in chapter three of Drag Strip. *Sierra makes a particular claim to her region in Florida, and she includes herself among the Florida panhandle locals, even though she is a Philadelphia, PA, transplant. The paragraph describes northwest Florida in a way only a relocated, assimilated, newly native*

Floridian can do: "Most folks consider Panama City to be a small town, despite its reputation as the Redneck Riviera. We get people flying in here all the time from L.A., but around here, that just means Lower Alabama. We are a village made famous by a strip of white sand beach and MTV. Most people drive right past the real town in their rush to stake a claim on the sugary sands, and that suits the locals just fine. Better the tourists should not know about the huge Victorians that line St. Andrews Bay. Better they should stay away from Uncle Ernie's or Joe's. Leave the good living to those of us who can appreciate it" (page 11).

I spent a lot of time in the quiet part of P.C. and fell in love with it. I rode with the cops and learned to shoot a Glock 9mm on their gun range (with wild rambling roses in bloom just behind the target, with spent bullet casings in my ears for sound-proofing because the storage shed was locked and we couldn't get earplugs). I have great pictures and home movies of my family staying in cheap strip motels so we could better *feel* the atmosphere, eat the food Sierra eats, and learn what it is to find her P.C.

What might lure you to write something else Floridian, and would you return to Panama City or somewhere else?

Well, Panacea always intrigued me... The swampy, marshy coastline that was particularly conducive to smuggling and dope dealing—Defuniak Springs also has such a great-sounding name. The very fact that the old north Florida (Monticello, Wakulla Springs, etc.) is so quickly disappearing makes me want to somehow capture the flavor and preserve that piece of history in a book. I want the rest of the world to know what they are losing, have lost in the name of progress.

What is distinctive about Florida and Florida writers, and how do you fit in?

Florida is a melting pot state. It melds newcomers like ingredients into a stew that slowly simmers to a spicy perfection. It accepts the oddball, rescues the hopeless, and yet does not suffer too many unhealthy, non-environmentally friendly idiots without taking action.

Florida writers use humor more than most, I think. And maybe it's the heat, but the humor is twisted. Florida writers are like a Jimmy Buffet shirt: colorful, rumpled and in-your-face honest.

How did you get into the business of writing mysteries?

I cut my teeth on Nancy Drew mysteries and from there went on to all the old classics. Having grown up with mysteries and having loved them so much made writing them a natural transition.

When did you first know you were a novelist?

I was too chicken to call myself a novelist, but just before my first Sierra was published I went to my oldest son's "Meet the Teacher" night. He was in second grade and they had all made posters about their parents. There I was, forever captured with a lopsided grin and curly brown hair, just as my son saw me. Beneath the picture, on that newsprint, pre-lined paper only first and second graders use, was a paragraph that began with "My mom is a mystery writer." In that one moment I realized he saw me as I wished to one day see myself. That night I became a say-it-out-loud novelist.

I'll admit it early on: Drag Strip *is my favorite book, and I can see a definite style development between* Drag Strip *(1999) and* The Miracle Strip *(1998). What happened to you between books? I'm guessing confidence, but Sierra Lavotini is simply sexier, wittier, and smarter in this book. Do you notice this, too, or is this just a matter of personal opinion?*

No, you are sooo right! *Drag Strip* and *Strip Poker* are two of my favorite books. *Miracle Strip* was my first novel. My very first. You know how I plotted that thing? I got a piece of notebook paper and on the first 23 lines I wrote down bad things that could happen to Sierra. The last three lines I used to tie it all together! That is such a foolish, ridiculous way to write a book! And I was scared witless of writing a book. Now, the plot changed as I wrote, but still, it was a first effort. Beginner's luck. I started *Drag Strip* with it already under contract. I was drunk on the high of selling my first novel and too naive to know what could go wrong in the world of publishing. I was into it and really going strong when my agent called. "Stop working on that," she said. "We've got to get you another contract for a second series. I mean, what if a stripper series doesn't make it? You want to earn a living, don't you? Go write me the first book in a new series!" That burst my bubble. I spent the next year writing *Your Cheatin' Heart*. By the time I got back to *Drag Strip* I was so homesick for Sierra and Panama City and of course, John Nailor!

How much attention do you pay to character and how much to plot? Which is the more difficult to develop, plot or character?

Plot, for me, is like math or balancing my checkbook. I hate it! The characters appear, fully formed most of the time, and begin talking. If I'm willing to let go and let them have their head, the plot comes trotting along as the characters begin moving and interacting.

*Nancy, I think you are the queen of opening lines: "What happened to Arlo shouldn't have happened to a dog" (*The Miracle Strip*). "John Nailor and Vincent Gambuzzo are trying to drive me crazy. If they were working together on this project, I'm sure I'd be in a straitjacket somewhere gulping down Prozac cocktails" (*Drag Strip*). "When Venus Lovemotion died it was a giant pain in my ass. Literally. I was bending over to unlock the door of my '88 Camaro when I heard the shot and felt a stinging sensation in my left cheek" (*Film Strip*). How do you get started writing these books? Do you know ahead of time how the story will work out, or do you just write one of these great opening lines and start from there?*

I mull the little seeds of plot or character around in my head, then shove them out of my consciousness and wait for the *pre-flashbacks* to start, little glimmers of the movie that will play in my head when it all begins coming together. But I don't write until I *hear* the first line in my head. After that, the book is truly gravy. I guess that first line signals the fact that I now know the characters well enough to *hear* them tell me the story. With Sierra it always feels like channeling—I know, I know *real* writers don't say that—they're always in control of the plot and the characters but honestly, I'm not! At least, not with Sierra!

You said that the Sierra books always come to you in a movie-type format, which you see before and as you're writing. Have you thought about writing a book like Drag Strip *into a screenplay?*

Well, *Drag Strip*'s been optioned, so I guess at least one other person saw it that way. But so far, no news (and it's been awhile!). A producer flew me out to L.A. to talk about a series for Sierra, but he wanted to set the movie in an apartment building in L.A. and make Raydean sane. My agent said an option was like going steady in middle school, it doesn't mean much, if anything. And as for the TV show, he says take the money and run—you don't want to see what they'll do to your work. But hey, maybe when I'm rich and famous I'll make my own movie!

All of your books are funny because your characters are either funny or they find humor in their situations. The books all have a focused story line, no doubt, but the ins and outs with Raydean, your alien-wary, Prolixin-driven neighbor is nearly the makings for a book of her own. Fluffy, the Chihuahua, is by herself a round character. Vincent Gambuzzo is the poster boy for Wanna-Be-Cool-But-Never-Will *magazine. Of course, John Nailor, my new imaginary boyfriend, is so perfectly handsome, smart, and self-controlled that he seems perfect fodder for a series of sexy detective-man books. How do you keep these people so vital through the series? I feel like they're my friends.*

From the moment Sierra entered my life, along with her entourage, I have always seen her life as a movie. I can *see* every single detail. I *know* these people. Maybe they came to me because my children were little and I was lonely for juicy, adult company. My dad says Sierra is my alter ego. I don't know. Like Sierra says when asked how she's able to get the tassels on her pasties swinging in opposite rotations, "It's a gift, either you got it or you don't!" Sierra's world is just a wonderful gift given to me in a moment of personal desperation!

How does someone meet Sierra Lavotini? I admit that I read Drag Strip *in one night, absolutely couldn't put it down. I also admit that my palms were sweating when Sierra and the detective were hiding in that closet, and I got choked up at the victim's funeral. I laughed at the way Raydean treated Nailor's partner, and I felt wonderfully uncomfortable when John and Sierra finally, you know. The point here is this: You have a nice sense of control in your work, a style that makes reading a potentially violent genre not so tense. Well, at least a style that offers a regular reprieve from tense, so who reads your books? Of course, I do now, but I probably wouldn't have had I not been given this assignment. I'd have missed a very fun spring, too, by the way.*

My first agent said she thought Sierra might be hard to sell because "Little old ladies don't like to read about sex." My mother begs to differ! Women read mysteries and women love a strong, sassy, sexy woman on top, so to speak. Of course, I do have my fan in prison... He reads Sierra and unfortunately thinks it's autobiographical!

Is writing fun or is it a job?

When I'm in "The Zone" it's a blast. When I can't hear the voices or "see" the movie in my head, it's a job... But even on the very worst day, it's still the best job in the world.

If you weren't writing mysteries, would you still be a writer? What else would you write? I ask this because your work, even your email notes and website, have a certain Erma Bombeck tone. Have you thought about creative nonfiction as another writing venue?

My aunt, Lillian Smith (also a Florida writer), wrote *Strange Fruit*, the first novel featuring an interracial relationship. It was banned in Boston and produced on Broadway. She went on to write many other novels and was very politically active in the '50s. So the bar is set quite high in my family and while they love reading mysteries, I get the feeling they're all waiting for the *real* novel, the literary masterpiece. I used to feel guilty about this and maybe sometimes I still do—but I also realize I'm just that, well, deep, I guess. I have ideals and goals. I'm an activist, certainly, but I choose to battle with humor.

My heroines are the underdogs. I make you love the characters that you'd normally pass on the street without a second glance. No, actually, I make you love the ones you cross the street to avoid, like Raydean. She's mentally ill. Hell, she's floridly psychotic, but she is also the wisest woman in the book. So, I know that if I didn't write mysteries, I'd still feel called to write. There are characters in my head and heart who long to have their stories told and they just won't shut up! How can I walk away from such a treasure?

I consult in three nursing homes and the pain I see there haunts me. We throw our elderly away like so much garbage. The people who gave us life, taught us everything, sheltered us, nurtured us—and we no longer see them as valuable when they need us. People don't know what gifts they're missing when they overlook these lonely souls. So, sometimes, when I just can't help myself, I disguise them a bit and write about my life with them on the website. Those essays don't get the *hits* that my funny pieces get, but I just find I need to write about them all the same.

Finally, what's going to happen to Sierra and John? Sierra says, "You put a cop and an exotic dancer together and there's a set of professional issues that immediately cloud the reality of the relationship." Tell me there's hope, Nancy. Before we sign off, can you say, "happily ever after," or even better, "wait until the next book, April."

Well, I'll tell you one thing, when there is a next book, it will be called *Landing Strip* and Big Moose Lavotini will reveal all, but don't give up on our John. He has *issues*, but who doesn't? He'll sort them out and when he does, he'll wake up and realize he's about to lose the best thing that's ever happened to him. Now, will he be able to win the lady and ride off into the sunset? We'll see!

Bibliography

Bartholomew, Nancy. *Drag Strip*. New York: St. Martin's, 1999.

_____. *Film Strip*. New York: St. Martin's, 2000.

_____. *Lethally Blonde*. New York: Silhouette, 2005.

_____. *The Miracle Strip*. New York: St. Martin's, 1998.

_____. *Sophie's Last Stand*. New York: Silhouette, 2005.

———. *Stand By Your Man*. New York: HarperTorch, 2001.
———. *Stella Get Your Gun*. New York: Silhouette, 2004.
———. *Stella Get Your Man*. New York: Silhouette, 2005.
———. *What Stella Wants*. New York: Silhouette, 2006.
———. *Your Cheatin' Heart*. New York: HarperPaperbacks, 2000.

James O. Born, Crime Novelist and Career Cop

by Steve Glassman

The backgrounds of Florida crime writers run the gamut of professions. Perhaps not surprisingly, among their number can be counted a fair number of literary fiction writers (and one poet). There is the rare building contractor and some lawyers, actually lots of lawyers, and a few journalists, at least one of whom made her name covering the crime beat. But there is just one working policeman, James O. Born. Although a relatively late comer to the crowded field of Florida crime writers, publishing his first novel in the new century, James O. Born was quickly recognized by his peers and literary critics as one of the most powerful voices writing about Florida crime. Much of the acclaim that has come his way can be credited to his background and the realism that imbues his books, but needless to say, James O. Born is also a talented writer. With the publication of *Field of Fire*, James O. Born has added four novels to his canon of Florida crime fiction.

STEVE GLASSMAN: *Thanks for agreeing to this interview, Jim. Let me start by asking how a nice policeman like you got involved in a shady racket like writing crime fiction.*

JAMES BORN: When I was new to police work, as an agent with U.S. Drug Enforcement Administration, I read a lot. On television, DEA agents are in shoot-outs and get the chicks, but in real life they follow suspected drug violators around until they can make a case. If you're a new guy, no one in the DEA much cares about family life or other interests, you just drive. I can remember sitting on people's houses (that's a slang for conducting surveillance) and waiting by their cars for hours with nothing really to do. This was in the late eighties. So I read Tom Clancy and W.E.B. Griffin because

I liked the idea of learning something about the military. I would read the occasional police book but felt the books didn't reflect my experience as a cop. I was not a CIA-trained assassin. I could not rip a shotgun out of someone's hands without suffering a catastrophic injury. I didn't crawl out of crushed police cars and shake off the injury. Neither did any cop I knew.

That's sort of unsettling to learn. Like most academics and writers, I like to think that the guy in the white hat gets the girl every time. But as you were saying...

During this time I met Elmore Leonard through a family friend. He was popular but not like he is now. We hit it off and he asked about calling me for technical advice from time to time. We talked frequently about guns and police work, and over the years our friendship developed. In providing him with realistic ways in which to complete many of his ideas for scenes in his novels, I found myself starting to jot down my own story ideas—especially after studying Dutch's work and that of a number of other writers. I started thinking that I'd like to write a police novel. One with realistic roots. Dutch Leonard and his assistant, Gregg Sutter, really supported me in this by reviewing my manuscript and offering advice. My first effort remains unpublished and resting at the bottom of a desk drawer. I wouldn't call it unreadable but my kids have instructions that if anything happens to me it should be destroyed immediately. But that was practice for my second novel, which used some of my experiences as an undercover agent at a Ku Klux Klan rally in Palm Beach County. Nothing really happened at the closed meeting. But my imagination supplied the intrigue that these ignorant rednecks failed to deliver. In real life these morons are not what I'd call a threat to national security but in my novel they are usurped by a local Nazi group and tricked into a deadly plan. This manuscript fared a little better, eventually landing me an agent.

But ultimately every major publisher declined. Most of my story ideas came while I was sitting on surveillance late at night with nothing to do and no one to talk with. Different scenarios for a particular case I was working on at the time would run through my head: If a smuggler we were following discovered his surveillance team and took action, how would we respond? Would I stay professional or sink down to his level? I found that running these storylines through my head were helpful in breaking the incredible tedium of following the same suspect for days on end with no obvious result.

Undeterred, although I should have been smart enough to quit, I started to work on my third novel, *Walking Money*. I used my experiences on a SWAT team during one of the larger Miami riots and incorporated them into the story of a FDLE [Florida Department of Law Enforcement] agent framed for a bank heist which occurs during the riot. Not wishing to relive the mounds of rejection from literary agents I had received on my previous books, I gave the manuscript to a friend in New York. He was a private editor and he said he'd look it over. He was so happy with it he gave it to a literary agent who liked the story enough to call me and ask if I needed representation. I agreed and within a few weeks I had a two-book deal from Putnam. The most exciting part was that my editor, Neil Nyren, was also the editor of my two favorite military writers, Tom Clancy and W.E.B. Griffin.

Or in other words, you were the typical overnight success story that only required two unpublished novels for one published one. So how about a little private background, where you are from, what was your major was in college, what you did in the service, if you were in the service?

I was born in West Palm Beach, a native Floridian whose parents were from Pittsburgh. Grew up in the south end of West Palm, then went to undergraduate school at Florida State, earning a BA in psychology. I went on to the University of Southern Mississippi, where I earned a Master's of Science in psychology. It was while I was in this program that I realized I wouldn't make a good psychologist or counselor. I always felt like the problems people were sharing with me were none of my business. I still feel that way.

I enjoyed physical activity and had become heavily involved in karate and thought a police career might work out. I applied to a number of agencies and was hired by the U.S. Marshals. The job was a little on the dull side and like many deputies, I transferred to another agency. I started in the U.S. Drug Administration in February of 1987. I attended the academy in Quantico, VA, and got to experience my first snowstorm. While all the recruits from up north were bitching about the cold and snow I was looking around thinking, "This is great." It was during my time with the DEA that I started reading more and more and considered writing my own novel.

Let's talk about a subject near and dear to your heart, the FBI. I know it is never a good idea to assume themes that crop up in a novel—or even a series of novels—are necessarily those held by the author. Nevertheless, the vituperation that occurs in your prose every time the acronym FBI appears leads me to take the plunge.

I like FBI agents. They do great work that helps a lot of people. The FBI as an agency tends to believe it is infallible and others are here to serve it. Occasionally some agents retain that attitude. The thing to remember is that FBI agents come form the same places as good detectives. A twenty-year Ft. Lauderdale Detective is every bit as capable and smart as a twenty-year FBI veteran. The detective probably has had a great deal more experience as well. The jokes I make about the FBI in my first two books are just jokes most cops make about them. In the end of each book, the FBI agent gets with the program and helps avoid disaster. Cops love my books. That's plenty of vindication.

I know I'm asking a lot. But try not to let this question make you self-conscious. Are you an escapist writer or are you trying to get at a deeper moral, aesthetic, or philosophical "truth"?

This comes back to "What is the theme of your books?" Theme is an elusive concept that some people say springs from books and that you cannot effectively consciously write a theme. I have never written a book with the idea of passing on my moral beliefs but if you are engrossed in the writing process and wish to tell an honest story sometimes those beliefs bleed through. I believe my books have to do with karma in that if you do the right thing, or even the wrong thing for the right reason, your life will work out and you will be happy. That's my experience. I'm not saying that all the problems are solved. It's more of a conscience thing. If you can sleep at night and know you did your best, then things can go to hell but you're able to continue to live and grow.

It sounds a little New-Ageish. But I'm tried of simple shoot-'em-ups and *Miami Vice* rip-offs. There are consequences to actions in police work. Sometimes emotional consequences, sometimes physical, sometimes legal, but you still have to answer every time you fire your weapon. You don't say, "Yahoo, I've got a vacation coming."

That being said, I want my stories to entertain. But that seemed too easy to say.

Why Florida? Sure you live here and grew up here and went to school here, but you could have chosen to place your fiction elsewhere, perhaps a place or a time you'd never been. Tell me why you chose to set your work here.

There are a number of reasons. Maybe the most important is that my main character is an agent for the Florida Department of Law Enforcement. But really, I wanted to show as much realism as possible and I know how things work here. I know the details of booking someone in at any of the main jail facilities. I know the cities and streets. I know the communities. I hear how people speak in places as diverse as Liberty City in the heart of Miami to Panama City in the heart of the Panhandle.

Florida also offers the greatest diversity of any state. We have Miami, a worldwide capital of trade and entertainment with a population that speaks several languages, is in the news constantly and is just plain exciting. The state also has north Florida, which is more similar to Alabama and Mississippi. Then we have the clash of these two cultures through central Florida. What a fertile area for any stories, not just crime fiction. In other words, you can write about Texas but the stories are invariably about Texans. You write about Florida and the story can involve New Yorkers, Colombians, Germans and Floridians all in one place for very plausible reasons.

Another benefit to writing about the Sunshine State that I never thought of until I started having book signings is that there is a big group of readers that love Florida crime novels. Some of them only want Florida crime novels. Some like the kooky characters. Some like the references to old Florida. But they all want stories about people in Florida. There's a cadre of authors these people line up to read.

What kind of TV do you watch? Any cop shows? How about A&E and Court TV? Do you think any of those shows are worth the bother, especially the one with the—oh, I love being able to ask this—FBI-trained profiler. I've noticed she claims to have been involved in cases that happened before she probably joined the force and that crucial pieces of the case are left out or rearranged for whatever reason, not always having more dramatic appeal so far as I can tell. What do you think of the concept of "profiling" in general?

I honestly don't watch any of those shows. None. I have never seen *NYPD Blue*, *CSI* anywhere, no Court TV, no A&E. Nothing!

The last police drama I watched was *Hill Street Blues*. I loved it in college. I also watched, and this is to prove I'm being honest, *Miami Vice*. Before I became a cop that show rocked. Then I saw it as unrealistic. Now I see it as silly. I worked as a technical advisor on *Karen Sisco* for ABC. That opened my eyes to TV. It was a good dramatic show but sometimes veered off into fantasy.

Between raising a family and writing, my time is limited on the TV I can watch. I've seen every episode of *The Simpsons, Sopranos, Deadwood, My Name is Earl* and *Seinfeld*. If I like a show I never miss it. I get a chuckle out of *Reno 911* and all the news shows on Comedy Central. And sports. From football to the dumbest, made-up competition on ESPN, I'm usually good for at least an hour.

As for the second part of your question, I have not had the broadest experience with profiling. I have watched the Court TV show with Dayle Hinman once or twice because she was a FDLE agent. I don't really know her personally. I have referred stuff to the Miami FDLE profiler and found her to be very helpful. I don't know if I ever saw a big case broken by a profile but they can help a stalled investigation. I make fun of profiling in my second novel, *Shock Wave*, but I make fun of everyone in my books.

What are your writing habits? Do you get up early in the morning and write daily? Do you binge write in days off?

I write every day. Never miss a day unless something catastrophic has occurred. I get up thinking about the scenes I want to work on for whatever novel I'm writing. I have an idea where it's going but like to be surprised while I'm writing so I don't know exactly what's going to happen. I make notes all through the day. When I get home, I sit out on my porch and work on a little PDA with a keyboard. I shoot for fifteen hundred words but if they don't come I don't push it. I also try to take advantage of little down periods. If I'm traveling, I don't waste airport time or flight time. With a family and police job I have to be efficient. On Saturdays and Sundays I edit on a full computer and start the whole process over on Monday. It seems to work since I've met my deadlines on the first four books.

Writers tend to downplay the importance of the art to themselves. How central is writing to you? What is your motivation? What's more important, the money you make from it, the gratification it gives—well, that didn't come out so well, but you know what I mean.

I believe that writing is an art. I get annoyed when people say, "Oh, I'm gonna write a book," without giving it serious consideration. I cannot even look at manuscripts anymore because I got overwhelmed and never read one that was publishable. As for what my motivation is to write a good book: I like the money. I like the people I meet, but I write because it's satisfying to complete a story.

Earlier in this interview you said you did a little writing in college. Did you even then harbor secret ambitions to be a writer? Such ambitions, of course, are not that uncommon. Think of all the folks who plan to write when they retire, but did you have that burning desire to write then? I ask this because writing a book—even an unpublished manuscript of book length—requires a great deal of discipline. Anyone who goes the distance—published novel at a New York house that is well reviewed—has a story worth telling.

I always thought it would be cool to be a writer without knowing how hard it was. Like everyone I pictured writing in a quiet place and then having people say, "Wow, this is brilliant." Then I got serious and it took two unpublished books and hundreds of rejections to really get it. Writing is hard. Typing is easy. My friend, novelist Tom Corcoran, says he always asks people if they wrote a book or typed a book.

I take the process very seriously and I work to improve. My editor, Neil Nyren, makes suggestions on each book but I treat them like lessons and carry them on to the next project. I also want to take some chances. That's why I wrote *Field of Fire*. It's not in the Tasker series and is a darker thriller that deals with serious issues. I think that's why I can work on a novel every day without getting bored. It's always fresh and exciting.

I've always been able to buckle down and concentrate on something if I choose to. I try to make up lack of athletic ability or talent with hard work. That's why I like running. I can compete in marathons because all it takes is discipline. Run. Run a lot. I can write novels because I know what is expected. Tell a story from beginning to end in about 100,000 words. There is no writer's block or time off. That kind of thing appeals to me.

Had you not the assistance or at least the model of Elmore Leonard, do you think you'd have succeeded as a novelist? Or was knowing him irrelevant?

Elmore Leonard encouraged me and suggested agents on my early books. The agent I finally landed and the book deal were separate from him. I called him after I signed with Putnam, but he was with Harper Collins. Like many writers, I read all his novels and stole some of his sensibilities. I would never say that knowing him was irrelevant to my career. He has made me a better writer.

What do your colleagues think about your literary career? How about your superiors?

The cops I work with get a kick out of my books. I have never met a cop who had read one of my books that didn't like them. To me that's one of the coolest things to happen to me. Even FBI agents have made favorable comments to me about the books. They get the joke. At least the ones that read the books. My bosses have always been supportive. From letting everyone know about a release to attending book signings, they have been very helpful. The agency heads have told me they like the national exposure and attention. The books have at least gotten FDLE's name out in other states.

There's an old maxim, "Never argue with a fellow who buys ink by the barrel," mean-

ing writers have their own way of evening up the score. Have you ever felt tempted to give professional enemies hell in print?

I've never had a beef with a writer or reviewer but my first novel, *Walking Money*, expressed a lot of cops' feelings about the FBI as an agency. I have more confidence to write editorials about things that bug me around my hometown.

If crime fiction goes cold on you, will you turn to other genres? Do you have any other type work in mind, either in the here and now or as a distant possibility?

I write crime fiction because I feel like I can add something to the genre. I have a couple of other ideas I'd like to pursue regardless of what happens with crime fiction. I don't read only crime fiction. I prefer science fiction and historical fiction. I may try that at some point but I hope I wouldn't jump to something else just because another genre is hotter at the moment. I hope I wouldn't do that, but who knows? I might.

Are you a cop that writes books or a writer who is a policeman?

I am a writer who still works as a cop. I actually resent a little when some says "Jim's a cop, oh, and he writes books too," like it's a phase I might grow out of. I may retire from police work but I won't retire from writing.

What is your advice to young writers?

I would advise young writers to take time to read. I hear too many writers say they don't have time to read. That doesn't cut it. Don't write until you've read a load of fiction. Don't tell people you're writing a book until you have a manuscript. Don't tell people what you'll do when you're published. Read, write and shut up. You can't go wrong.

Bibliography

Born, James. *Escape Clause*. New York: Putnam, 2006.
_____. *Field of Fire*. New York: Putnam, 2007.
_____. *Shock Wave*. New York: Putnam, 2005.
_____. *Walking Money*. New York: Putnam, 2004.

Nancy J. Cohen, Writer of Soft-Boiled Mysteries

by Steve Glassman

Nancy J. Cohen began her publishing career writing futuristic romance novels as Nancy Cane. Her first book, *Circle of Light*, won the HOLT Medallion Award. She wrote four more romances before switching to mysteries with the series debut of her hairstylist sleuth, Marla Shore. Nancy's titles have been nominated by *RT BookClub* for a Reviewer's Choice Award and have made the Independent Mystery Booksellers Association (IMBA) Best-seller List.

As author of the popular Bad Hair Day mystery series, Nancy is listed in *Contemporary Authors*, *Poets & Writers*, and *Who's Who in U.S. Writers, Editors & Poets*. She is an active member of Mystery Writers of America, Sisters in Crime, Romance Writers of America, Novelists, Inc., and The Author's Guild. She has served as President of Florida Romance Writers, Inc., and as Secretary for MWA—Florida chapter. As a featured speaker at conferences, bookstores, libraries, and local community groups, she enjoys meeting readers and booksellers. Additional activities include writing non-fiction articles for *The 3rd Degree*, *The Kiss of Death*, *Romance Writers' Report*, *The Literary Times*, *Mystery Readers Journal*, *Romantic Times*, and *Mystery Scene Magazine*.

STEVE GLASSMAN: *Thanks for agreeing to do this interview, Nancy. I know you had a life before becoming a full-time writer and that you had a writing career prior to turning to mysteries. How about filling us in a bit on your background?*

NANCY J. COHEN: I was born and raised in New Jersey, where I lived until I went to college. I got a bachelor of science degree in nursing from the University of Rochester in New York, then I worked for a year as a staff nurse (R.N.) at Massachusetts General Hospital in Boston. Tired of the miserable winters, I moved to Florida, where many of my cousins lived. It was like coming from night to day.

My writing during these formative years consisted of some poetry, short stories, and a Shakespearean play which I convinced my bunkmates to perform during one summer at National Music Camp in Interlochen, Michigan, where I studied ballet.

After three years working in a coronary care unit at Doctors Hospital in Coral Gables, I decided to get my master's degree and moved to San Francisco to attend UCSF. Here I earned my Master of Science degree. And this is where I wrote my first published book, which was a spy novel.

I moved back to South Florida to work as a clinical nurse specialist counseling heart attack victims. More full-length novels followed, along with many rejection slips. Then in 1988, I joined the Florida Romance Writers, got an agent at the first conference I attended, and found a critique group. My writing improved greatly, but I still couldn't sell. It wasn't until a fellow writer suggested I combine two genres I loved, science fiction and romance, that I succeeded at selling my first novel. *Circle of Light*, a futuristic romance, won the HOLT Medallion Award in the paranormal category. I wrote three more romance novels before switching to mysteries. As for quitting nursing to write full time, I retired when our son was born and haven't looked back since.

Given your early work in the romance genre, I suppose cozy mysteries seemed a natural step. In that regard you are pretty much odd-woman-out in Florida crime fiction, as most Florida women crime writers would be termed hard-boiled or at least soft-boiled. What are your thoughts about your genre, and the state of women's crime fiction generally? Maybe first we should define the term "cozy."

A traditional or cozy mystery usually involves an amateur sleuth in a confined setting with characters who know one another. There is no overt sex or violence. The focus is on personal relationships, not crime scene analysis or forensics. Serial killers, terrorists, and world domination have no place here. The killer is motivated by personal reasons like jealousy, greed, protection of a loved one, etc. Agatha Christie's novels and the TV show *Murder, She Wrote* are examples of this genre.

I do feel out of place in the Florida crime scene because there are only a couple of other mystery authors writing cozies in this state. I don't think we get the respect we deserve because people regard this subgenre as if it's of lesser import than serious crime fiction. We are serious about our writing, and we don't treat murder lightly in our stories, but we aim to entertain and leave our readers with a smile on their face. Sisters in Crime was formed to give women mystery authors a voice, and that applies to readers and reviewers, as well as other mystery authors. On the other hand, I find my books have broader appeal because people who don't normally read mysteries think my covers are cute and are willing to give the book a try. My readers range in age from pre-teens to ladies in their 80s. And if I can get someone started reading who might not have picked up a book otherwise, I'm happy to keep writing these stories.

What writers do you read and admire?

Oh, my. I have a whole list written up that I bring to book signings, so when I get asked this question, I can just hand it out. I like genre fiction, and I read romance, science fiction, and humorous mysteries. I switch around for variety and often read more than one at a time.

Like most of us you started off somewhere else, New Jersey and points north in your case, and ended up in Florida, and much of your work is set in Florida. Many hard-edged writers find Florida a good locale because, frankly, of our state's abundant crime and a climate, both geophysical and psychological, that seems to encourage a moral laxity. But what about the writer of cozies? Do you reformulate Florida to be an idyllic paradise just right for your kind of murder mysteries?

Enough authors show Florida as a pit of depravity with weird characters, or their stories focus on serious environmental issues. My books may be light and funny, but I apply some lessons too. Topics I've addressed include child drowning, animal testing, melanoma prevention, and illegal migrant labor. As for Florida itself, I try to showcase the parts I enjoy, like the unique small towns, the tropical greenery, the food and ethnic flavors. Marla has chased suspects to Tarpon Springs, Mount Dora, and Vero Beach, for example. There are so many interesting enclaves she can explore, and it's led me to some fun research adventures as well.

I think the title of your series Bad Hair Day Mysteries is a hoot. How'd you come up with such a clever idea?

I wanted a concept with universal appeal, and who hasn't gone into a hair salon or barbershop? Plus I have no talent whatsoever to do my own hair, so I greatly admire stylists who have the skills I lack. I was actually getting a perm when I came up with the idea to murder off one of the customers in a salon and make the sleuth be the hairdresser.

Do you know any hairdressers personally? The few I've known have been outstandingly creative, and the names of beauty parlors always struck me as being more clever than other businesses. Do you feel your protagonist Marla somehow incorporates any of this, or am I just blowing smoke?

Of course Marla is clever! She uses her people skills to find out information that eludes her boyfriend, Detective Dalton Vail. A good stylist knows how to start a conversation and is a good listener. People gossip in salons, making it the perfect backdrop for a mystery series. And a hairstylist has a mobile profession. She doesn't have to confine her activities to a salon. When I started the series, I asked my hairdresser—who also owned her salon—lots of questions, followed her into the back room to watch her mix solutions, and subscribed to *Modern Salon* magazine to learn the lingo. I really do respect the occupation and try to be as accurate as possible, and I'm especially thrilled when I get fan mail from working stylists.

Let's talk about Nancy's work habits as a writer. How many times do you write a week? How much do you try to write during a session?

My goal is to write one chapter a week. I plan out my titles with 20 chapters per book. At 75,000 words, that's about 15 pages per chapter. Each week, I set myself a daily goal of 5 pages a day. This means I have to work three days a week to complete my chapter. The rest of the time, I'll either get ahead on next week's quota, or work on promotional activities. Since I'm an early riser, I write best in the morning. My brain is fried after lunch, so that's when I work on promo stuff.

It's axiomatic nowadays that character is more important than plot, but in a mystery, plot still is a necessary ingredient. Tell us how you develop yours. Do you outline or just sit down at the word processor and let it rip?

I'll do whatever preliminary research is necessary before formulating the plot. Usually this relates to the setting. Then I draw a spider web, with the victim in the center. The spokes of the web are the suspects, people who relate to the deceased. This is the character development phase. I give each suspect a secret and/or a reason to want the victim dead. I've devised a character development tool to help further this process, and I'll often cut out pictures from magazines for visualization. These notes get put into a ring binder; I have a separate notebook for each book in my series. Once the characters and opening premise are in my head, I write the synopsis. This is a necessary sales tool since I sell my books on the synopsis now. It acts as a writing guideline once I start the story. However, this outline is not written in stone. Sometimes new characters pop in to surprise me, or the plot takes a different twist than what I'd expected. That makes it more interesting for me as well as the reader.

You have a fair number of zany standing characters in your series. How did you develop them?

Whoops, I think I just answered that above. But here are some other things my character development tool includes besides the usual Name, Career, and Physical Characteristics. I'll add in Favorite Speech Phrases and Mannerism, Lifestyle Preferences. Then we come to the Dark Secret and Ruling Passion. What's most important, though, is the character's GMC, and if you don't know what this is, run out and buy a copy of Debra Dixon's book *Goal, Motivation and Conflict*. This is why the character acts the way he does. Strengths and Flaws come next, and finally the Realization Leading to Change if it applies.

Is writing fun or is it a job?

It's both. Storytelling is fun. Sitting down in the chair every day to write my quota is part of the job. So is sending out postcards, doing book signings, conducting myself in a professional manner, and dressing well. Why else would I have an excuse to go shopping at Nordstrom Rack every few weeks if not to search for snazzy conference attire? Seriously, writing is a business, and you have to keep records just like for any small enterprise. You also have to work hard at marketing yourself. That's probably the toughest aspect. Writers want to stay home and write, but that's not enough anymore. Publishers expect you to be a good promoter or you'll get overlooked in the crowd.

I know you work hard at being a successful writer because I have met you at several book signings and similar "author events" around the state. How much of this kind of promotion do you do and how important do you consider it?

I do a lot of promotion because I consider this an extremely important part of an author's career. Take a look at the bookshelves. So many books are out there. How can you get readers to pick up one of yours? It's our responsibility to contact readers and booksellers with the goal of name recognition. Conferences, articles in trade journals, postcards and bookmarks, blogs and web sites—the things you can do are endless. Deciding where to put your money and how much time to spend on this aspect is difficult because no one has the right answer. It's a judgment call for each author on their comfort level. I believe in niche marketing too, so I try to reach hairdressers, salon owners, and others in the industry. I'm hoping people will spread the word if they enjoy my books because then I'll know I am doing something right.

If you weren't writing mysteries, would you still be a writer? Of what? What else would you be, if not a writer?

My book of the heart right now is a futuristic romance. But my dreams, the good ones I have that I am compelled to write down, are pure science fiction. This is how I got the idea for *Circle of Light*. It started as a dream, but when I woke, I didn't want the story to finish, so I wrote the rest of it. That was my first book that sold. And yes, I confess that I'm a Trekkie. I'm also a fan of *Stargate* and *Star Wars*. Love that space opera stuff. *Galaxy Quest* is one of my favorite movies. I'm also tempted to write a story when what I want to read isn't out there. And I'm always taking notes. I have travel journals going back to my early days so I guess writing has always been in my blood. It's who I am, even when some days I swear I'm going to retire.

Let's get back to the topic of Florida. You live here for a reason. Do you set your stories here because you live here or is there another reason? I mean a hair stylist in New Jersey could be every bit as interesting, and heck, maybe even more so, than one in Florida.

It's a lot easier writing a story that is set in my backyard. And it gives me an excuse to explore different places in Florida that I want to visit. I love the tropics, and I hope to share my enjoyment with readers.

Cozies are rather naturally suburban or even exurban. Do you consider Marla an urban protagonist or a suburban one?

A little bit of both. She lives in the suburbs, but South Florida is such a cosmopolitan place with multinational influences. Many of us here are transplanted northeasterners, Marla included. She's on a career track, even when she meets a handsome homicide detective who becomes her love interest. So there's nothing provincial about her. At the same time, she enjoys the foliage, walks her poodle around the block, and shuffles about on errands like a good suburbanite.

Of the issues you have covered in your series, only melanoma prevention could really be linked to the Sunshine State. What other possible issues do you see as Florida-specific that might be worth writing about—and that interest you?

Child drowning prevention is the core of Marla's behavior. In South Florida, child drowning is the number-one cause of death for children age 4 and under. When Marla was a babysitter at age 19, the toddler she cared for drowned in the backyard swimming pool. This motivates her to prove herself because she seeks redemption, and she is involved in a child drowning prevention coalition.

The citrus canker eradication program came into play in *Highlights to Heaven*, which also mentions exotic bird smuggling. With all its waterways, Florida is a great entry point for smuggling of all kinds. I dealt with illegal immigrants in *Dead Roots*. I'm not going to hit upon the bigger targets like the sugar industry or drug smuggling, because my books focus on personal relationships, not terrorists or the mob or serial killers. Environmental concerns also play a role in my books. I've talked about mangrove preserves, tilapia farming, aquaculture. And now I'm into orchid cultivation for the next story. I love the parks in Florida and I want to take my readers with me vicariously down the lushly shaded paths.

Where is this state heading? Is the quality of life getting better or worse?

Worse, with the taxes and insurance zooming upward. Pretty soon, no one will be able to afford to live here. Our electric bill was over $400 last month, and our insurance increased astronomically. So the cost of living is going up, but people's salaries are not keeping pace. I don't know how young people afford housing anymore. It seems as though the next generation will have more of a struggle than we or our parents did, and I don't know how that will end.

Would you think about living elsewhere or setting a series or a book, stand-alone or series, elsewhere?

I'm sticking to Florida. I hate the cold weather, and as I said, I love the tropics. As for other books, I'd rather stay a part of the Florida mystery scene. Although I'm not averse to setting stories on other planets!

What's your favorite part of the state and why aren't you living there, assuming you aren't?

I am happy exactly where I am, although we like Orlando a lot. We go up there often and have found lots of places to explore besides the theme parks.

What Florida writers do you admire and why?

Gee, I don't want to play favorites, or I'll make someone mad at me if I forget to mention their name. Suffice it to say I'm partial to female mystery authors, and I have pals who write romantic suspense, science fiction, and historicals. I try to read a sampling from everyone I meet. My selections are all popular fiction. I studied the literary stuff in college, when I took courses in Shakespeare and Tolstoy and read Molière in French (which I've mostly forgotten). Now I want to read books that entertain me, are fast-paced, and have a happy ending. I'd rather close the book with a smile on my face than a frown, and that's my goal for my readers.

Thanks, Nancy, for talking with me. Do you have any final comments?

Thank you, Steve, for your interest in my work and for such thorough questions. I can be contacted through www.nancyjcohen.com or mysterygal.bravejournal.com. For aspiring writers, I offer this advice.

Remember to follow your P's along the road to success:
Be Polished, Productive, and Purposeful.
Seek Preparation, Passion, and Perfection.
Maintain Persistence, Patience, and Professionalism.

Bibliography

Cohen, Nancy J. *Body Wave*. New York: Kensington, 2002.
____. *Crew Cut*. New York: Kensington, 2007.
____. *Dead Roots*. New York: Kensington, 2005.
____. *Died Blonde*. New York: Kensington, 2005.
____. *Hair Raiser*. New York: Kensington, 2005.
____. *Highlights to Heaven*. New York: Kensington, 2005.
____. *Murder by Manicure*. New York: Kensington, 2005.
____. *Perish by Pedicure*. New York: Kensington, 2005.
____. *Permed to Death*. New York: Kensington, 2005.
____. "Three Men and a Body." In *"Wicked" Women Whodunit*. New York: Kensington/Bravura, 2005.

Futuristic Romances Written as Nancy Cane

Cane, Nancy. *Circle of Light*. New York: Dorchester Publishing, 1994.
____. *Keeper of the Rings*. New York: Dorchester Publishing, 1996.
____. *Moonlight Rhapsody*. New York: Kensington, 2005.
____. *Starlight Child*. New York: Kensington, 2005.

Tom Corcoran, Key West Crime Writer

by Mary Beth Ellis

"[His] lifestyle absorbs his natural surroundings, family, friends, work, books, travel, art, food, and fun, and layers it with social responsibility." Mystery writer Tom Corcoran could have written this remark about himself, but he was discussing his friend and former co-writer Jimmy Buffett in the liner notes of Meet Me in Margaritaville: The Ultimate Collection. In addition to crafting the songs "Cuban Crime of Passion" and concert favorite "Fins" with Buffett, Corcoran, who has lived in Florida since 1970, has steered his creative skiff far from the stereotypical waters of tropical thrillers.

Best known as the author of five novels (soon to be six) that trace the adventures of Key West photographer Alex Rutledge, Corcoran has also written three nonfiction books on Shelby Mustangs and co-owns The Ketch & Yawl Press. Like his protagonist, Corcoran is an accomplished photographer, but he is truly a Renaissance man with a Swiss army knife in one hand and a cold beer in the other: he has also worked as a disk jockey, travel counselor, bartender, and officer in the U.S. Navy. Corcoran's dynamic plots always have time for a drink at Sloppy Joe's and some thoughtful ocean-gazing, for he is careful to firmly plant his wild stories in a very real, very Floridian Key West.

MARY BETH ELLIS: *Who do you like to read and which authors are your biggest influences?*

TOM CORCORAN: Authors I have enjoyed in recent years—all for different reasons—are Ian Rankin, Janwillem van de Wetering, Alan Furst, James Sallis, Louise Erdrich, William Gay, Michael Connelly, and Edwidge Danticat. I probably read more frequently when I'm working on a manuscript—as many as 20 books in the course of completing one of mine. I've never feared "subliminal plagiarism" or other creative intrusions, and my mind is energized by others' efforts at twists and tone and mood. (Hell, if I'm going to unknowingly steal someone's work, why mess with simple words and sentences? Go for the "architecture!") I've made a point of reading at least one Ross Macdonald mystery while writing each of my novels. I also keep a fat, forty-pound nonfiction book nearby—such as Tim Ferris's *The Whole Shebang* or one of Peter Guralnick's rock-and-roll bios. When I fear that my dialogue is going flat, I'll pick up anything by Elmore Leonard or—akin to mainlining—a James Ellroy book. Either will kick me back to real-world-speak (as best done in print form). When I'm stuck with, say, an outdoor scene description, I'll often reread passages from Jim Harrison or Peter Matthiessen or James Lee Burke—again for tone and mood. If I need a refresher on realistic female viewpoint, I'll look to Sujata Massey, Ellen Gilchrist, or Joyce Carol Oates. It may sound odd, but I use my fiction shelves as a reference library—in search of ambience and subtlety.

My influences, aside from every writer I've mentioned so far, cover the gamut from Chuck Berry for his humor, vocabulary and rhythmic words (Google the lyrics to "Nadine" to see what I mean) to Hitchcock movies for techniques in building suspense through editing and camera point-of-view. As to other authors I call influences, I must invoke the names Nabokov, le Carré, Pynchon, and O'Hara. From more recent years I've appreciated Barry Gifford for his believable surreality, Hunter S. Thompson—despite his offbeat reputation, he was a brilliant journalist who taught me much—Walter Mosley for his senses of era and setting, and Charles Willeford for leading the way to the pits of paradise.

You have truly stepped out of "the ivory tower" as a writer and bring your many real-life interests and talents (photography, classic cars, etc.) to bear in your writing. Please discuss how you bring these traits to your characters. Do you find a blurring between yourself and the people in your novels?

From the day I began *The Mango Opera* in 1994, I've wanted my readers to think that the action on the pages was physically possible. By doing that I could ease their journey into the realm of believing my invented tales. My job description, at its core, is to force people, most of whom I've never met, to keep turning pages filled with inventions from my skull. Keeping things "real" improves my chances of doing that. Turned pages, in an ideal world, equals job security—at least within the limits of my abilities.

As regards the fiction I create, reality is the sum of my reading, viewing, listening, and life experiences. Whatever blend works best is what I use;

blurring is mandatory. I try to ignore the fact that Alex Rutledge, my protagonist, was smart enough to buy a Key West home in the 1970s, plus he is younger, more agile and more courageous than his inventor. In effect, I've put Alex in his own ivory tower—his luck, timing, fortune, experience and talents all play major parts in his sleuthing and surviving.

Characters in your novels sometimes discuss development and change in Key West; in fact, it was a major backdrop in Bone Island Mambo. *Where do you feel the island is headed? Is it a good place?*

Key West has undergone huge adjustments during its 180-year existence as an active seaport and trade center. Its economy has bounced from wrecking to shipping to coaling; sponging to shrimping to sport fishing; salt to cigars to turtles to tourists. Change has been forced by storms, the Depression, the Civil War, a sponge blight, the migration of the cigar trade to Tampa, the Cuban Missile Crisis, the building of the railroad, the later building of the Overseas Highway. What is happening today—with insurance rates and the long-term effects of Hurricane Wilma equal in impact to property prices and development—is the biggest change since the Navy reduced its presence in the early 1970s. Add to that the immediate impact of the building boom in Homestead and Florida City—homes that will require water sold for decades to the Keys—and something must give.

Where to? Key West will remain a haven for artists and writers. Local politics will remain a spectator sport. Much of the island's character will survive the years. Big money, in the hands of individuals and corporations, will flow inward until some huge event discourages it. Tourism will maintain its influence despite the island's dwindling count of restaurant and hotel workers. Ten years from now there may be no water available, making desalinization mandatory. Havana could open to tourism (with, gasp, gambling), drawing revenue away from the Keys; the middle class could be displaced by both the wealthy and the homeless; or, the weather cycle (including rising sea levels) could discourage habitation.

Is Key West a good place? In coming years it may not be an easy place to live, but goodness is defined by humans. As long as good people are drawn to the Keys, people who care, its chances are better than most. If all the good people do a Big U-Turn, I will start to worry.

Along those lines, I was charmed that at one point in one of your books, Alex Rutledge considers taking a side trip to Epcot, which seems at odds with his predilections for an unspoiled, unbothered Florida. What are your views on the "Disneyfication" of certain parts of the state—of presenting "fake history" or a purified version of Florida?

Alex is an optimist. I fear that his author will sound like a total pessimist on this because I believe that the concept of an unspoiled, unbothered Florida is complete myth. Each day over 1,000 people move to this state. If we (disingenuously) assume that these folks come in family units of four each, almost 7,000 new homes, condos, or apartments are needed every month of every year. Paradise is already paved. In some parts of the state, traffic is awful and getting worse, and the building of roads is an intrusive game of catch-up. (Alex will learn this first-hand in the next Rutledge novel.) Except for sunsets, overcrowding will force the compaction of our notions of history and pristine nature.

All that said, the population of Key West has an odd way of remaining almost constant. Alex is allergic to crowding; he already lives in his ideal Florida city. Finally, as tourist destinations go, Epcot is probably educational and probably okay—as long as it stays near Orlando!

Tourists don't usually come off very well in your novels. What do you think is the impact of so many visitors to the vacation destination that is also your home? Do you feel invaded?

In the early 1970s we had a brilliant idea. We could spend more time at the beach if the Chamber of Commerce put a lookout on the Seven-Mile Bridge who would call ahead if a car carrying tourists was seen heading south. We could all run to Duval Street and open our shops, look ready for business. That's how few tourists came around. Now, after years of promotion, we got our wish. More tourists than any island really needs. But in this regard, Key West is not alone.

America, over the past thirty years, has fallen in love with beachfront living. From Maine to Miami, Vancouver to San Diego, Texas to Tampa, we all want paradise with an ocean view. Those who blame Spring Breakers, treasure hunters, Jimmy Buffett, and cruise ships are missing the point. Americans everywhere have more disposable income, more leisure time and, for now, a great desire to get sand in their shoes. Try to drive to Clearwater Beach on a Saturday. Talk about an invasion. Try to stroll Miami Beach during tourist season—it's like trying to walk through a packed airport. All the old Conchs are moving to central Florida. Floridians are moving to the mountains of north Georgia and North Carolina.

Hell yes, we feel squeezed and invaded. And the number-one reason I pick on tourists in my novels? Most of them leave their brains back in Michigan.

Your characters do a lot of meeting and drinking at Key West restaurants, and you often mention specific menu items. What is it about the atmosphere of such places as the Blue Heaven, Sloppy Joe's, and Mangoes that lend themselves to novel settings?

Each of these spots has its own personality; collectively they represent a portion of the Keys mystique. I want my characters to exist in a setting that is unlike any other—not just in North America, but the rest of the world. Such is the uniqueness of the Keys. Not only do my characters have to make certain lifestyle adjustments to live in Key West, but they also reap the benefits of being in a location that's (almost) impervious to homogen[iza]ation.

Do you feel boxed in by such labels as "Key West writer" or "detective/mystery novelist"?

Some labels have an odd way of really saying nothing. No "Key West writer" would be published if he or she didn't offer a "product" unlike any other. The writers I might see any day in Key West—at the grocery, in a restaurant, at a sporting event—are as diverse a group as you could imagine. If you wanted to discuss the work of Annie Dillard, Ann Beattie, Robert Stone, John Leslie, Harry Mathews, Judy Blume, Barbara Ehrenreich, Richard Wilbur, or Alison Lurie, you might not bring up any of the others in that list as contrast or comparison. Each has his or her own "voice" and audience, and I certainly couldn't be compared to any of them. I guess "mystery novelist" is closest to what I do, though each of those terms has multiple subgenres. So what then is my label? I write books, they're set in the Keys, people get hurt and justice usually is done. Say what you like—just spell my name correctly!

What is it about Florida that you feel is so, well, crime novel worthy?

To cop a well-known book title, *To Have and Have Not.*

Florida is a state of contrasts. The ultra-wealthy; the poverty cases. The old establishment; the immigrant who arrived yesterday. Rolls-Royces next to beater Yugos at a traffic light. Trailer homes within sight of mansions. Culture clashes between races and nationalities, ex-cons and grad students, Florida natives and newcomers. Of those 1,000 people who move to Florida each day, one may limp down I-75 in an '84 Oldsmobile on bald tires while one may land in West Palm in a privately owned jet. As long as we have "thems that got" and "thems that ain't," we have crime, we have novel fodder, we have in-your-face reality.

Your books and articles about Shelby Mustangs are decidedly nonfiction. How did you make the transition from the genre of magazine and special interest writing to the plot-heavy world of mystery writing? Which do you enjoy working with more?

I couldn't be writing fiction today if I hadn't spent seven years as an automotive magazine editor. Editing technical, somewhat repetitive text—usually written by someone else—gave me a great overview on editing my own work. Writing a monthly column, often at the last minute, gave me a confidence in my ability to project both information and entertainment from paragraph to paragraph, page to page. That editing experience was primary in my development as a novelist.

It was, however, repetitious. Writing fiction allows one to avoid repetition because, while the details that make it real must be factual, the chapter-to-chapter events that carry characters through a plot are an author's fabrications. At this point in my writing career (and my life) I enjoy the freedom that fiction offers.

That said, I will admit to falling off the wagon during the last three months of 2005. I wrote and edited an entire "one-shot" magazine called *Mustang Milestones* that covered the race-driving and car-building career of Carroll Shelby, the 83-year-old genius behind Ford's 2007 Shelby Mustang GT-500. I wore myself to a frazzle but learned a lot and reacquainted myself with the automotive hobby.

How has your work in the visual arts impacted your work as a verbal artist? What do photography and writing have in common—or are they worlds apart?

As a photographer I learned to notice small details, fluctuations in color tones, vertical and horizontal edges and lines, oddities in the structure and design of objects. I paid attention to perspective, to what photographers call "convergence," which is visual overcrowding, and to the effects of lighting and shadows. I also paid attention to people and faces, body language and comfort zones. I am sure that all of that knowledge boiled itself down to a sense of surroundings—not so much instinct as learned—that carries into my work. It doesn't just affect my descriptive passages; it informs my mental pictures as I work through scenes in my fiction. I allow Alex Rutledge once in a while to describe these visualizations as a way of telling another character what's on his mind, why he's reaching certain conclusions, or why "facts" don't match "evidence" (or vice-versa). My experience pressing all those shutter buttons is a fundamental factor in my writing.

The music and general presence of your friend Jimmy Buffett crops up from time to time in your novels. In some places you even quote from "Cuban Crime of Passion" and "Fins." A little wink and a wave to the Parrot Heads, or do you feel that a cameo from Buffett is what people would expect from a novel set in Key West?

Friendship aside, any discussion about Key West these days requires the mention of Jimmy Buffett. As his fame grew and as the island's reputation as a destination grew, they became co-conspirators in drawing people to the tropic mystique. I catch myself mentioning his name too often; but walk down Duval Street any day of the year and look at the T-shirts and listen to people talk and the music blaring out of storefronts. Jimmy's a fact of Key West life as much as rising and falling tides.

As I mentioned earlier, my writing is the product of my experiences and knowledge. Jimmy and I became friends in late 1971 or early 1972. We hung out with a group of folks who enjoyed the ocean, the parties, restaurants and bars. And that group of friends—or those of us who've survived—has hung together, at least to the point of staying in touch. We like to think that, during those great years in paradise, Jimmy was writing the soundtrack to our lives. We were the first ones to hear most of his early songs, in our back yards, in the Chart Room Bar, or anchored offshore in a motorboat or two. So it's natural that I would invoke the spirit of "I Have Found Me a Home," and the other great tunes from Jimmy's career. As far as freely quoting the occasional lyric from "Cuban Crime of Passion" or "Fins," I suppose I was daring some music industry exec to sue me—after all, I co-wrote those lyrics. I wanted to see if they'd come after me for "stealing" my own work.

Alex Rutledge is quite a well-defined lead character. How do you balance the development of him and his supporting cast without sacrificing plot?

Alex and his friends tend to sort that out book by book. In *Bone Island Mambo*, for instance, Sam Wheeler is almost as important as Alex. In *Air Dance Iguana*, Sam is absent throughout the book but his girlfriend, Marnie Dunwoody, plays a major role. The best way to describe the balance is to say that his friends are always available and on his mind, and he calls them for assistance as the plots require. Kind of like real people with their circles of family members and friends.

Please discuss your methodology. How much plotting and outlining do you take on before drafting?

As I launch into each book I have a short list of topics to discuss, concepts to approach. In *Octopus Alibi*, for instance, I knew that Sam Wheeler would have to deal with the possible murder of a family member, and he would call on Alex for support. Also, Alex would have to confront the death of an elderly friend, and the city of Key West would be shocked by the death of its mayor—by suicide or murder. That was enough to get me started.

I don't outline a complete novel but, as I move along in the manuscript, I try to think two or three chapters ahead of myself. Later in the book, I might try to think myself right through to the end. That helps direct the plot and lets me know what each chapter needs to accomplish in revealing new clues, resolving old clues and furthering the suspense.

What are the most difficult and enjoyable aspects of setting crime novels—which typically require a fast-moving, high-adrenaline plot—in famously laid-back Key West?

As an author, I love it because the action stands out so well against the "easy-life" background. It's a contrast that makes the tropical life more desirable and the dangerous aspects all that more ironic and edgy. For Alex Rutledge, it's a different deal. He strives every day to capture the laid-back essentials, but is challenged again and again by circumstances that require high-energy work. As each book draws toward its conclusion, I wonder if he doesn't think that his life might be more peaceful in Miami! I sincerely hope that he never finds the chance to get revenge on me for the hell I've thrown his way.

Bibliography

Corcoran, Tom. *Air Dance Iguana*. New York: St. Martin's/Minotaur, 2005.
____. *Bone Island Mambo*. New York: St. Martin's/Minotaur, 2001.
____. *Gumbo Limbo*. New York: St. Martin's/Minotaur, 1999.
____. *Hoofbeats: The Pulse of the Mustang World: A Collection from the Pages of Mustang Monthly*. New York: The Backlash Press, 1994.
____. *Mustang 65 1/2-68*. Osceola, WI: MBI Publishing, 1993.
____. *Mustang 1964 1/2-1973 Restoration Guide*. Osceola, WI: MBI Publishing, 1992.
____. *Octopus Alibi*. New York: St. Martin's/Minotaur, 2002.
____. *The Mango Opera*. New York: St. Martin's/Minotaur, 1998.

Tim Dorsey, Satirical Crime Writer Extraordinaire

by Richard McKee

With the 1999 publication of *Florida Roadkill*, Tim Dorsey roared into the fast lane of Sunshine State crime and mystery fiction. Over eight books later, he is still full throttle and not looking back. From the beginning, his stories prompt comparison to the likes of Carl Hiaasen, Elmore Leonard, and even Thomas Pynchon, but Dorsey's strengths and narrative tendencies lean toward the farcical and outrageously satirical more so than any of his peers. In addition, through the voice of his recurring and loveable serial killer Serge Storms, Dorsey's books are a veritable catalogue of Floridiana, on one level zany tour guides that are passionately and meticulously researched and expounded. The novels are fast-paced, episodic, hilarious, and generously riddled with calculated disorder, dark truths, and scary wisdom. Dorsey's Florida, and the world of his antihero Serge, is resplendent with whackos and weirdos deserving of a clever and violent demise. In that respect Serge is very accommodating. But there is a passionate thread to the antics of Serge, and that is an undying thirst and reverence for all things purely Florida.

The following interview took place as I rode with Tim around Sarasota in his 1996 Cadillac DeVille, November 17, 2005. He insisted that the best way to talk about his work would be to drive about the town and visit some of the sites he places in his novels: local institutions like motels, bars, bookstores, endangered landmarks, and so on. He was correct.

RICHARD MCKEE: *Why do you set your work in Florida?*

TIM DORSEY: This is where I grew up. It has tremendous emotional value to me. I have all kinds of memories. It's what I know. I left the state for a little while, came back, and that's when I realized how lucky I was and how much I loved it. This was in the sixties, so everybody was a transplant. I don't remember anybody who was a native. There was no sense of culture, or belonging, or where you were, or cultural or regional identity. That has changed. Because the state was so young it seems that now crime writers and other fiction writers are writing the history of Florida in real time.

Do you have a preference for geographical regions of Florida, such as urban, or rural, or coastal; or do you just love it all, just like your main recurring character, Serge?

Florida geography is so versatile. You can stay within Florida and find it all. My books are set all over, so I guess I don't have a favorite region or area.

Which Florida writers do you admire? Which ones that you read best capture Florida for you?

My favorite Florida book of all time is *Ninety-Two in the Shade* [Thomas McGuane]. It's bone deep. I was making regular trips to the Keys back when I was at the *Tampa Tribune* as copy editor. I would walk around in the Keys and take photographs, and that novel just hit the nail on the head. I remember watching the movie that starred Peter Fonda, and then I visited the blimp hangar of the novel and it conjured so many memories.

[We pass on U.S. 41 the Cabanna Inn, and Tim points out that he had to stay there once so he could get it right for one of the scenes in the novel he was writing at the time.]

If you could live anywhere in Florida other than where you are now, where would it be, and why?

There are a couple of answers to that. The family changes everything, but if I had a vacation home somewhere it would be in the lower Keys. I'd have a house overlooking the water and the mangrove flats, and I'd have a little boat and dock. But with family, it's exactly where we are. Tampa is so convenient for the things we need, so I'm there.

What do you think shapes the state today as far as where we are headed?

The main thing that shapes the state is all of the money to be made, greed. It's almost unlimited, real estate prices are sky-high, and Florida is probably the last place the bubble is going to burst because people just keep coming here. We get a disproportionate number of those people that retire or migrate, so there's all of that housing, jobs, retail... It's amazing. I mean, look at this, there's a new Border's we're going by. That wasn't there a few months ago.

Can you imagine setting your work someplace other than Florida? I know you had a few episodes in New York, et cetera, and there's a portion in Hollywood in your next novel. But can you imagine using someplace other than Florida?

Only in the limited context that you mention. I'll sometimes start in Florida and come back, but I can't imagine doing a whole novel in, say, Chicago. Like in *Orange Crush*, I may use another place briefly for a change of pace. Florida is my primary inspiration, and with *The Big Bamboo* I probably tested my limit as far as how much I can stand being out of water. This fish had to come home. I had to take extra trips to California to get it down right. I'm used to writing from unconscious familiarity when I'm writing about Florida, and here I am in *The Big Bamboo* doing all of this stuff out in Los Angeles and Hollywood. It wasn't natural. It lends to the book, though, because that's my main character's feeling being out there. Serge feels unnatural in California, and he comes back.

[Tim pulls up to Brant's Used Books, a Sarasota institution since 1956, that still inhabits an old World War II army barracks built in 1942.]

When I first came down here, they had a big trove of *National Geographics*. I went to the indexes and I bought every copy of *National Geographic* since 1927 that had articles in it about Florida. They almost always contained maps and I would use them to take trips around the state.

[We are greeted inside by Barbara, the owner. She recognizes Tim and is happy to see him. She tells us about the store's architecture, which sections of roof and floor are original; Mr. Brant also dealt in art and antiques in the old days. Prior to '56 the barracks were used as a church—her parents were married there—and a lunch room for Sarasota County. Tim decides to take a "walk down memory lane," so we browse the store for about fifteen minutes. We talk with Barbara on our way out concerning the rapid growth of Sarasota County and the daily razing of old landmark buildings, the demise of family-owned bookstores, often victims to rampant population increases.]

This interview is intended for a book with the working title Florida Crime Writers Speak. *What do you want to speak out about? Is there something I haven't asked so far that you want to address?*

Yes, we're losing all of the wonderful places. John D. MacDonald and Carl Hiaasen have done an excellent job on that. What I'd like to do, before things are gone, I'd like to place scenes in books and chapters in some of these places that might be at risk, to get some enthusiasm going for them. On a more realistic level I guess I'd just like to tip a few people off so they can visit these places before they disappear. I almost feel as if my books are the kiss of death because so many places that I've already set scenes are gone now. And although I see a lot of these places being lost, I also see a lot more people caring about it.

Do you have any pet environmental issues? I've seen a lot of that in your books, Serge raising hell about a lot of things disappearing.

I feel, as I've already said, that Hiaasen and MacDonald have done that a lot better than I could. But one thing is that visually Florida is so intoxicating, so I hate litterbugs. I've held off, but I think Serge is going to have to hold a small massacre on them. Littering is the ultimate spit in the face to the community, the attitude that someone else can clean up behind me. The landscape is sacred. That's the micro level. On the macro level, these old electric power plants that use coal and have been grandfathered in so they can get away with pouring all of this shit in the air. If you wear polarized sunglasses, as I do, and you're driving around you can see the long streaks of pollution trailing out from their smokestacks and how the dust and soot travels and settles and messes everything up. You can tell because I'm running at the mouth that this is one of my pet peeves.

What about the Everglades? Has everything been said that can be said about the debasement of the Everglades?

They haven't said all there is. There's more. I'm saving mine for a future book. But as far as saying anything about the ecology now, I will only say how much I enjoy the Everglades.

How did you get into the business of writing crime novels? Had you always been interested? Were you an avid crime novel reader?

Well, I am now. I have to confess I was a latecomer as a fan. Specifically I can recount how that developed. I was a big fan of satire, Kurt Vonnegut, Joseph Heller and those types, *The Catcher in the Rye*... And that's the type of book I wanted to write. Being in Florida, from Florida, and a lover of Florida, I wanted to do that type of book about Florida. And I actually started this book many times and it wasn't going to be a crime or mystery novel at all, rather a sort of picaresque, wandering, *Don Quixote* kind of thing. Then I accidentally started reading a series of Florida mystery novels, starting with *Ninety-Two in the Shade*. I rented the VHS movie, actually, and saw that it was based on a novel. I went and grabbed the novel. Even after reading it I didn't realize it was a mystery. Then I saw *Miami Blues*, read the book, and I didn't realize that that was a mystery. Meanwhile I'm writing chapter one of this picaresque Florida thing over and over again. Then I read a review in the *Tampa Tribune* of James Hall's *Bones of Coral* that raved about how it captured Florida's sense of place, although the review didn't call it a mystery. So I read that and found it more structured. It had all of the Florida things that I loved. I realized then that it was a mystery, and that the previous books I had read were mysteries, and that's where I was making my mistake. I realized that I had a reservoir of stuff similar to that in James Hall's book from being a newspaper reporter and an editor. That's when a light bulb went on. I devoured Hiaasen and realized I should have been reading Florida mysteries a long time ago. Naturally I then got into MacDonald, and that's how it happened.

The tags that booksellers put on these books—crime novel, mystery novel, detective novel—are they helpful or necessary? Of course I guess a detective novel has to have a detective.

I was up in New York having lunch with some booksellers, near a mystery bookstore. And one of them gave a definition of *mystery* implying that "mystery" covers all of those things: hard-boiled, soft-boiled, detective, all of these subsets, and they're all mysteries. We have these big major booksellers, you know who they are, and one always puts me under fiction, and the other under mystery. So, go figure.

Why do you think mystery/crime novels are so popular?

I'll tell you why Florida ones are. When you can connect with someone's sense of humor, they love it. I find in reading [Tim makes a hasty stop at the busy Ocean Boulevard intersection, realizing that cross traffic is getting a quick jump on their stop sign. "Sorry," he says. "I was just concerned for your life." I reply that it's OK, and that I had had numerous close calls here during my Siesta Key days of the early '90s.] that, that if you ask people about all the books they've read, and specifically ask what are the funniest, they can name them. And you can connect with them if you can make them laugh. And that answers another question as to why there are so many former newspaper people in this field, and why there's so much wacky material in these books. It's because, hey, this is Florida. It really happens here every day.

The mystery novel has a huge audience nationwide, and a lot of them don't have a sense of humor. Why do you think they are popular?

The ones that I like are springboards into something additional. John D. MacDonald and Carl Hiaasen took the mystery book to somewhere else. They weren't close-ended. You can do this with settings other than Florida. [We pass the Crescent Club, a legendary Sarasota County watering hole. *Florida Roadkill* has a scene in it. Tim notes that he very accurately describes the bar's interior in his book. Then a car passes us on a double line and Dorsey observes, "There's another crazy Sarasota driver."]

How do you prepare for a novel, with notes and a general road trip? Bad dreams?

A road trip is definitely part of the preparation. At first I started out not having a real plan. But then I started thinking about how I had previously done it. It's kind of like an artist when he starts a painting. I ask myself where I would I like to set my easel up? It could be a combination of location, time, and event. Part of *Cadillac Beach* is Miami Beach in the early sixties. I didn't have a plot or characters, nothing. It was just, "Where are we going to start setting up the canvas?" I just drove over there. The books are not plot- or character-driven; they're location-driven; they're Florida-driven. I'll just pick a different location, or I'll pick a different route, because sometimes I'll link up a bunch of locations through a journal, reminiscent of the methods of Mark Twain, like Huck Finn, or something similar. So many American novels go back to that, journeys like Huck's on the river. *Torpedo Juice* winds up in the lower Keys. But there was the journey to get to the Keys; then there was the location, once you got there, that picked up and drove the story.

So it's as if place is the driving force in that once you get there it produces the characters and the theme for you, although Serge is a constant in your books, but place dictates what Serge does or what he's up to that week?

Yes, I have Serge coming back, and I have choices from a number of other things. So I pick the location and start thinking about what news stories are from that area, what the people are like, what are the regional distinctions. For instance, if I set the story in Apalachicola I'd have oyster fishermen and whatever they might be involved in.

Do you think, then, that having your books pigeonholed as mystery or detective keeps some people from picking them up and reading? Does it help you, or tie you down?

Any pigeonholing, at the beginning of your career, probably helps you because there are readers looking for a particular type. But some authors, like Carl Hiaasen, eventually create their own category. Then you get readers who spread the word and explain to others what you're all about. In the beginning I picked up a lot of people who read mysteries, then I started picking up an audience who loved general fiction and Florida lore, which is not somewhere you can readily position a book. So the tour-guide aspect of the books absolutely helps sell some of them. Some reviewers call my books painless history and geography lessons. I coat the informational tidbits with some entertainment.

Can you see yourself writing in a genre other than mystery/crime, and if so, what might that be? If you're bored, where would you go from there?

The easy answer to the first question is no [laughs]. But if it was yes, I'd have to ask myself what would be entertaining for the reader and still self-indulgent. I don't know. [Tim slows the car, looking for a driveway that may lead to an old Siesta Key fish market, which we decide has been swallowed up by new condos dotting the general area.]

Let's talk about Serge. He's certainly taken off as a popular character. You're probably in a situation now where you couldn't get away with writing a book without Serge in it.

Not only that, but that's now mandated in my contract; it's an additional clause.

I know you've been asked this before, but let's try it again. Why is he the main selling point? Why might people not want to read one of your books now if he's not in it?

Basically, he makes people laugh. As I've said, when you can do that you get some very loyal and appreciative readers. And there's a number of dynamics going on. One has to do with what George Carlin calls repressed laughter, like laughing in church or at a funeral. Probably one of the most common responses or takes on the books are, "I can't believe I'm laughing at a serial killer."

Yes, but you know satire often has that very serious side. There are some things that Serge is very serious about: history, preservation, the Florida environment, and ironically enough, consistent moral behavior, his neighbors. Do you think that aspect of him is appealing as well?

That lends to the humor. The fact that he's a killer, and vicious, and immoral on one level puts him off the chart. Therefore anything he says along the moral lines doesn't come off as preachy. Yes, he's crazy and goes around doing some horrible things, but in the middle of it all he says or does something that rings true and we say, "Wait a second. That last thing makes sense, yet nobody's saying it." You sort of get in some of your pet peeves without being shrill. That's why I kill those people.

Can you paraphrase some of the more impressive things that Serge has ever said, or done?

His commencement speech at the University of South Florida, where he'd been impersonating a professor and lecturing [in *Triggerfish Twist*]... He just pulls up to the auditorium in the middle of a crime spree and chase, and it just comes out of nowhere. When I wrote it it was the end of the day and I was a little tired and a little loose and I told myself to just free associate and say things that are on your mind. It just kept going and it became a three-page paragraph. I wasn't trying to write real hard and thought, OK, this is the first try and I'll probably just throw it out. But it just came out, and as far as expository writing goes, it's a mess. There's no thesis, no organization... It just goes on and on.

Let's stick with the topic of Serge. I take it that most of the responses and reactions you get concerning Serge are positive, in spite of his erratic and often horrifying behavior?

Almost too positive, to a point that they are sometimes scary. I get emails. Guys say he's a role model. Women ask, "Where can I marry this guy?" I think of him as a marriage of a couple of things. There's the criminal side, but then there's the humor, the entertainment value. I'm a huge fan of traditional American humor, and I think if you take Mark Twain and Groucho Marx, and if you could gene-splice those two guys together and make them a serial killer... That might be where we're heading.

I'm sure you've gotten some bad reactions to Serge. Do any of those come to mind as well?

Oh, those are almost better! I get enjoyment out of the fact that I'm pissing those people off. I want to ask them, don't you have a life? The uptight people help to make it worthwhile. At one book signing for a very small store they had to rent a hall at a Catholic church. I was talking about Serge and I had some video taken and there's all of this stained glass around me, and religious paintings and big crosses. It was beautiful.

Did you ever consider having Serge being caught or killed, although I guess your contract won't allow that now?

In the first draft of *Florida Roadkill* I killed Serge at the end because I figured it was going to be one self-contained book. I think he was dead throughout the third and fourth draft, but I started liking the guy so much I said, "I'm going to have to unkill him because this might get published and I'd like to make this a series." I never really entertained a serious notion that it would get published until after several drafts and I saw it getting there, so I unkilled him.

So where does Serge go from here? How long can you keep him going until he has a thousand-man posse after him?

The more you spend time in newspapering, and especially the crime beat, the more you realize the insane things that are possible. People wonder how some criminals can remain at large for so long, but having talked with police I'm aware of the limitations of law enforcement and the sheer luck that factors in favor of the criminal. You had the terrorists hanging out in South Florida in those dirtbag motels and people asked how come they weren't noticed? But they were probably the finest tenants on the block compared to all of the lunatics that hang out on such strips. Florida is also a perfect camouflage, and at any moment there are thousands of stupid criminals getting by on sheer luck. Serge is actually smart, so to me it's no stroke of luck that he can remain at large. If people realized how many fugitives were living around them and crossing their paths every day in daily life, they would never stop throwing up.

Some Florida crime writers are said to write the kind of books designed to scare or keep people away from the state. Do you think that's true? Could your books be taken that way?

Actually, I've heard Hiaasen make that remark, and I've kidded about that too. However, to be honest, it's hard to say that other people shouldn't come here because I love it here. So come on down. I'm not trying to scare people away, but get questions as to whether the chamber of commerce or tourist bureau officials hate me. Basically I think it's just the opposite because there's no such thing as bad publicity, some say. I remember that before *Miami Vice* started there were chamber of commerce types down there saying it was going to ruin their image. I said, "What image? You've got the worst image in the country right now." But the show actually helped. They ended up painting and preserving all over the place.

I recall that the Stuart Kaminsky interview for this book has a similar thread in that he would seem to agree with you. You've said it, and Carl Hiaasen too, that every time I write something that seems like the sickest thing I've ever come up with it gets topped by a story in the newspaper that week.

I feel like the books can't come out fast enough. I can't count how many times I've had something in a book, waiting to come out, and it gets topped in the newspaper before publication. *Orange Crush* [Dorsey's novel of political corruption and fraud at the polls] couldn't come out fast enough for me. My publisher practically stopped the presses and had me rewrite the last chapter to include something about hanging chads.

Do you work on a word processor all of the time, or do you do some longhand drafts?

The only longhand I do is if I'm writing on a clipboard in the car.

So, is it fun, a job, or a little bit of both?

Oh, it's a blast. Anyone who bitches at all about doing this should be taken out and shot. This is a dream come true. Sometimes it's work when you're putting in a lot of hours, which is sometimes necessary to maintain continuity. When you get near the end of a novel, and you're fatigued, and it's the end of the day and the kids are home from school—and you need to concentrate—well, sometimes I'll get into the car and take my laptop to Tampa International Airport and find a quiet corner.

Bibliography

Dorsey, Tim. *The Big Bamboo.* New York: Morrow, 2006.
____. *Cadillac Beach.* New York: Morrow, 2004.
____. *Florida Roadkill.* New York: William Morrow, 1999.
____. *Hammerhead Ranch Motel.* New York: Morrow, 2000.
____. *Hurricane Punch.* New York: Morrow, 2007.
____. *Orange Crush.* New York: Morrow, 2001.
____. *The Stingray Shuffle.* New York: Morrow, 2003.
____. *Torpedo Juice.* New York: Morrow, 2005.
____. *Triggerfish Twist.* New York: Morrow, 2002.

Carolina Garcia-Aguilera, Award-Winning Hispanic Mystery Novelist

by Cynthia Davis

Miami is a city of waterways and beautiful women. From the windows of Miami Dade College, host of the Miami Book Fair where I have come to hear Carolina Garcia-Aguilera speak, one glimpses the glitter of Biscayne Bay. Nearby, the aquamarine Intracoastal links the Atlantic with olive-green canals and secret backyard lagoons. In the room, Garcia-Aguilera's green eyes sparkle as she regales a rapt audience with stories of her family, her writing career, and her fictional sleuth, the smart, sexy Cuban-Floridian, Lupe Solano.

Garcia-Aguilera, the author of eight novels, including the Lupe Solano mystery series, just celebrated her 20th anniversary as a licensed Private Investigator (P.I.) in the state of Florida. Carolina's family left Cuba a year after Castro came to power, lived briefly in Palm Beach, and ultimately settled in New York. She attended Miss Porter's School in Connecticut and Rollins College in Winter Park, FL. After graduating with a double major in history and political science, Garcia-Aguilera pursued a master's in languages and linguistics at Georgetown University. She lived in Hong Kong, Tokyo and Beijing, where her first two daughters, Sarah and Antonia, were born, and returned to the University of South Florida in Tampa where she studied for a master's in finance. Her youngest daughter, Gabriella, was born in Miami, where Carolina had begun working towards a Ph.D. in Latin American affairs at the University of Miami.

Garcia-Aguilera has always considered herself a storyteller; instead of reading to her daughters at bedtime, Carolina concocted entertaining and complicated tales, some with so many characters she had to create a chart to keep track of them. When she began writing her first crime novel, she drew on her expertise in plotting and storytelling. Wanting to bring the highest degree of credibility and technical accuracy to the book, she interned at a detective agency where she eventually received her P.I. license. Her books include the six Lupe Solano Series (*Bloody Waters, Bloody Shame, Bloody Secrets, Miracle in Paradise, Havana Heat* and *Bitter Sugar*), as well as *One Hot Summer* and her most recent novel, set in Miami and Las Vegas, *The Luck of the Draw*. She just finished writing her ninth book.

After meeting at the Miami Book Fair, we arranged a series of interviews which took place over the next several weeks. Carolina is witty, unpretentious, and generous with her time. Like many working women, she is adept at multitasking, and she conducted our last conversation while bathing her five dogs and packing for an upcoming trip to Peru.

CYNTHIA DAVIS: *As the first Hispanic in Florida to win a Shamus award for a full-length novel, do you feel a certain responsibility for being a trailblazer? Does being a Hispanic "role model" influence your work in any way?*

CAROLINA GARCIA-AGUILERA: Actually, I've been told I'm the first Hispanic ever to win the Shamus Award. I won for the best private eye novel written in 2000 for my fifth book, *Havana Heat*. But in terms of being a role model—that carries a heavy responsibility. I don't claim to represent all Cuban-Floridians because we are a much more complex and nuanced community than we are portrayed in the popular press.

I also wanted to introduce the Catholic perspective in my work because not many crime writers focus on that. But really, I feel I have been very fortunate because I've been able to do what I love, and to do well at it.

Tell me about your family history in Cuba.

Well, I was born into a family of fighters for freedom and independence. Francisco Vicente Aguilera, my great-great-great-grandfather, fought against Spain in the Ten Years War, during the 1860s. As a result of his courage and leadership, his face appeared on the Cuban $100 bill.

Since this is Miami, can we talk Cuban politics for a minute?

Well, people always try to peg me and they can't! I'm anti-Castro but I'm not particularly right wing. I'm a registered Democrat, although I don't always vote that way. Not all Cubans in Miami are fanatics and rabid right-wing crazies as some of the media would like you to believe, although if I were in Havana today, I would certainly be in jail!

What bothers me is that Castro has gotten a free pass in the U.S. press. He and Che Guevara are portrayed as romantic figures, and they certainly are not! When I see individuals wearing that Che T-shirt I feel sick; I really want to throw up. Che was Castro's executioner but people don't understand that, or they'd rather not acknowledge it.

You see, I am a firm believer in human rights. As a matter of fact, I'm on the board of Amnesty International, and therefore I know about such human rights violations in Cuba. It's very sad.

Is it fair to say, then, that one purpose of your detective novels is to write/right the record about Castro and the Cuban history?

[*Laughs.*] My books are to educate and entertain, so yes, I definitely try to do that, in both senses of the word. For example, in the Elian Gonzalez situation, when that little boy was rescued from a raft at sea, the press had a field day. They stereotyped the Cubans in Miami. In reality, the community was very, very divided about Elian; people had conflicting feelings about whether he should return to his father in Cuba or stay with relatives in Miami. Then, something like ten people burned a couple of tires in a back street and that incident was shown over and over on national television, implying that mobs of Cubans were out of control. I'll tell you one thing, the press could never stereotype the Jewish or the black community in such a way without a real outcry! For some reason, Cubans are considered fair game, though.

If a desire to portray the Cuban community accurately is the purpose of your work, what is the central theme of your novels?

Well, certainly my books deal with the idea of loss, the search for something lost, for something interrupted, the sense of longing for the past.

When I taught Havana Heat *to my class in the detective novel, the students found a lot of symbolism in the book. Several of the students thought that Lupe's dead mother symbolized Cuba, the lost motherland.*

[*Laughs.*] Now that is deep! But I have to tell you that students, academics and psychiatrists seem to find all kinds of deep inner meanings in my work.

For example?

Well, a young man from Arkansas told me he had written his dissertation on my books. Apparently they are used in courses at Yale and at the University of Hawaii. A geography professor from Dartmouth told me recently that when he teaches the geography of Miami, he uses my books because the book is so accurate in terms of streets, landmarks.

I want to get back to your description of Miami and the sense of place in your books since that is such a hallmark of crime writing, but what do the psychiatrists say?

A few years ago, I was doing a reading and a psychiatrist in the audience asked me how I chose Lupe Solano's name. I explained that Lupe is the nickname for Guadelupe, as in the *Virgin de Guadelupe*, and because that is a part of her Catholic and Hispanic culture I wanted to bring it out. I chose Solano because that name is easily pronounceable in many languages, and also because in Coral Gables, where I was then living, there is actually a street, Solano Prado, along which I always liked to drive. But he informed me that Solano must have come from "Solo" because Lupe was actually a loner, and that I was referencing the hard-boiled detectives like Sam Spade and Philip Marlowe who always work alone!

Are you influenced by Raymond Chandler and Dashiell Hammett and the hard-boiled tradition? After all, Havana Heat starts out with the lines: "I should have been born a man. I think like one, I act like one, I live my life like one." Lupe is a pretty tough lady, isn't she?

Oh, sure, the hard-boiled writers, Chandler and Hammett, are definitely some of my influences. Another writer whose work I admire is Elmore Leonard. No one writes dialogue like Elmore Leonard. So human and so crisp. And funny.

Certainly, the ironic humor of the hard-boiled tradition comes out in Lupe's comments and thoughts.

Well, she is funny but she does not take herself too seriously; she accepts herself just as she is and she can laugh at herself.

Of course, with Lupe's expensive tastes, her designer shoes, and those gourmet meals at high-end Miami restaurants, she is very different from the Depression-era detectives who enjoy a nip from a hip flask, or at most a dry martini and a steak.

Of course, but that is part of her charm. Lupe does not diet and she certainly does not deny herself a good meal or an excellent bottle of wine. Lupe is tough but always has a perfect manicure and pedicure. The reader learns early on that she hates to use her gun because it ruins her manicure!

Getting back to sense of place and specific urban geography—why is that so important in your books and in the hard-boiled tradition?

Well, geography is vital to any detective story and Chandler and those writers knew that. If readers believe the geography, if they see the writer really knows his or her way around the streets and the city, then they believe the plot. They will trust whatever the writer tells them in the story.

You have lived all over the world, in New York, in Asia... Why do you always choose Miami as your setting?

There are endless pockets of culture in Miami. For example, I just discovered that there is a large Russian community here. I'm a boxer, you know, and I follow boxing. A couple of years ago, there was a Latino-Russian match and the only place the tickets were being sold was up in Golden Isles in North Miami. I was totally amazed because I was in a different world there: the food, the shops, the signs, the language. Completely Russian—the people were from what was Soviet Georgia, actually.

My students are impressed at how you cross cultural boundaries and write with authority about so many different aspects of Miami.

Miami is a very complex, nuanced city. Working as a P.I. you realize that things are not what they seem. You learn not to make unwarranted assumptions and not to stereotype people.

What comes first in your crime fiction, plot or characters?

Oh, they go together; the characters drive the plot through the things they do, and the plot hinges on the characters' being believable in order to move forward. As I have said, my characters talk to me and tell me what they would do or not do.

Is storytelling an important part of your Cuban background?

Well, yes, but storytelling is important in every ethnic group... There are great storytellers in Appalachia and in African-American culture; it is all part of the oral tradition that so many cultures share.

Speaking of African-American culture, you also introduce elements of the Afrocentric tradition, the Santeria tradition into your books. Lupe's powerful, cigar-smoking pilot friend, Barbara, seems to represent Yemaya, the Yoruba goddess of the sea, and the principle of the "eternal feminine."

Oh, yes, Santa Barbara is the equivalent of *Yemaya*, in the way that Catholicism absorbed the West African deities.

Do you find that the Santeria religion is another element of Cuban culture that people stereotype?

Yes, people think it is all about sacrificing chickens and goats, but there is a very strong, complex belief system among *some* elements of the Cuban community. Barbara comes from that particular tradition. She was in my first book, Bloody Waters, you know, and I brought her back in Havana Heat.

I think people are drawn to her. My students certainly were. And that strong, matriarchal tradition that Barbara represents is reinforced by Lupe's strength. You include a lot of powerful, assertive women in your books!

Well, Lupe is strong but she is also very feminine and petite; I made her five-foot-one so I could always have her in sexy high heels!

In what ways is Lupe like or unlike her creator?

[Laughs.] Let's see... I'm taller... I'm older than Lupe, obviously, and I have children. But we both have a wicked sense of humor—quite irreverent!

Speaking of children, do any of your daughters write?

Gabriella, my youngest, just finished her first novel; it takes place on Miami Beach and is all about the nightlife and the clubs: basically, sex, drugs and rock and roll!

My students love the recurring descriptions of Lupe watching the parrots building their condo-nests in the avocado trees outside her office. Someone suggested that they represent the need to rebuild a Cuban homeland in a new environment. Would you agree with that?

Well, again, that's reaching a bit for symbolism—although it's always interesting to hear readers' interpretations. Actually, I'm fascinated by nature. In fact, just now there are some birds building a nest in a telephone pole outside my window (wait until FPL [Florida Power & Light] sees that!). I love seeing how nature goes on undisturbed in an urban setting. But I'll tell you a story about the parrots: soon after my first book was published, in 1986, I received a letter from an ornithologist who informed me that parrots would *never* nest in an *avocado* tree because if they ate the fruit, they would get sick and die! So how do you like that? You see how careful a writer has to be! This is fiction but readers insist that every fact be exact.

Let's talk about Lupe's relationship with the police. I used to teach Elmore Leonard's Rum Punch, but my students who were in the police force complained because they said he made fools of the police. It really bothered them so I had to select a different book with a Florida setting and that is how I discovered Havana Heat.

You know it really upsets me when I read crime fiction that shows a lot of conflict between the private investigator and the police. It just doesn't happen. I learned early on as a P.I. that working with the police is really essential. Each can contribute something to the solution of a case and they need to work together. In certain cases, we help each other. When I read about P.I.s badmouthing the police or doing blatantly illegal things like breaking and entering, or tampering with a witness, or lying, I know that the writer has just not been in the trenches. That's stupid: in real life, that would never happen, at least not with experienced private eyes. It's just a case; no reputable P.I. is going to compromise his license for a case.

You ran a successful detective agency for ten years before turning to writing full-time. What did you learn as a P.I. that gives your books verisimilitude?

How to shoot.

Really? Who taught you to shoot?

My partner. He taught me the ins and outs of being a private eye—among them, how to conduct an investigation while staying within the law (which is *very* important); how to do moving surveillance; and especially how to interview witnesses. That last skill is vital, critical in both civil and criminal cases. I was always very good at interviewing witnesses.

What do you think of when you reflect on your "life of crime"?

Well, I just renewed my P.I. license; after surviving in the field for 20 years, shouldn't I get an award...? Keys to the jails, maybe?

Any high points in your writing career you would like to share?

Some years ago, my daughter, who is now a lawyer in New York, was an undergraduate at the University of Pennsylvania. She had joined the Hispanic Students Association, and every year they invited a speaker for Hispanic Heritage Week. Well, unbeknownst to her, the group decided to invite me, and when she arrived at the meeting, they were all discussing ways they could contact Aguilera and whether or not she would accept, and my daughter spoke up and said: "You know, I can just about guarantee that she'll come." Of course, they had no idea who she was, since I use my maiden name to write, but when she told me that, I felt wonderful about my career, about my family... It all came together.

Bibliography

Garcia-Aguilera, Carolina Garcia. *A Miracle in Paradise*. New York: Morrow, 1999.
____. *Bitter Sugar*. New York: Morrow, 2001.
____. *Bloody Secrets*. New York: G.P. Putnam's Sons, 1998.
____. *Bloody Shame*. New York: G.P. Putnam's Sons, 1997.
____. *Bloody Waters*. New York: G.P. Putnam's Sons, 1996.
____. *Havana Heat*. New York: Morrow, 2000.
____. *Luck of the Draw*. New York: Harper Collins, 2003.
____. *One Hot Summer*. New York: Harper Collins, 2002.

James W. Hall, Maverick Master of the Keys and South Florida

by Rick Hofer

"Thorn parked the Fleetwood and sat for a few minutes with the headlights blaring at the side of Kate's house. Finally, he pushed in the light plunger and sat there, breathing in the darkness. There was a thunderstorm out in the shipping lanes, explosions of lightning muffled inside black cumulus. The wind was beginning to quicken already, blowing the mosquitoes back into the Everglades. And the stand of tall Australian pines was moaning. Clouds sped past the moon."

This passage, which appears in *Under Cover of Daylight* (1987), James W. Hall's first novel, also anticipates the fourteen novels Hall has published since. It mentions Thorn, who becomes the recurring hero of Hall's fiction, and it presents Florida in the naturalistic detail Hall characteristically supplies when turning his narratives from the complexities of character and culture to the motiveless conditions of place. This passage looks out and up, past several deliberated elements—Thorn's waiting, the interior of a Cadillac, a house, hypothetical lines drawn on the sea—toward Florida's natural forces and forms.

Consistent with a tendency in American writing that goes back at least as far as Irving in fiction, and Emerson and Thoreau in nonfiction, Hall looks to the natural environment, for him Florida generally and the Keys specifically, as a repository of admirable and durable value. Hall's fiction, like several of his essays, encourages readers to recognize that Florida's water, its fish and its birds, its clouds and its storms, and even its light, deserve attention and respect. Those characters who lack or exploit either—polluters, aggressive developers, or even those who just do not pay enough attention—become those whom Thorn battles and Florida's light betrays as empty and, often, garishly evil.

RICK HOFER: *Why do you live in Florida? Chance? Choice? Some of both?*

JAMES W. HALL: In January of 1965 I came to Hollywood, Florida, to attend military school (my senior year in high school). I took one breath of the air and promised myself I'd live here. I went to college in St. Pete, then after getting a Ph.D. in northern climes, I applied for teaching jobs only in Florida. I'd decided if I couldn't get a teaching job in Florida, I'd do something else rather than teach in some other place. Luckily, I got a job in Miami and have been here since.

What do you think is distinctive about Florida?

The air, the light, the birds, the water. But mainly the light.

How important to you is Florida's history?

I'm reading it all the time. I'm reading A Land Remembered by Patrick Smith right now. I loved Les Standiford's Last Train to Paradise. Most of my novels involve the power of the past, and mingle that with the power of the place.

How does the past seem to you to assert itself in Florida?

Literature and psychology are about rendering the past into the present. It is all we have. To understand our present moment we have to have a full understanding of our past. For the thousand people entering Florida every day, A Land Remembered should be required reading. Florida has a rich and complex and kinky past. In our current age of cultural amnesia, a failure to honor the past is partly what has caused the sprawl and loss of wetlands to continue unabated.

About the future—for many people Florida seems to be a place to start over, to write new chapters. How does a sense of the future, what may yet be, seem to you to be at work in Florida?

Florida is the land of eternal youth, the fountain of youth Ponce was looking for. A place where you can start over with a new identity. It's the end of the road, literally and figuratively, for a lot of folks.

Why do you set your work in Florida?

It's the sea I swim in.

Can you imagine setting your work elsewhere?

Maybe for a page or two.

What do you like or dislike about the way other writers use Florida?

I will speak no ill of my fellow writers.

What parts of Florida do you especially like or dislike?

I haven't found a place I didn't find fascinating.

If you could live anywhere in Florida, where would it be?

I'm there. The old shady streets of Coral Gables.

What do you think is, and of, the state of the state today?

The state of the state is overburdened and underappreciated. Too many newcomers who lack the appreciation and commitment to the place. I see my job as a fiction writer, partly, to inform some of those folks what it is about this place that should stir their passion.

Overburdened by what?

Overburdened by insensitive exploiters.

If New Yorkers are pushy, Californians spacey, and Texans brash, what are Floridians?

Pushy, spacey, brash, and silly.

Silly how?

They wear Goofy shirts with great élan and regularity.

We're so varied that a shorter version—What are Floridians?—may be the better question.

There's about a dozen Floridas I can list off the top of my head. I think it's dangerous to categorize the state in a one-liner. It's complicated demographically and in almost every other way that matters. It's an amalgam of a lot of other geographic regions of America. Drive fifty miles you're in Ohio, another fifty you're in the Deep South, or Mexico, or New Jersey.

One of Thorn's allies, at times a reluctant one, is Sugarman, formerly a sheriff's deputy and more recently a private investigator. In Off the Chart (2003), Sugarman and his daughter Janey do some bird watching, and by the end of the novel Janey stands considerably better off for the experience. How does something as quiet and even gentle as bird watching fit into a fictional world of crime and punishment, violence and passion, or simply the conflict between good and evil?

From John J. Audubon to Dick Cheney, Americans see birds as more than simple objects of beauty. They're game. They're plumage. As a kid growing up in Kentucky, I was surrounded by blue jays, robins and mockingbirds. I still find the birds of Florida to be of Martian wondrousness.

In your essay "Poet Sinks to Crime," from the collection Hot Damn *(2002), you praise suspense writers for their "complex plotting and rousing good yarns." As you plot your novels, what do you remind yourself makes for a good plot?*

People wanting things passionately is what makes a good plot. It helps if two people with fairly equal power and ability are posed against each other. I think of plot not as something extrinsic, but a causal connection between events that grows out a character acting consistently to achieve a certain end. Scarlett wants to marry Ashley, and everything she does for most of the novel is driven by that want.

In the same essay you point out that "Mystery novelists are practically alone in preserving rich regional settings." What advantages does regional culture provide, in books, and/or in itself?

If it weren't for living and loving Florida I'm not sure I'd be working on my fifteenth novel right now. I'm lucky to live in a region that enough people in the U.S. and around the world find fascinating that it helps sell books. If I'd wound up in Missouri, well, I'd probably be selling insurance right now. This place resonates so profoundly with others not just because it's exotic, but because it's a nexus for so many of the larger social struggles going on in the U.S. And because it's damned gorgeous and changing so damn fast.

In "Poet Sinks to Crime" you make a further point: Our novelists of suspense are indeed the only group of writers today who consistently fulfill Tom Wolfe's view of the novelist's true responsibility: to write works with a wide social scope that are populated by people of all classes and to tackle the great moral and political issues of the day. What is there about your novels and their hero, Thorn, that helps you meet that responsibility?

Thorn is like a man-from-Mars sociologist. He's so isolated and such a hermit that when he's forced to go out into the world, he sees people against bigger backdrops. He can talk to the banker or the street bum with equal curiosity, partly because he's so innocent and in some ways naïve. He's an outsider and because of that I think he sees the world more vividly and correctly.

In another essay, "Guns," you express the concern that the violence in your fiction "can be both numb and numbing." In the essay "Hemingway," you acknowledge your deep admiration for Hemingway's work, which often contains violence and killing. How do you think Hemingway's work redeems its presentation of violence?

Hemingway is deeply ambivalent about violence. A Farewell to Arms is one of the great anti-war novels just as some of his short stories, like "Hills Like White Elephants," are great feminist statements. He doesn't celebrate violence, but looks at it with more brutal frankness than almost any writer I know, except perhaps Tim O'Brien.

In the essay "Fresh Starts" you state: "I don't know if we can truly change or if we only fool ourselves into believing we do." Earlier in Hot Damn, *in "The Hardy Boys," you point out that by rereading* The Missing Chums *you were "reminded again of the magical, transforming power of books, their ability to transport us beyond our puny lives and to shape the very texture of our personalities." Can this power of books bring about what you consider "true change"?*

It's as close to true change as anything I know.

A final question: Apart from matters that are your business alone, what satisfactions do your novels bring you?

Letting the voices in my head speak freely, taking me places I never guessed at.

Bibliography

Hall, James W. *Blackwater Sound*, New York: St. Martin's, 2002.
_____. *Body Language*. New York: St. Martin's, 1995.
_____. *Bones of Coral*. New York: Knopf, 1991.
_____. *Buzz Cut*. New York: Dell, 1997.
_____. *False Statements* (poetry). Pittsburgh: Carnegie Mellon University Press, 1986.
_____. *Forests of the Night*. New York: St. Martin's, 2005.
_____. *Gone Wild*. New York: Delacorte, 1995.
_____. *Ham Operator* (poetry). Bristol, RI: Ampersand, 1980.
_____. *Hard Aground*. New York: Delacorte, 1993.
_____. *Lady from the Dark Green Hills* (poetry). Pittsburgh: Carnegie Mellon University Press, 1977.

_____. *The Mating Reflex* (poetry). Pittsburgh: Carnegie Mellon University Press, 1980.
_____. *Mean High Tide*. New York: Dell, 1995.
_____. *Off the Chart*. New York: St. Martin's, 2004.
_____. *Paper Products* (essays). New York: Norton, 1990.
_____. *Red Sky at Night*. New York: Dell, 1998.
_____. *Rough Draft*. New York: St. Martin's, 2000.
_____. *Tropical Freeze*. New York: Norton, 1989.
_____. *Under Cover of Daylight*. New York: Norton, 1987.

Vicki Hendricks, South Florida Noir Specialist

by Ellen Smith

Vicki Hendricks was born in Covington, Kentucky, and raised in Cincinnati, Ohio, although she fled the cold weather thirty-three years ago for South Florida, and now considers herself a native Floridian. She spent fourteen years in Catholic school, where she was told, early on, that her idle mind was a devil's workshop, and this trait has served her well in recent years. She eventually finished her undergraduate degree at Ohio State University with a B.S. in English education and later received a master's in English from Florida Atlantic University. She found her calling at Florida International University, where she was graduated with an M.F.A. in creative writing. Currently, she is in her twenty-sixth year of teaching writing at Broward Community College. Her love of travel and adventurous sports, such as SCUBA diving, skydiving, and sailing, have provided much material for her fiction, although the roots of her dark side remain unaccounted for.

ELLEN SMITH: *What is your familiarity with Florida?*

VICKI HENDRICKS: I consider myself nearly a native, having moved to South Florida thirty-three years ago. I was drawn by the climate, like most people—after a spring break in Ft. Lauderdale during my college days—and my interest in water sports, boating, and marine life. I had grown up on novels about shipwrecks and stowaways, and Jacques Cousteau documentaries, despite the fact that the Ohio River was the only body of water I had occasional access to. It was extremely polluted with raw sewage in those days, but that didn't stop some of us from water skiing or hanging out on the banks. Beer helped kill the germs! Even though I was extremely poor when I moved here, I was able to indulge in enough snorkeling off the beach and camping in the Keys to keep me happy. When I finally made enough money to try out the rest of my dreams, I became obsessed with SCUBA and later learned to sail, filling out my knowledge of the ocean and the Bahamas considerably. I discovered much beyond what I'd expected, for example, diving in the underwater caves at Ginnie Springs, swimming with the huge ugly/cute manatees in the Crystal River, and kayaking the clear water of springs all over the state. I'm still stunned by the haunting beauty of Spanish moss and titillated by lurking gators, although I'm being more careful these days. Over the last eight years, through skydiving, I discovered the less populated areas of the state, orange, sugarcane, and cow country, along with becoming part of the wild skydiving subculture that thrives on year-round jumping weather. Lately, in addition, birding has taken me to most of the swamps all over the state, besides the Everglades, Corkscrew Swamp and the infamous Fakahatchee featured in *The Orchid Thief*—don't go there. Yet, there's still more to be experienced and learned in this state. I've barely touched the panhandle.

What is it about the state that has particularly suited your work as a fiction writer?

Everything is useful in fiction, and since I much prefer to do research firsthand, living in Florida has made it easy for me because there's so much to choose from. In my search for fun, I find ideas for fiction. I have utilized skydiving in *Sky Blues* and SCUBA in *Iguana Love* to the point where those novels have been dubbed "sport noir." Writing the novel *Voluntary Madness* allowed me to recreate all the zany and bohemian characteristics of Key West and its inhabitants that I adore. I don't think a person needs to be surrounded by the wild and exotic to turn out interesting fiction, but "researching" provides a good excuse for spending money and creating excitement—then I pass it along to others.

What is it about the state (apart from the scenes in your books) that especially speaks to you?

Apart from the tropics and activities I use as background, the diverse people from all over the world, who live and visit here, make South Florida fascinating. I'm not comfortable writing about other cultures in depth, for fear that I don't have enough insight, and we have many good writers to do that for themselves, but I love to use the variety of languages and styles as details to make my stories and novels vibrant, contemporary, and unique for the particular mixture.

What Florida writers do you admire?

I'll assume I'm not limited to mentioning crime writers, because we have many wonderful writers of all kinds here. I'd say, first, my mentors and instructors from Florida International University, Lynne Barrett, James W. Hall, Les Standiford, John Dufresne. I not only admire their work, but also their skill in explaining the creative process and specific technique. Learning to write fiction under their guidance opened a new world for me and enabled me to get beneath the surface of this tropical paradise to the places where only writing can take you.

I'm also a big Harry Crews fan, having read all his books before I started to write. And then I'll add my former classmates, amazing writers in the mystery field, Dennis Lehane, Barbara Parker, Christine Kling. I also admire Carolina Garcia-Aguilera, the only Cuban female detective writer, and Brian and Robert Antoni, literary types I've met through becoming a "Florida writer," both unique for their styles and interests. I wish Brian Antoni would get going on his second novel, because his first was a knockout! Tom Corcoran, S.V. Dáte, Tim Dorsey, and Randy Wayne White are just a few of the others I admire and have been privileged to meet on the book trail. Now Michael Connelly has joined the crew for the last few years by moving to Tampa, another fabulous writer that we can claim for the state. I'm looking forward to the publication this fall, 2006, of *Miami Noir*, edited by Les Standiford, stories from many of my Florida crime-writing friends. Being a writer in Florida really has its perks when it comes to socializing. You can't help rubbing shoulders with interesting and creative people, and I always figure it's contagious.

If you were to categorize Florida writers, where would you place yourself (tart noir, police procedural, hard-boiled)?

Is tart noir a respected category now? If not, let's make it so! I've only heard the phrase used as the title of a collection of short stories I'm in, edited by Lauren Henderson and Stella Duffy, two brilliant writers from the U.K. I think I must have been the original tart noir writer in the states, in the mid-nineties, although it took the Brits to find a nice word for the kind of sex, violence, and tough female combination I put into *Miami Purity* and *Iguana Love*. I can't think of any other Florida writers who use the lengthy sex scenes I'm fond of or the dark narrators, so I might still be alone here. It's probably because most writers want to sell books and make money! I do also, but so far I've been too stubborn to change. Contrary to what people say, sex doesn't sell, and unsympathetic characters are possibly an acquired taste, so far acquired by very few! However, I write what I love best, which is always the obsessive and sexually passionate unraveling of a psychologically twisted individual. I don't really care who dunnit or by what intricate method, so my murderers are always the narrators, putting me into a very small category of writers. Most of my stories examine why an individual might commit murder and the effects thereafter. The crime is solved before it's committed, thereby inhibiting mystery and plot twists, keeping me out of the hard-boiled detective and police procedural categories. My sister has a degree in experimental psychology, and when she was doing her doctoral study, she told me she didn't want to "get stuck with a project involving 'normals'"—that made perfect sense to me. I'm not interested in creating normal people who solve crimes or normal people who commit crimes for money. I'm only happy with strange combinations and aberrant personalities. I'm sure it's my interest in pathological behavior that keeps me writing and puts me into the very small category of noir tarts.

How do you account for your popularity outside the state and the U.S.?

I think my writing appeals to people everywhere who are interested in the gritty characters I produce. The Florida atmosphere encourages European readers and people up north, of course, since they need a dose of sunshine, swaying palms, and coconut oil now and then. Popular is not a word I would use to describe the extent of my celebrity, however—but thanks! I always say, if I could just get a commercial on the Independent Film Channel, I'd be all set. That's my readership, the strange people. No amount of sunshine can blind the world to the fact that I write dark stuff in a limited scope, and it's difficult to reach the low numbers of people of weird taste. Writers seem to like my books more than the reading public, which is complimentary, but there just aren't enough of them buying books so I can quit my day job!

Do you believe Florida mystery/detective/crime novels have influenced or will influence any actions or attitudes in the state?

Certainly not my books. I hope not, or the crime rate will zoom upward! However, Florida seems remarkable to me by the fact that we have so many mystery writers who incorporate regional and social issues into their fiction. Carl Hiaasen is the most striking example, of course, in representing our threatened ecology for all age groups, using humor and excitement to get people's attention. I'm sure his dedication has and will continue to help the state. Also, Jonathon King's beautiful re-creation of the Everglades in *The Blue Edge of Midnight* must inspire appreciation for this unique place and motivate many people's concern. Lately, Christine Kling has brought attention to social issues through her remarkable novel *Cross Current*, which deals with problems in the Haitian community while portraying the Florida boating scene. Carolina Garcia-Aguilera, of course, offers insight into the Cuban community. Many Florida writers use their skill to expand the knowledge of Florida cultures and keep alive concern for the needs of the state.

What impelled you to start writing crime novels?

I think you're always inspired to create something out of love. I fell in love with the writings of James M. Cain when I was just beginning my master's in creative writing, so the timing was right to go in his direction. I admire his ability to keep the reader riveted to the characters throughout, with the lively action and his use of animal passion in human nature—implied to some extent, because it could not be written at that time. *The Postman Always Rings Twice* was my favorite Cain novel, and I modeled *Miami Purity* after it in many ways, especially in the passion, the compact nature of the story and the use of a dark narrator.

What kind of preparation did you have? Did you ever study the history of the genre? Did you have a mentor?

I guess I studied the history when I taught it in Mystery Lit class, but that had nothing to do with my writing. However, I wasn't new to crime and mystery. I read all the Nancy Drews as they were published—besides shipwreck stories and classics—graduated to Agatha Christie in high school and some Dorothy Sayers, and then rounded out my education with classics like Chandler, Hammett, Ross McDonald, and others in college. Eventually, I ran into Jim Thompson. Besides Cain, I think he was most influential, since his dark characters and crude toughness appeal to me more than the detective seeking to restore order. I also loved Camus' *The Stranger*, from high school on, and found out after I'd written *Miami Purity* that Camus had also used *The Postman Always Rings Twice* as a model, so it all made sense.

Lynne Barrett at FIU was my fiction mentor—still is. She is the person who recommended Cain originally, and the instructor whose logic and analytical ability impressed me the most when I was struggling to understand the basics of writing technique.

How do you work? What can be the "germ" of an idea that sets the book in motion?

I work from sentence to sentence, I'm afraid. My "germs" come from people I meet, a place I've visited, or something somebody tells me. I seem to do very well with secondhand information, either about friends of friends, or incidents. I think getting the "tip of the iceberg," so to speak, from other people, allows me to develop the rest of the story without being bogged down in too many details of reality. When I'm working on an idea that comes from my own experience, there's always the feeling that I should stick to the facts, when it's generally more useful to stay loose in order to create structure and plot. However, the skydiving and SCUBA hobbies worked well to give me interesting details that also helped form plots.

One recent example of a "germ" of an idea came from Shirley Murry, an instructor in the office next to me at the college. She's Jamaican and told me that when she lived on the island her house had been burgled once, jewelry stolen, and the police couldn't figure out how the guy had entered. She didn't learn the answer until she moved out some months later and discovered that a hole had been cut in the wood floor under her bed. When Les Standiford asked me for a story for *Miami Noir*, I was holding that idea in reserve. It was easy to move the wooden structure to an old section of Miami and create the personality of a character who would choose this sort of crime, a small, quiet, and likable guy, with limited goals, not too heavy on the brains, but unusual. All I had to do was fix him up with a big, smart, ambitious woman to lead him farther astray.

Do you outline the plot ahead of time?

I tried that once on *Iguana Love*, but I couldn't follow the outline, just kept changing it. Somehow, that novel turned out to be the least plotted of any I've written. I also made index cards with scenes for that novel, but I felt nervous all the time because I kept changing them. Now I find I was doing something similar to what Robert Olen Butler recommends in his new writing book, *From Where You Dream*. However, in his method, once you know what your main character yearns for, you enter your dreamspace, tapping the unconscious to find sense images for each card that call up a scene, instead of using plot points, as I was trying to do. It's important to add, change, and rearrange the cards as you go along—nothing to worry about. It's fascinating, especially as Butler explains it in detail. I've tried this to some extent in writing short stories this past year and plan to use his method in writing my next novel. I highly recommend it, and have used it as a text in my fiction class for the more advanced students. I've always been told that you have to let your subconscious do the creating in the beginning and then go back with a rational mind to structure and make everything consistent, and this way the cards help to keep your mind working. I certainly enjoy when my subconscious can take over. Sometimes in short stories the characters nearly have to "hit me over the head" with the climax, for example, in "Stormy, Mon Amour" in the *Tart Noir* collection. I just kept writing along and was smack into the climax before I understood the psychology of the character I'd invented and the deeper level of the story. Then everything fell into place. I had to go back and do a little tweaking to make it all consistent, but I love when that happens. One minute I'm disgusted because I'm lost, a deadline is approaching, and the number of pages is nearly to the limit, and the next moment I feel like a genius. Stupid to brilliant in a flash! If only the outcome was guaranteed. I usually like to have a bit of irony in mind that I'm working towards because it's too frightening to work completely in the dark, but if I knew exactly where I was headed I would bore myself to death trying to write out those scenes.

Which is more important, character or plot?

Both are necessary, if you want anybody to read the novel or story. I think it's the amount of character and plot that are flexible, depending on your taste and beliefs. Personally, I like a heavy dose of character development through a plot that grows out of the protagonist's need and goal, which cause him or her to make choices. It's all intertwined. This is what I've been taught as the basis for any good fiction, regardless of genre, and my taste already ran in that direction in reading before I learned it as a method for writing. It's the psychology of the character that keeps my interest, the human emotion and variety, and I get perturbed if there are too many plot twists. There's a limit to how many times you can twist the plot, without having to cheat somehow, either by being untrue to your character, breaking your own established rules for point of view, or adding coincidence. The popular reading audience generally doesn't care about point of view inconsistencies and loves the surprises and extreme emotions that occur through the use of coincidence and sentimentality, such as you find in some best-sellers, in order to pack in the thrills and chills. However, I'm always irritated by these devices, especially if strange surprises take the place of logical and meaningful outcomes. Fiction has to be perfectly logical in its use of cause and effect to be artful; so coincidence, although interesting in nonfiction and life, degrades the form of fiction.

Do you strive for local color?

Adding details from nature, culture, and the landscape that I know so well is the fun part of writing. I'm sure every state has many interesting aspects of life to choose from in order to create backdrops for fiction, but especially

Florida, because of the attraction of the tropics and its reputation for crime and insanity, perfect for crime stories. To create the reality of place and time and bring the scenes alive, a writer always needs a sense of detail, and it has to come from the particular area where the story takes place. The details emphasized must be used to develop the plot, not to seem extraneous, so everything works together to create something original and revealing of the locale at the same time.

What different requirements do you see between novels and short stories?

The depth of the idea is the main difference. A writer must develop a sense of what ideas are suitable for poems, essays, short stories, and novels. Otherwise you waste a lot of time starting things that don't have enough interest or complexity to get you through. Or, when there are no scenes and no story you can write to dramatize an idea, it must be told straight out, in an essay. A short story is short because of the limited amount of scenes that it will take to get the protagonist from one place to another in life. A novel must contain more than one simple complication, and might involve several plots working simultaneously. I remember Barry Hannah's panel at the Associated Writers Programs Convention, 2005, called "This Dog Won't Hunt." The members of the panel talked about works in their past, or of their students' works, that finally had to be tossed out because of innate problems. Sometimes years were spent trying to jazz up things that were not fixable, because of lack of complication, until finally the number of rejections became overwhelming or somebody of knowledge and respect clarified the reasons to give up. It's terrifying to know that this could occur, since it's sometimes a fine line to cross. I think it's easy to fool yourself. So far, I haven't had a problem in figuring out if my ideas will work for novels or short stories. When I start to write I generally know by instinct the approximate length of what I'm setting out to do, even if I don't know what will happen, but this has developed with experience—and luck! One of the most terrifying aspects of being a fiction writer is the fact that you do not truly know how to keep doing what you do successfully. You fear you'll lose the magic on each new book. At least, that's the way I feel after five novels and quite a few short stories.

Why has Florida produced so many fine writers?

This is anybody's guess. I'm not even sure that we have more fine writers than any other state, and many authors have moved here after already having been published elsewhere. Of course, we have FIU and its amazing faculty to add expertise. Of course, I could further theorize that the same adventurous and creative spirit, and the insatiable curiosity, that gives people the courage to move from the familiar to the unknown, and compels them to leave the comfort of family and friends to discover something new, is part of the basic psychology of a writer. Florida is still somewhat wild country, in psychology and geography, and the pioneers keep coming, the writers. Maybe that's true.

Why are mysteries so popular?

I don't know. If I did, I might be writing some and selling more books! To me cleverness of plot and puzzle-solving are not nearly as interesting as something malodorously human and ambiguous. I only read mysteries if they have characters that I can crawl inside, and I don't care how everything is tied up at the end, so long as there's no cheating. I don't read many series books because I want a completely new personality to intrigue me every time. The taste for mysteries and plot twists is probably genetic. Just generalizing, I think mystery readers and writers enjoy more highly structured activities than I do. They delight in creating the most complicated web they can imagine and then being able to straighten it out. Underlying that motivation must be the belief that you can make sense of the world if you know the rules. Or, at least, it's fun to pretend you can! Personally, I'm not attracted to crossword puzzles, jigsaws, solitaire, gambling, playing or watching games of any kind—although I enjoy recreational sports without rules, like skydiving, SCUBA, sailing, hiking, rock climbing, dogsledding, all open-ended activities. Instead of trying to find a pattern in the world or figure out the rules, I would rather observe and, hopefully, enjoy the processes as I discover them. Part of my love of skydiving has come from learning about my own psychology, mainly effects of fear on my mind and body that I would never have imagined. This is not to say that I reject the cleverness of mystery. I greatly admire the ability to make scattered pieces fall into place with planning and strokes of genius. I'm just not thrilled to the core when I read those stories, the way I am with Cain and the simple unraveling of demented minds.

Bibliography

Novels

Hendricks, Vicki. *Cruel Poetry*. London: Serpent's Tail, 2007.
    _____. *Iguana Love*. New York: St. Martin's Press, 1999; also published in Germany.
    _____. *Miami Purity*. New York: Pantheon, 1995; also published in the U.K., France, Italy, Germany, Holland, Japan, Korea, Israel.

____. *Miami Purity*, new edition, with a foreword by Ken Bruen and an afterword by Megan Abbott. Houston: Busted Flush Press, 2007.
____. *Sky Blues*. New York: St. Martin's Press, 2002, also published in France.
____. *Voluntary Madness*. London: Serpent's Tail, 2000.

Selected Short Stories

____. "Boozanne, Lemme Be." *Miami Noir*. Ed. Les Standiford. New York: Akashic Books, 2006.
____. "Gators." *Flesh and Blood*. Ed. Max Allen Collins and Jeff Gelb. New York: Warner Books, 2001.
____. "Must Bite." *Dying for It: Tales of Sex and Death*. Ed. Mitzi Szereto. New York: Thunder's Mouth Press, 2006.
____. "Purrz, Baby." *Deadly Housewives*. Ed. Christine Matthews. New York: Avon, 2006.
____. "ReBecca." *Best American Erotica 2000*. Ed. Susie Bright. New York: Simon and Schuster, 2000.
____ "Stormy, Mon Amour." *Tart Noir*. Ed. Stella Duffy and Lauren Henderson. New York: Berkeley Prime Crime, 2002.
____. "West End." *Murder for Revenge*. Ed. Otto Penzler. New York: Delacorte, 1998.

Chapter

____. *Naked Came the Manatee*, Chapter 10: "Dance of the Manatee." New York: Putnam, 1996.

Stuart Kaminsky, Midwestern-Florida Crime Master

by Cal Branche

Stuart M. Kaminsky is the author of fifty-one published novels, five biographies, four textbooks and thirty-five short stories. He also has screenwriting credits on four produced films, including *Once Upon a Time in America, Enemy Territory, A Woman in the Wind,* and *Hidden Fears.* He is a past president of the Mystery Writers of America and has been nominated for six Edgar Allan Poe Awards including one for his short story "Snow" in 1999. He won an Edgar for his novel *A Cold Red Sunrise,* which was also awarded the Prix du Roman d'Aventure of France. He has been nominated for both a Shamus Award and a Macavity Readers' Choice Award. Kaminsky writes several popular series including those featuring Lew Fonesca, Abraham Lieberman, Inspector Porfiry Petrovich Rostnikov, and Toby Peters. He has also written two original Rockford Files novels.

His nonfiction books include *Basic Filmmaking, Writing for Television, American Film Genres,* and biographies of Gary Cooper, Clint Eastwood, John Huston and Don Siegel. Kaminsky holds a B.S. in journalism and an M.A. in English from the University of Illinois and a Ph.D. in speech from Northwestern University, where he taught for sixteen years before becoming a professor at Florida State, where he headed the Graduate Conservatory in Film and Television Production. He left Florida State in 1994 to pursue full-time writing. Stuart Kaminsky has written two novels set in Sarasota; these are the first two installments in the Lew Fonesca series. He brings to this series a rich background which has featured series characters set in very different times and locales, from Moscow in current times, to Hollywood in the '30s and '40s, to contemporary Chicago.

CAL BRANCHE: Among the Florida authors in this book you are, perhaps, the most prolific: Lew Fonesca, Inspector Rostnikov, Toby Peters, Abe Liberman, and Rockford, to say nothing about your film publications. All are very popular and you continue to be successful with each new book. Why so many series characters? Did you set out to have this many, or was it an accident of writing, that you were interested in different locales and time periods, and the characters were created for each?

STUART KAMINSKY: I did not set out to write as many series as I do. I started with Toby Peters. My plan was to do Toby and non-series books. Simply couldn't make enough money doing this. Rostnikov came after I had done extensive research on what I thought would be an epic multi-generation stand-alone novel. Not a mystery. I did the outline and wrote one hundred pages. My agent couldn't sell it. No American had, at that time, written a mystery set in the Soviet Union. I suggested that I might try it. I did not anticipate a series, but that's what happened. By the way, Martin Cruz Smith's *Gorky Park* came out a few months before my first Rostnikov (which was a paperback original). We were obviously writing our books at the same time.

Lieberman was a character in my stand-alone novel *When the Dark Man Calls*. By this time I was looking for a series set in Chicago, where I lived. I tried a novel about a young Mexican-American private eye in Chicago who does most of his work for his extended and demanding family. I had a contract, started the book, and found that I couldn't get the voice right. I asked my publisher if I could switch and do a police novel using Lieberman as the central character. Rockford came about because the producers of the series and the publisher wanted a series of novels featuring Jim Rockford. They knew I was a fan and came to me. I did two books, loved doing them, and that is probably the end of Rockford novels.

Lew Fonesca came at first in a series of short stories published in various magazines. I was, by this time, living in Sarasota. I did not intend to do a series of novels. However, one of the short stories, "Find Miriam," began to win awards and was nominated for an Edgar. The same year another Fonesca story was nominated for an Edgar. Thus, two of the five nominations that year were not only my stories but my Lew Fonesca stories. Publisher interest soon followed, as did a contract and a series. I plan no new series characters, but one never knows.

Do you juggle different manuscripts at the same time, or finish one, and then take up another?

I always finish one before I start the next, though I start thinking about the next one long before I start writing.

Since you do not live in some of the geographical areas you are writing about, how do you prepare? Is it enough to know landmarks and some history, or must there be more personal involvement?

Well, I do live in the geographical area I write about in my Lew Fonesca novels set in Sarasota. I did, for most of my life, live in Chicago, where Abe Lieberman and Bill Hanrahan work and live. I have spent a great deal of time in Los Angeles, where Toby Peters and Jim Rockford reside and try to make a living. I have spent less than two weeks in Rostnikov's Russia. My research for Sarasota is done by getting in my car, reading the newspaper, talking to people. For my Chicago books, I refresh my memory of places by making visits and staying in touch with people—family, cops, criminals. Moscow is all research and Los Angeles is mostly research, memory and imagination. For me it is important to see, at least in my imagination, the specific locales about which I write. For me, the places are not vague. They are tangible. I know what can be seen from a particular spot. I know what kind of floor or street my characters are standing on. I know the weather. All places are different and each place interacts with my characters. Place affects how a character will think and behave.

Why choose Sarasota as a setting for the Fonesca series?

Simply put, I live here. After living in Florida for thirteen years, I've developed a perspective on the state in general, the west coast of the state more specifically and, even more specifically, on the greater Sarasota area. I didn't feel comfortable even venturing into my first short story set in Florida till I had lived here five years. The prologue to *Retribution* indicates clearly (or maybe not) why I am fascinated by Florida and my part of it. Florida is a state of contrasts.

Florida is a state of contradictions. Florida is a state of mind.

For the mystery writer, that state of mind includes sandy coastlines; red tides; hurricanes; inland swamps; the wealthy Keys; Canadian and European tourists; retired elderly; natives in pickups who are often unkindly called rednecks; hustling stereotypical politicians; the crowded, automatic, massive theme parks of Orlando; the colossal noise and size of the Daytona Speedway; the now–Hispanic city of Miami; gators (both real and those who play football in Gainesville); spring training; land speculation; boat people. The list goes on.

Retirees, tourists, writers and speculators flock to Florida, but so too do drug smugglers, child abusers and teen gangs who rob and kill each other and tourists. Ted Bundy made his way here. The most famous female serial killer, Aileen Wuornos, made her way here.

Florida is ripe for the mystery: the promise of Paradise, the reality of broken dreams. The contrast between Paradise and consequences is fertile material for the mystery writer. The shark, the jellyfish, the alligator, the drug dealer shooting wildly, the kid with a knife and no conscience, the old man driven mad by broken dreams. They're all out there and they're very real. I like it here. In Sarasota I'm comfortable. I find the city and county endlessly fascinating.

Readers of this book on Florida mystery writers should come away with a good knowledge of contemporary writers in the Sunshine State. You know most, if not all, of the writers. Care to hazard a guess on some themes common to each? What should readers expect in books such as this one?

Tough question. I'd say Florida mystery writers tend to have the following in common:

1. A sense of the unexpected, the quirky in human behavior. There is a zaniness to living in Florida that comes through in mystery fiction and attracts writers to the genre.

2. Florida mystery writers tend to deal with protagonists who live on the fringe, usually because that is what they want to do. They are marginal.

3. There is often a sense in Florida mysteries that time does not pass, one day is like the others, there are no seasons. Heat permeates the tales, heat and water. The weather seems to be of particular interest to us, as it is to most people who come here.

4. Florida mystery writers tend to like to visit not the bright orange tourist world of theme parks, beaches, resorts, etc., but the dark underbelly of violence, corruption and downright evil that lies beneath. I don't think most of us write mysteries that would make people want to move to Florida.

I'm sure there is more.

What is distinctive about Florida as a state which makes it fertile ground to serve as a setting for mysteries?

It is a cultural, political, historical mess. It is constantly growing in confusion. I love it. My character Lew Fonesca was headed for Key West when his car dropped dead in Sarasota. Lots of people are heading for the furthest southern end of the United States and finding themselves elsewhere.

Given the variety of your books and series characters you must do a lot of research. How do you make sure your characters and settings ring true to the time?

I do the research which gives me a sense of the place and time and then I plunge my characters into the world my research has revealed. Imagination, however, not research, is the thing that makes the character live. I see them, hear them in the places I have done the research about. I want to know what their lives—day-to-day—are like in that time and place, and then I just let it happen.

In the conclusion to Doctor Zhivago *two generals are sitting on a balcony, looking down on Moscow streets. They talk about Moscow as the protagonist in the story. Given your sense of place could any of your settings serve as the protagonist? (Perhaps the setting is always an implicit protagonist?) You have talked about "plunging" your character into the place you have created after completing research, but each of those places—Moscow, Chicago, Los Angeles, and Sarasota—have uniqueness, I think, as settings for a mystery-crime-detective novel. Any thoughts on this premise?*

I do think that each place I write about—Chicago, Moscow, Los Angeles, Sarasota, and the imaginary town of Little Man Flats—has its own identity, flavor, personality, and I like traveling from one to the other and letting my story, characters play out the portion of time I spend with in each book in the city or town which has that identity.

After reading a few thousand mysteries, and teaching about some of those for several years, I know that "place" is very important to me, and to readers with whom I have discussed this subject. We lived in England for a year, and have visited many other times—so when I begin a Reginald Hill, P.D. James, Ruth Rendell, Jonathan Gash, or Colin Dexter novel, for example, I am also reading to remember the sounds and feel of England. Always in the background is the history of place, both locally, and as a country.

For me, good writers do more than mention some place names, they imbue their stories with that special sense of "place," and you have managed to do this in your stories on a consistent basis.

Yes, I too want the locales of my tales to be tangible to my readers as they are to me. When I write of a street, a park, a store, I see them, smell them, hear them and I want the reader to do the same.

The Toby Peters and Lew Fonesca books contain characters not unlike those Steinbeck created in books such as Cannery Row. *Fonesca and Peters are not complete loners such as Sam Spade, for example. There is a sense of family in the Fonesca and*

Peters books. Is this a conscious decision on our part to "people" these series with a type of family?

Yes, I am very much aware of the importance of family—direct relatives, extended family—in my work. Actually, it becomes more and more important as I keep writing. My characters may start out as loners (Lew), but they soon find themselves in close relationships which are definitely familial. Thanks for noticing.

I remember a blurb on the back of a John O'Hara novel that suggested that future historians of mid-twentieth century America would do well to read O'Hara for an understanding of time and place, and how people talked.

For example, in one part of the United States you would refer to a "fifty-cent piece," whereas somewhere else it would be a "half-dollar." It is often said that good writers have a good ear, and that seems to be the case with you.

I happen to like O'Hara very much. He is, unfortunately, an almost forgotten novelist and short story writer. William Saroyan is another almost forgotten writer who I like very much. Both are very much in tune with time and place, diction and vocabulary. Whatever ear I have for authenticity I had even before I started my Ph.D. work. I hope it continues to develop with each thing I write.

I believe you know John Cawelti and you probably have read Northrup Frye; their writings on the "hero" have affected me quite a bit as teacher and reader. I wonder if you could discuss your protagonists in terms of your understanding of the "hero"? I am particularly interested in how you think each protagonist views himself.

I'm very familiar with Northrup Frye and he was, indeed, a great influence on my academic writing and, far less consciously, on my fiction. John Cawelti was and is extremely influential. John and I have been friends for about 30 years. One of the running characters in my Toby Peters novel is named for John. I saw John and his wife in New Orleans in April of 2003, where I was given an award by the American Culture/Popular Culture Associations for my contributions to scholarship in those two fields. I am sure John was instrumental in getting me named for this honor. By the way, the book by John that most influenced me was *The Six-Gun Mystique*.

Does Toby Peters think of himself as being a hero, for example?

Definitely not. Toby doesn't think of himself in the slightest abstract way. Life is a day-to-day adventure for him. When a job comes along, he does it in the hope that he will enjoy it and be reasonably paid. He definitely gets a rush out of danger and satisfaction out of seeing a job through to the end. He'll risk his life to get the job done, but he doesn't see this as heroic. Determination is his primary vocational virtue and he while he takes pride in it, he certainly doesn't consider it heroic. As for the other characters, Abe Lieberman and Bill Hanrahan certainly don't see themselves as heroic. They are working cops doing their jobs. They go beyond the limits of what is required of them because they both have a strong sense of right and wrong, but they do not consider the actions required to "do the right thing" as heroic. Porfiry Petrovich Rostnikov views the human condition essentially as a sad one. He gets caught up in the humanity of each case assigned to him and sees himself as one who tries to restore the very delicate balance of Russian life when a crime occurs. He is more concerned about surviving than about being heroic.

Lew Fonesca not only doesn't see himself as heroic, he would like to turn his back on any attempt that would result in his committing an heroic act. He reluctantly helps people in trouble because he identifies with them. He is a man in trouble fighting his demons and memories, his nearly clinic[al] depression. He simply wants to give peace to those who come to him for help. He does not view this as heroic. Jim Rockford probably does view himself as heroic, but while I wrote two Rockford novels and love the character, I did not create Jim.

I think my protagonists can all be viewed as heroic archetypes by the reader but never by themselves. I think that many protagonists in mystery fiction do view themselves as heroes. Holmes, Poirot, Marlowe, Archer, the Continental Op, Spenser, V.I. Warshawski, etc., clearly, at least to me, consider themselves heroic. My characters tend not to have a terribly high opinion of themselves and their motives. They don't look like heroes. They don't talk like heroes. They don't think like heroes. But they do act like them in spite of themselves.

I wonder what it would be like to be a fly on the wall if each of your protagonists were having a drink at a bar and sharing their world views.

Now that is a tough one, but I'll give it a shot. Toby: "I don't think much about the world beyond the people I deal with day-to-day, beyond the immediate job. I like to keep moving, acting, not thinking much, enjoying myself though what I enjoy might not be what other people would enjoy. I like the thrill of danger. It makes me feel alive. I think the world is a quirky place and people are all a little off base. Every day is a new adventure. Is there a

God? I don't know. Don't think about it." Rostnikov: "People are born into a sad world and strive to survive and derive some satisfaction from their work, their families, their jobs. People are frightened, desperate, afraid of the unknown. Is there a God? If there is, he or she is definitely Russian and not terribly happy. He probably weeps a great deal." Abe: "People live as if they are swimming upstream and not knowing what will be at the end the journey. People are afraid and try to hide it but the masks they wear are fragile and behind each mask of confidence, anger, humility is the face of a frightened human being who will do what he or she can to preserve the fragile box of life in which they live. Is there a God? Yes. The irony which surrounds us couldn't be simply a matter of chance. Is God ever wrong? All the time. Am I willing to tell Him? Yes, and to do other than what He wants if I think it is the right thing. I'll argue it out with whatever God may be when I have to face Him." Lew: "The world is chaos. There's no foundation. If you step out the door one morning and there's no world out there, don't be surprised. We cling to each other because we're afraid but then we lose each other. Maybe the best we can do is hold someone's hand who's in pain and tell that person, 'I know what you're feeling.' We've all been there. I'm there right now."

I have asked many mystery writers the following question, and would like your response as well. As you are writing are you conscious of your reader? And as a follow-up: Do you write for yourself, or is it a combination of merging the creative self with a desire to please the reader? Some writers have noted the compulsion to write, a need to tell a story. Nicolas Freeling once said that to me in a letter. He said that need must be satisfied.

I write primarily for myself though I am aware of the reader. Therefore, things that may make perfect sense to me often set a small bell ringing which signals to me that I should be sure that I am giving the reader what I am getting for myself. I agree with Freeling. I have a compulsion to tell stories. I would write them even if no one were there to listen. I write to amuse, mystify, frighten and intrigue myself. The stories are there crying to be released so I will have these sensations and satisfactions. Of course I hope my readers feel the same way.

What are your work habits? And what do you suggest as preparation for those who are preparing to write?

I work mornings if I can. My goal is at least ten pages a day. If I have nothing scheduled in the afternoon and the writing is going particularly well I'll write until late afternoon. If I'm on a deadline, I'll write for eight hours or more. I suggest that those who are preparing to write stop preparing and start writing. Trust the voice within you that wants to speak, wants to tell a story. Listen to that voice and write down what it is saying. If you don't hear that voice, you are probably not a writer.

Does a good writer read other writers? If so, why? And do you have any favorites?

I don't know what all other writers do, the good and the bad. The writers I know read a great deal. I read other writers. I advise students and those who attend my workshops to read. How can you know what is new if you don't know what has gone before? How can you write in a particular genre if you don't love the genre? Reading is both fun and an act of learning. I learned to write from reading, not textbooks on writing, but novels and short stories. I have lots of favorites, people whose novels I read as soon as they come out. I'm reading Larry Block's *Small Town* now. I regularly read James Lee Burke, Joyce Carol Oates, Donald Westlake, Larry Block, Dean Koontz, Joe Wambaugh, Michael Connelly, Jonathan Kellerman, Faye Kellerman, John Lutz, Bill Pronzini, Tony Hillerman, Ann Rule, Lisa Scottoline. This list could go on into near infinity.

Does mystery fiction have any formulaic models one might use?

Yes, there are models, conventions for various subgenres within the broad spectrum of the mystery. The conventions exist because readers, including me, have come to expect them, find them satisfying and meaningful. One can create quite comfortably within these conventions or one can violate or tinker with them. For example, conventionally private eye novels have been written in the first person; police procedurals have been in the third person; locked-room mysteries are in the third person. There are many successful exceptions to this and other conventions. One more convention: Private eye tales usually withhold the identity of the perp until the climax of the tale. In police procedurals, we usually know who the perp is early in the tale. Classical tales involving a superior detective—Holmes, Poirot, Dupin—are dependent upon the superior intellect surprising us with his or her revelation of the criminal. In classical tales, a small, familiar society substructure is restored and the world is ready to move on. In private eye novels, the assumption is that the world is too dark and deep to restore. What the detective does is try to rescue someone from the depths. The police tale, on the other hand (I guess that it would make it the third hand), involves cops who are neither trying to save someone [n]or restore an ordered world, but to keep the ever-growing jungle of crime from completely taking over. The cop's victories are measured by how well he or she can endlessly hold back the night.

Sometimes it seems as if current writers allow research and what they have learned therein to overwhelm the story. How do you suggest keeping plot, character, scene, and theme balanced?

As far as I am concerned, all fiction is grounded on character. Research exists to create an interesting milieu in which living, breathing creations of the author can act. Research builds the stage on which the actors come to life. As far as keeping the elements balanced that you list in your question, character is foremost. Plot exists so they can act in a way I, and I hope my readers, find interesting. Scenes are the blocks of time-space in which my story is told. Those I can outline before I begin and play with as my characters come to life. I don't think about them. I am a story teller. I believe whatever meaning my stories have come[s] from within me and will emerge if I have interesting characters in interesting situations.

Do good writers make good readers, and possibly vice versa?

In my experience, good writers make very good readers. Good readers, unfortunately, do not automatically make good writers. Imagination, talent, determination define who is and who is not a writer.

Why do you think mysteries have become mainstream in the past twenty-five years, when before there were many who turned up their noses at such "writing"?

I still run into those who proudly announce, perhaps with a slight or more than slight tone of condescension, that they "don't read mysteries." However, your basic question is a good one and mysteries have become more mainstream for the following reasons:

    1. Readers of mysteries have always been among the best educated and brightest readers, readers who read them for pleasure and ignored "best-sellers" because they found the latter dull, pretentious or not well written. These bright readers began coming out of the closet more than a quarter of a century ago and declaring that not only were mysteries fun to read, they were, on average, better written than what was considered mainstream fiction. I like to be identified as a mystery writer. It separates me from the often third-rate best-sellers and mainstream books which hold no interest for me.

    2. More and better writers have embraced and entered the genre because they like writing mysteries and like the rewards of doing so. I truly

believe the quality of writing of "mainstream" mysteries, especially those identified as best-sellers and even mid-list, is far better on average than mainstream fiction. I think Danielle Steel and Belva Plain and their ilk are capable mainstream writers but they don't compare in simple quality of story, meaning, writing to James Lee Burke, Joyce Carol Oates, Jonathan Kellerman, Tony Hillerman, Larry Block, Don Westlake, Elmore Leonard—the list goes on and on.

3. People always read and bought mysteries, but the acceptance of the quality of mysteries by readers, critics and reviewers gave those who determine such things no real choice than to accept the simple fact that people love mysteries, especially well-written ones.

4. A small part of the breakthrough, but a significant one, came when highly educated people began to write mysteries. It was hard to ignore the credentials of all those lawyers, physicians, psychologists, and people with Ph.D.s in everything from biology to English Literature who were writing about what they knew best.

5. The academic community—at least significant parts of it—began, about 25 years ago, to take mystery writing seriously as a subject for academic attention as literature and cultural phenomenon. It became okay for college students to read, study, enjoy and talk about mystery fiction. It became acceptable for them to write in the genre.

6. Oddly, too, there have been a great many brilliant mainstream novels that simply failed to gain an audience. There was nothing the public could grasp that told them what they were going to read for their twenty-five dollars or more. Romances, mysteries, science fiction gave the reader a sense of the world they were going to enter and those genres began more and more to deal with issues not only in the headlines but in moral, political and philosophical discussions.

How do you work? Outline, no outline?

Outline, usually about twelve pages double spaced, fourteen point (Courier New). I think about the outline while I am finishing another book. Then I write the outline. When I actually do the first draft I use each paragraph of the outline as a chapter. However, if I get a better idea than the one I had in the outline, I revise the outline. I usually revise the outline more as I get closer to the end of the book.

Publishers and reviewers invariably categorize mystery/detective/crime fiction as a genre. Are those qualifications—"mystery" or "detective" or "crime"—limiting?

No, I don't think they are limiting. This is a very popular genre—in its broadest definition—and it provides a framework of history of the literary form (mystery in its various incarnations). One might say they are limiting if the goal of the writer is to achieve literary consideration from scholars, but even that is no longer a real consideration. The holdouts against mysteries as a viable, serious (and, God help us, fun) literary genre are dwindling in number, for which I am profoundly pleased.

What do you see as the difference between crime novels, detective novels, and mystery novels?

I have an answer. It is too long. These are not parallel concepts for definition. If by "mystery," you mean whodunit, then most of the others, but not all, fit within it. If by "crime" you mean a novel in which a crime occurs (usually murder), then detective fiction—hell, almost all fiction—is crime fiction. If you want subdefinitions within the broadest scope of mystery, then each subgenre—hard-boiled, cozy, locked-room, great detective, cop tales—has its own definitions, or rather, its own conventions.

How do you work? Is writing fun or is it a job?

Writing is both a job and fun. I think that's what jobs should be if we are lucky.

How much attention do you pay to character and how much to plot?

I don't draw a distinction between character, plot, story, dialogue when I am writing. They are all important, all require attention. As a reader, however, I think character is most important.

If you weren't writing mysteries, would you still be a writer?

Probably. I'd write more horror or I would go back to being a journalist. I always enjoyed that.

What else would you be?

A basketball, softball or soccer coach.

How do you develop your stories and/or story elements? Where do they come from?

From snatches of conversation, the news, books I read (both fiction and nonfiction), things that happen to me or I observe.

Please talk about your work in other genres, nonfiction or film. What kind of carryover is there? Is that work more or less satisfying to you?

I don't make distinctions. I just write. Yes, there is carryover. Writing screenplays and television episodes affects my novel and short story writing and vice versa. Writing for television is very satisfying because it pays so well.

Can you think of any metaphors in your work, especially those you have written deliberately? Sometimes writers are not aware of some things they have written. Later interpretation may reveal a writer's unconscious thoughts along these lines. Then again, some can read too much into a story.

Off the top of my head I can't think of any metaphors in my work but I do put them in and am conscious about doing so. I agree fully with Steve Glassman's comment that sometimes writers are not aware of some of the things they have written. I think it works best that way. As far as later interpretations revealing a writer's unconscious thoughts, I think interpretations are just that, interpretations, one person's interpretation of meaning, not necessarily what the writer's unconscious thoughts were. As far as people reading too much into a story, I agree that it happens far too often. Stories work at a mythical level. There's nothing wrong with analyzing those myths and how they play out in a particular story, but it is certainly not essential to appreciating the story.

Given all that you have written and experienced over the years, what in your writing reflects your overall view of mankind? Put in another way, I am asking how you feel about the condition of mankind. Freeling's last mystery reflected his life-long attitude that crimes against children were the most horrendous of all human criminal acts. How is your philosophy reflected in your writing?

In some ways, this is a tough question. I certainly do not intentionally infuse my work—novels, movies, short stories and so on—with a moral or philosophical view of life. However, I recognize that since I am doing the writing, what I believe must surely be in those pages or on that screen. With this in mind, I submit the following: I believe that life is ultimately a tragedy which can be endured and even savored by people who behave with compassion toward others, who have empathy for others, who have a determination and a sense of wit. I have never forgotten Faulkner's description of Delsey in *The Sound and the Fury*. He simply said, "She endures." To endure with dignity and invest oneself with true affection for others is what we can do to create a meaningful life for ourselves on earth. I, and my central characters, find joy and take solace in small pleasures. Evil exists. It comes from selfishness, madness and fear. Those who perpetrate evil should be identified by those of us who endure with passion. They should be identified and isolated, separated or eliminated from society. The lesson of the Bible for me is that we never know what fate or God or the gods will do nor why. The Bible teaches us, if we are willing to learn the lesson, that we must be prepared for and accept anything that happens.

The day may come when a lengthy critical work is done on your writing. What would you like to be found?

I would like the author to find something that resembles reasonable interpretations of which I may or may not have been conscious. I don't want the author to find what he or she wants to believe is there because they are projecting or because they have a pre-formed idea of what I tried to do.

Bibliography

Kaminsky, Stuart. *Always Say Goodbye.* New York: Forge Books, 2006.
____. *Denial.* New York: Forge Books, 2005.
____. *Midnight Pass.* New York: Forge Books, 2003.
____. *Retribution.* New York: Forge Books, 2002.
____. *Vengeance.* New York: Forge Books, 2000.

Jonathon King, Edgar-Winning Mystery Novelist

by Cal Branche

Jonathon King exploded onto the Florida mystery scene with his first book. Since then he has shown his literary promise to be one realized with each new book. Jon is a former journalist and author of three critically acclaimed, award-winning novels. His debut, *The Blue Edge of Midnight*, won the Edgar Award for Best First Novel and was a Los Angeles Times best-seller.

With his first novel, *Publishers Weekly* said: "King jumps into James W. Hall territory and lands firmly on his feet. The author's stylish prose and insider's knowledge of the sinuous, dangerous Everglades give a fresh twist. King uses descriptions of places and environment to reveal character and attitude, much as Hall, James Lee Burke, and Robert B. Parker do. Skillful writing, original characters and evocative settings initiate a welcome new series."

Jon was a journalist for over twenty years. He covered crime and then became an award-winning news feature writer for the *Florida Sun-Sentinel*. In 2004 he gave up journalism to write fiction full-time. He is married with two children and lives in Florida.

CAL BRANCHE: *Why do you set your works in Florida?*

JONATHON KING: I've lived in South Florida for the last 20 years. I was married here. My children were born here. Most importantly, I was a newspaper reporter here for those two decades so it is a landscape, both urban and wild, that I know best.

From my days as a cop and courts reporter I know the city streets. I've stood under a metal roof with a group of cops on New Year's Eve and listened as the roughest neighborhoods explode with gunshots in the air at midnight—and waited out the gravity return. I've been in the back of a patrol car when narcotics agents busted a Colombian midget with a duffle bag of cocaine. I've followed officers into an apartment building when they brought down a marijuana hydroponics operation and been on scene too many times when homicide detectives showed up for yet another killing. Same with the courts. I covered the trial of one of our most notorious human smugglers, who forced his Haitian cargo into the surf, leading to the drowning of two children and adults. I reported on the murder conviction and subsequent release of a 12-year-old who was brought up by her mother to be a crackhead. And I wrote about a family wiped out by a drunk driver on Christmas Eve and then, months later, covered the DUI trial of the surviving father, who went off the deep end after that tragedy.

But as a magazine writer in South Florida I have also spent 48 straight hours on a stone crab trawler on opening day, held a baby bald eagle in my arms while writing a story about the unmanned keys in Florida Bay, taken many memorable night canoeing and kayaking trips in the Everglades and got a personal tour of the whiskey-still encampments from a denizen of the Ten Thousand Islands in Southwest Florida.

Florida and its people are endlessly fascinating to me and their stories are what I use as raw material when writing my books.

Which other Florida writers really "capture" the state?

In no specific order: John D. MacDonald, James W. Hall, Peter Matthiessen, Marjorie Kinnan Rawlings, Carl Hiaasen and Randy Wayne White in fiction. Gary R. Mormino and Jeff Klinkenberg in nonfiction.

Whom do you read, and why? Not just mystery writers, but I hope they are on your list.

James Lee Burke for the luster of his language. Michael Connelly for his engaging and brilliant police plots. Raymond Carver for the poignancy of his short stories. Richard Price for his descriptive urban writing and ability to capture the dark side of the city. Russell Banks for his flawed and truly human characters. Laura Lippman for her insights into character from a woman's point of view, Flannery O'Connor for her dark wit, and the list goes on and on...

How did you get into the business of writing mysteries?

Of all the reading I had done, both fiction and nonfiction, I kept coming back to well-written mysteries. The best of the good ones carried me along and showed me the kinds of places and people that I knew existed through my own newspaper work and spun deeper stories than I could in the confines of a 600-word daily report or even a 3,000-word magazine piece. I yearned to do that kind of writing but was afraid of giving up the paycheck for my family. Then in 1999 I worked twelve months straight. As reward I was given my '99 month of vacation in January and my 2000 vacation in February. For 60 straight days I wrote, all alone, at my in-laws' North Carolina mountain cabin and finished the first draft of The Blue Edge of Midnight. The book was sold in nine months and won the Edgar Award for Best First Novel by an American Author. It don't get much better than that.

What was your preparation for being a writer? And when did you first know you were a novelist?

It's hard to even call myself a novelist out loud. I revered those who were for so long. I think the reading was my first preparation. I am a slow reader, very careful and meticulous. Since I was a teenager when I would read a paragraph in which the language made my heart trip or made me see an unforgettable image behind my eyes, I would stop and reread that passage, study it, roll it around on my tongue. I even rewrote a chapter from Hemingway's *Old Man and the Sea*, copied the words on my own typewriter to actually feel what it was like.

Then, I studied people. On my job, certainly, but also in crowds and public venues and while listening in on conversations. When I first sat down to write a novel in 1982 at the age of 28, I failed after a few paragraphs and said: Novels are about people! And I don't know shit about people yet! After 20 years in the newspaper business, I knew about people.

Were you aware of the history of the form? Has that awareness affected your ideas of plot, character, theme?

Without consciously being aware of it, I believe the form simply soaked into me. When I was a junior in high school we had a reading class for jocks. They put the basketball and football players in a classroom on Friday game days and told us to pick a book out of a box, read it and shut up. I stuck my hand in and came up with *The Deep Blue Good-by*. The next Friday I searched for *A Tan and Sandy Silence*. The following week I paid $1.95 for *A Purple Place for Dying*. When I finished John MacDonald I asked the store clerk for more and he passed me Robert B. Parker, then James Crumley and on and on. Then on my own I went back to the classics of Chandler and Ross Macdonald. Those ideas of plot, character and theme, and more importantly, the rhythm of rising and falling action, seeped into my head. To this day I still feel that rhythm while I am writing my first drafts.

When you began to form your two main characters how did you go about doing it? And why have a character with a stutter? What are the characteristics of your main characters?

Max was my first creation and as I have said he is an amalgamation of several cops, detectives, and literary heroes I've known and admired. His pursuit of truth, however you define it, and justice, if that concept even can be defined, are also borrowed from those folks. He follows a loose mold of crime series protagonists but he is my own. His background in Philly and movement to South Florida flowed from the images of places I know best and have personally witnessed.

Creating Billy as a sidekick was a bit more calculating. I wanted an opposite to Max and someone whose characteristics and strengths would complement his friend. I specifically made him a black man because I liked the juxtaposition of his characteristics—cerebral, educated, wealthy, handsome and successful—against the stereotype.

Billy Manchester also has his beginnings in north Philadelphia, a poor, black and totally different world that I got to know as a police reporter for the *Daily News* and as a student at Temple University, which is an odd anchor to that area of the city. I met kids like Billy when I did a story on a national chess champion team of middle-schoolers who came from this area. They were poor, black kids who went to an inner-city school and they were brilliant. The school had kept this national chess team rating up for several years. I thought it was fascinating then, back in the early 1980s, and kept an image of the kids in the back of my head.

The other influence in the creation of Billy was a well-known black attorney in South Florida who came to wealth and renown through his own brilliance at law. He came from a poor agricultural background in the Glades and rose to prominence. Like Billy, his attorney has a high-rise office in West Palm Beach. Unlike Billy, he is loud and boisterous and a bit of a traveling-fair barker.

Billy is both Freeman's opposite—black, rich, connected to the internal workings of the business and lawyer world—and his psychological brother—raised by mothers of abusive fathers in Philadelphia, quiet and somewhat isolated (Billy in his tower, Max in his shack), and most importantly sharing an ethical outlook that guides them.

I also needed Billy as a conduit to bring Max out of the swamp in future books. Max was not going to find enough adventures in the Glades to sustain a believable series, so I knew when I started the first book that Max would need to become a quasi–P.I. in the future. Who better to work for than Billy?

Billy's background was amazing in that it simply grew out of the writing process. He actually was created at the tip of a pen. The stutter was actually an afterthought. Once I had created this nearly perfect character, I realized Billy had to have a flaw because otherwise he is simply a cartoon. So in a moment of inspiration, I recalled a character that my stepfather told me of years ago: a military subordinate of his who was immensely bright and efficient and capable, but one who could not speak directly into anyone else's face without stuttering. But, as my stepfather related, he could call you on the phone from the other side of the warehouse or even speak from the other side of the wall and speak with perfect diction. I some how plucked this description out of a twenty-year-old memory and gave the stutter to Billy: a perfect flaw for a lawyer in that he could be brilliant but never able to become a trial attorney. Billy had a cross to bear.

Has there been a gradual development of Max Freeman as your protagonist? Any significance to "Free-man"?

"Freeman" was indeed a thought-out character naming. Max is a man running free after a lot of family and police-officer angst. Although some readers have asked me why I selected a Jewish protagonist, they need only to read Max's backstory in the first two books to find out there's nothing Jewish about it. Max is a blend of many different cops and detectives and private investigators I have met as a newspaperman. I don't consider him heroic, or necessarily bright. But he does have this doggedness to his personality in which he grinds away at problems looking for the truth, which we all know is forever elusive.

I would be the first to admit that I used Travis McGee's DNA to begin my Max character. And whereas John D. put Travis alone as a bachelor on the water at the Bahia Mar in Fort Lauderdale, a place where two disparate cultures—boaters and drylanders—came in friction with one another, I put Max on the edge of the Everglades in his lonely cabin where two cultures—urban and outback Glades dwellers—create that rub. But then I layered on a dark past to Max, gave him a legitimate knowledge of police work and gave him some axes to grind. Each book I try to bring him along a bit in his development with the characters he meets, with his love interests past and present, and with his friend, Billy.

How do you prepare for writing? How do you do research? What are your "writing" work habits?

The preparation has changed for me over the years. My first three books were written while I was on vacation alone in a mountain cabin in North Carolina. I had sixty days—a month of regular vacation and a month of unpaid leave. I grocery shopped on my way up the mountain and then did not turn the ignition key for 60 days. I wrote all those first drafts with pencil on legal pad, the idea being that I needed to change my physical style since I was writing fiction, not journalism. For three hours each morning I worked, then took a walk along the cold mountain roads (it was Jan./Feb.), ate lunch and then wrote until I had 1400 words each day. In the evenings I watched college basketball and read nonfiction.

Those habits changed over the years. Most of my fourth novel was written on a laptop in the library across the street from my newspaper office. I'd go there after work and write until the place closed. After that novel I quit my reporting job and now I write at home, sticking with that 1400-words-a-day pace and sticking with that midday break for walking, nowadays along the beach.

As far as research, I do most of it as I go along. As during my journalism career, I'll do fact-checking, read nonfiction books on subjects I'm writing about, and use some Internet sites to make sure I'm as factual as possible. But most of what I write is coming out of my head from my days as a police and court reporter. I also consider my books to be character-driven rather than procedurals. So I'm really just writing about human beings. You research that throughout life.

Publishers and reviewers invariably categorize crime/mystery/detective fiction as a genre. Are those qualifications limiting? Should we distinguish these works from "novels"? How do you classify your work so far?

Man you're pushing my buttons! Categorization is the root of evil. It just breeds prejudice, intolerance, religious persecution. In my opinion, when you categorize you stereotype.

So why do that to anything or anybody? Seems pretty incongruent that a creative endeavor like writing novels—meant to enlighten, entertain, take readers to places they'll never go, introduce them to people they would never see or listen to—should be subject to categorization. James Lee Burke writes prosaic descriptions of nature as well as Cormac McCarthy and better than Theroux. Michael Connelly writes scenes about corrupted governmental systems as well as Robert Penn Warren.

Yeah, yeah, I know the reason for categorization: easier marketing, better chance of getting a browsing reader to find something similar to what he or she already likes, narrowing a "target market" among the book-buying public. But just because that's the reality doesn't mean I like it.

As far as limiting? No. I write what I like to write. No one is asking me to stick to any formula. No one is outlining my stories under "protagonist vs. bad guy, three maximum dead bodies and the good guy gets the girl" dictates. I like to say I'm simply writing stories about people, some psychologically or physically wounded, some searching for truth, some wreaking havoc for reasons even I don't understand, most getting through during extraordinary circumstances. That's human drama. I'm writing in the Human Drama genre! Aisle Nine!

Writers—knowingly or not—reflect personal philosophies in their work. Now that you have spent many years in reporting, and a few solely writing novels, what is your philosophy in terms of crime and punishment and good vs. evil?

Hey! I write Human Dramas! We all hold the same possibilities of human emotion in each of us—love and compassion, fear and hate. I am reminded of a line by John Barth:

"For ages the fault creeps secret through the rock; in a second, ledge and railings, tourists and turbines all thunder over Niagara. Which snowflake triggers the avalanche? A house explodes; a star. In your spouse, so apparently resigned, murder twitches like a fetus."

Good guys can be bad. Crimes can be committed in the name of good. Evil might look just plain tasty to the guy sitting next to you on the subway. On the subject of crime and punishment, I've seen killers go free and innocents go to the slam many times as a reporter. So if I'm writing believable fiction, I'll include all those possibilities, with one exception.

One absolute for me is that any character in my books who commits domestic violence gets it in the neck before the last page. That comes from being raised around that horrific family dynamic and in the world of my novels, the world I create, those guys don't get away with it. They get their asses kicked.

How careful are you in preparing for character change/development?

If I was careful at all it was in not revealing too much about my main characters in the first books of the Max Freeman series so that I would have room for them to grow. I gave some background, but not too much. Same with his friend Billy. I had lots to tell about their childhood, their family members, the cases that they'd worked on, but I was leery of letting too much go all at once, first of all to keep the story tight and on point, but also to hoard other story lines. I also knew I was writing a series so I made certain selections in preparation. The location of Max's stilt shack on the edge of the Everglades was, I think, wonderfully exotic and captures a part of Florida few people know much about. But I also knew that Max was not going to have a dead child float up every few weeks to launch another quest for an unknown killer. I knew in the future he would be sucked into the city for further adventures so I couldn't put him way out in the boonies. I set Billy up with the stutter as we have talked about, but I didn't really challenge him until the fourth book when he has to overcome it to save Max's friend. Max doesn't make love with Det. Sherry Richards in the first book. It just didn't fit his style. But that omission also gave me a wonderful chance to deepen their relationship in the next book. I think that sometimes those preparations are deliberate and sometimes they simply follow in the character's natural development. There are a lot of things I don't know about Max and Billy yet. Discovering them will be my pleasure as well as yours as a reader of the series.

You noted in an earlier answer that you "study people." Many will say this, but what separates you, and authors in general, from the average person who says this?

I think I've learned, from the years of being a reporter, to watch and study people with a particular eye for detail. In my first years I thought the broad descriptive terms would do: He was tall, broad-shouldered, sandy-haired. She was blond,tanned, shorter than the other three women in the group.

Not good enough. Not for a newspaper story or magazine piece. I learned I needed every precious word when I only had 600 to use, or even 3,000. If the descriptive terms didn't help me tell the story, then I had to ditch them. That meant studying more carefully, looking for telling detail. Once I was doing a story on a transplant surgeon and when he stepped out of his office, I walked behind his desk to see the things that were facing him, like photos and such. From that vantage point, I noticed an open pack of cigarettes behind a book. A lung transplant surgeon who smoked! Later we talked about it and he admitted the habit and went on to discuss the tremendous stress involved in standing for hours over a patient doing such delicate work. I used it.

I watched a Cuban woman one day making café cubano across the room and noted that from the time she first opened the bag of sugar to measure out what she need for the coffee, she would continue to lick her finger and poke it back into bag. Sweet tooth. Could I use that detail somewhere?

Doing a story about the hot weather in South Florida, you've got to include the sheen of sweat you noticed in the hairline of the lady from Buffalo you're quoting. At my favorite pub I watch a guy take his money from a beat-up wallet that is held together with rubber bands and carries an odd odor of rotted leather as it sits on the bar top. Do others note that when they study him? Maybe. But I'm going to use it to describe a character clinging to something in his past, or one whose superstitions guide him.

Another guy sits down next to me to have a beer. For whatever reason I start studying his hands, thickness of fingers, maintenance of nails, quivering of the wrist as he raises the glass. Without much trouble I notice the callous on the outside edge of his thumb. "Bic Thumb" the cops call it down here, from the rub of the small metal wheel of a disposable lighter used over and over again to keep a crack pipe going.

Telling detail is what I think good writers look for when they study people. It's all possible grist for the stories forming in our heads.

And what makes a good, or great storyteller?

I'm going to cheat here and use a line from John Updike, a grand storyteller. I kept this quote prominently displayed on my computer screen for many years as a journalist. "I want stories to startle and engage me within the first few sentences, and in their middle to widen or deepen or sharpen my knowledge of human activity, and to end by giving me a sensation of completed statement."

My only addition to that statement is that I want a great storyteller to take me on a trip and show me what it looks, smells, tastes and bleeds like.

We all know that a given number of people can view the same scene and walk away with different impressions and memories. How has your reporting background trained you to "see" and then translate what you have seen into words?

Again, I think my background as a reporter has trained me to cut down on the clutter and then render in the image on the page only those things that are important to the story. I learned real early from newspaper editing that all that gilded-lily stuff was going to get cut. As writers we're not supposed to be cameras. Once you try to write like that, including everything you can see into a scene or image, the clutter will overwhelm the point.

Can you offer any hints to a future writer who does not have that background similar to yours?

Stories are about people. You don't have to have been a reporter to observe and study and come to know people. The furniture around your characters can be researched and copied and set down in the appropriate places. It's the people you create and what they do in the situations you set up that make the story. Make them love, make them hurt, make them scared shitless or courageous. Make them do both ordinary and extraordinary things. People want to read about other people. It's been that way since we started painting on the cave walls. It's not going to change.

And a follow-up to the above: There are many reporters and lawyers who have turned to writing and made a success of that transition. Does their training give a strong assist to the effort? How do we explain the successful writers who did not have either background? What are the essentials for the writer to have prior to starting to write?

I know some reporters who tried to write fiction and failed miserably at it. I don't know that many lawyers, but I would guess the same. I believe you have to have a sense of story. A sense of beginning, middle and end. Neither one of those professions necessarily gives you that. I think I got that simply from reading, reading novels, soaking up a sense of story from them. When I wrote *The Blue Edge of Midnight*, even during that first crack at this novel thing, I believe I had a sense of when the story was losing rhythm, was starting to sag and needed the action to pick up. I think stories need to have that rhythm. Sometimes I think a better training for writers is in music composition rather than journalism or law.

Question: Readers love to figure out a writer by seeing what he is saying about things. A writer has a mental construct of a character, e.g., you and Max Freeman. At some point a writer may insert his own views into the mental construct of a character. How difficult is it to be aware of that "insertion" process? How do you keep Max's character consistent? How do you prepare the reader so that when Max "thinks" something it is consistent with what we already know?

I would certainly be lying if said that Max and I are not alike. His character comes from my head, even though it is more truthful to call him an amalgamation of several real people I have known in the news and law enforcement business as well as those literary characters I have read over the years. Yes, you heard me, I borrowed some of Travis McGee, some, though very little, of Spenser, some of even Harry Bosch.

One of Max's most intriguing and perhaps most destructive traits is his inability to just forget things and move on. I've called it his propensity to "grind" at the stones in his head. That is a trait I share and is perhaps the most significant mental construct that binds us.

I will also admit that my editor at Dutton, Mitch Hoffman, is often much better at finding places where Max has become inconsistent and points it out to me. I particularly recall a passage in *Shadow Men* when Max confronted a couple of hired guns in an isolated spot in the Glades where he was searching for the burial spot of the lynchpin character of the story. One of the guys mouthed off to Max and Max simply shot him to make his point. During editing Mitch asked: "Would Max actually do that? Shoot an unarmed man because he was pissed?"

No. I had to admit. That was me stepping into his character. I would have shot the son-of-a-bitch for his mouth and defiance. Max wouldn't have. So I changed the passage and had the bad guy actually pull a hidden weapon so when Max fired it was in self-defense.

As far as preparing the reader, I just hope that the simple rules that drive Max are reinforced in each book and what he thinks and does are always driven by those simple rules.

I recently completed reading James Lee Burke's latest Dave Robicheaux. At one point Robicheaux alludes to Shakespeare, but I didn't recall ever knowing that Robicheaux had studied Shakespeare. How did he know about that quote? Do I assume correctly that the writer must be constantly aware of how his character thinks, and how his mind has been conditioned by his experience?

I like the idea of making Max and Billy out to be realistic characters because those are the kinds of books I want to write; tales that could and in a sense do happen.

In my most recent novel, not in the Freeman series, I had a character quote General William Tecumseh Sherman. Now, it wasn't some obscure quote, one that people aren't generally aware of, but I looked it up and had the character speak it in total and exact. My editor once again asked: Would this guy really know a Sherman quote with such perfection? Did we set this up with his education or a military hobby of such reading? So I ended up rewriting the scene and only had the character speaking the part of the quote that most of us know, "war is hell," and paraphrased the rest.

That being said, I would also emphasize: This is fiction, folks. We make shit up. Burke is one of my favorite writers and if he lets Dave quote Shakespeare or see Confederate ghosts out in the cane fields it will not for even a second stop me from enjoying his work and in some cases will enhance that pleasure.

I think we may have talked of this before but given your protagonist's background was there a conscious attempt to place him in the Everglades, not unlike Shakespeare did in A Midsummer Night's Dream: *escaping to the Green World—nature, as it were—to heal?*

Yeah, I did want to transplant Max into an environment that was completely unfamiliar to him. He was trying to leave that which he knew so well and was so familiar with and had become painful to him growing up in the inner city of Philadelphia. As so many of us, he thought by getting away from it all he could leave the past behind. Going into the Green World was his attempt. But I was also calculating enough to put him right at the edge of the Everglades, not so far away that he wouldn't have access to the evils of civilization and not so far that I wouldn't have access to future story lines involving him as a private investigator for Billy.

What is distinctive about Florida writers? And how do you fit in?

What I find distinctive about my favorite Florida writers is their descriptive powers to capture the state as it is, during the time period of their writing. I can still recall a Travis McGee soliloquy of the sunrise bubbling out of the Atlantic and the heat growing in the sand and giggling barefoot girls running at the edge of the surf. When Thorn has tied a fishing fly and wrist-whipping it out onto the surface of Blackwater Sound in the Keys, that description is a delicate Florida music. So too when Doc Ford feels the salt spray in his face as he runs his boat south through the wind-churned water of the Gulf hard against time to get to the docks and trouble. The best Florida writers describe the unique environment of the state in ways that most mystery writers in, say, L.A. or New York or Boston don't because those places don't have our unique landscape. That uniqueness of water, temperature, humidity and humanity soaks into the best Florida writers.

As far as my fit? I think I do the Everglades justice when I write about her. But I have also spent a lot of time on the urban streets of South Florida, in the alleys and projects and cookie-cutter suburbs and the police stations that oversee them. So I believe my fit as a writer is on that edge between urban and Edenic Florida, where Max lives, and where things rub together and cause friction and heat and emotion and stories.

Has the history of Florida influenced you in any way in terms of your writing? What are the main forces shaping Florida today, and what things do you try to address in your books?

I am very much an amateur historian of Florida. I spent much of 1999 researching and writing a month-by-month history of the state for the *Sun-*

Sentinel newspaper where I was working as a general assignment reporter. And if I came to any one overall theory of the state it is that Florida is only 100 years old and that small lifetime has been an all-out sprint to catch up to the rest of the country. In its haste all foibles and corruptions and inherent discriminations and political skullduggery and simply human joys have all been packed into a small space in time.

Florida was a relatively unknown land until the late 1890s when Henry Flagler brought his train to Miami. You could already take a train from New York to California by then. There were streetlights in New York City before there was a single burning bulb in a South Florida household. In 100 short years we went from palm frond roofed huts on Palm Beach Island to twenty-story condos on every ocean and gulf view beach in the state. We went from an appendix surgery in the street outside a Miami livery documented in 1896 to one of the most sophisticated cancer research hospitals in the country only a mile away from that spot. We went from being an unknown, mosquito-infested swampland to the fourth largest state population in the country.

Because of that densely packed history, I believe the people of Florida and their institutions all rub up against each other in a different way than in the rest of the country. And the rubbing creates friction and heat and emotion and those are the basic elements of great stories. Those stories are what I try to duplicate in my books.

The answer to your second question is really an extension of the first. The forces shaping Florida today are the increasing population, the continual blending of cultures, the constant struggle of natural environment versus the seemingly unstoppable development of land. Yet, just as has happened in states much older than ours, I see hope in the maturing of generations of Floridians who can now rightfully call themselves native Floridians, born here and raising their families here and not just visitors who come for the winter and leave. These generations will stay and take care of their home.

How difficult was it to write a novel with a new protagonist, and do you have any plans for additional stand-alone novels? Any unexpected benefits starting out with a new creation?

It wasn't hard. I cheated. The stand-alone, *Eye of Vengeance*, is a novel with a South Florida journalist as the protagonist so in many respects I knew him pretty damned well already. The secondary character of this tale—which is really basically a two-character morality play—is a SWAT officer turned military sniper turned cityscape assassin. The shooter begins targeting bad guys in south Florida who either got away with murder, or in his eyes didn't do enough time for their crime. I wasn't too creative in that all of those crimes and the background of the victims and the perps themselves are fictional recreations of real cases that I covered as a journalist, so my research was basically already in my hands. The plot builds when Nick Mullins, the journalist, recognizes that each bad guy who gets inexplicably assassinated by a sniper's bullet is someone he did an extensive story about. Then the sniper's eye falls on him.

So, even though I had to find a voice for Nick that was different than Max, I think I cheated by giving him a large chunk of my voice. I let Nick take some shots at the ethics of journalists, something that again was not a fictional stretch considering my own background. And I had to give him some heartbreak, which again I drew from recent experience. The part of Nick's character that was difficult to write was the interaction he has with his daughter and the grief and adjustment both she and he are making after the death of family members. I recall Michael Connelly saying once that after his own daughter was born he couldn't bring himself to write of children as victims in his books. I have two kids—ages 13 and 10—and in this book I create strong motivations for Nick that are directly related to a family tragedy that includes the death of one of his children. There were scenes I found hard to create, but I think they made Nick both a sympathetic and a real, emotional character who comes off the page.

The benefit of doing the stand-alone is the challenge I suppose, of starting from a clean slate, giving a new protagonist a whole new world and background and sense of humanity. Yet, I didn't find it any more difficult than when I work to make Max grow and change from book to book with each new chapter of his fictional life.

I do have another stand-alone that I've started that is actually a Florida historical but I need to flesh it out some more on paper before I submit it to a publisher.

Bibliography

King, Jonathan. *Acts of Nature*. New York: Penguin Group, 2007.
____. *The Blue Edge of Midnight*. New York: Penguin Group, 2002.
____. *Eye of Vengeance*. New York: Penguin Group, 2006.
____. *A Killing Night*. New York: Penguin Group, 2005.
____. *Shadow Men*. New York: Penguin Group, 2004.
____. *Visible Darkness*. New York: Penguin Group, 2003.

Christine Kling, Writer of South Florida Nautical Crime

by Dan McGavin

Christine Kling, a graduate of the Florida International University's program for creative writing with an M.F.A. in creative writing, has written four novels, all about the people and waterways of South Florida. Each novel is centered around Fort Lauderdale. Her novels, *Surface Tension*, *Cross Current*, *Bitter End*, and *Wreckers' Key*, introduce us to the characters of Seychelle, a determined young woman who is making on her own way in the world by owning and operating a salvage boat business. We become acquainted with her two brothers, her family's past (including her deceased father and mother), BJ, a unique love interest, and Jeannie, her fearless but motherly lawyer, among others. As Seychelle encounters murder, kidnapping, and an assortment of other criminal activity, she is compelled to sometimes desperate action based on her compassion and determination. Interestingly, even Christine Kling's main characters change over time and take on a three-dimensional life as the series of novels moves along. This recent and expanding series adds significantly to the literature of crime and especially the crime literature of South Florida.

DAN MCGAVIN: *Why Florida?*

CHRISTINE KLING: I became a crime writer here in Florida, but that is not to say that I think it is the only or best place to set a crime novel. I grew up in Southern California, in Orange County, and I did grow up reading and loving mysteries. However, I first really decided I wanted to write after reading Hemingway. I thought that to be a writer, you had to visit exotic wonderful places—like Hemingway's Paris—and I took off at age 17 to spend a year in Paris. It never occurred to me that I could write wonderful books set in my hometown. T. Jefferson Parker proved me wrong. But there is something about being an outsider that makes me appreciate Florida in ways that others don't.

Can you elaborate on this last thought a little? What is it that an outsider brings to an environment that insiders might not see?

Outsiders see and appreciate small details about the environment that locals just take for granted without realizing how unique they are to the area. For example, down here on a winter morning right after a cold front, you'll awake to see steam rising off the New River or the Intracoastal. Locals sometimes won't realize how fascinating that is because it just is a part of the world they've always known. Yet, when I include that in a story, a person who has lived here will have this feeling of recognition of the truth of it, and the reader from outside Florida will see it as a unique detail about life here. Likewise, I really enjoy reading outsider writers like Michael Connelly and Robert Crais who pick out details about Southern California that had always just blurred into the background static for me as a local Californian.

What makes Florida uniquely suited to your work?

I have always liked the quirky, gritty, unique when it comes to setting. When I arrived in Florida in 1984, I had seen my home in SoCal turn the orange groves into strip malls and suburban housing developments. I call it the franchization of America. Florida still had Hollywood Beach with the grimy little gyro places and roadside stands that sold twenty kinds of citrus marmalade and chocolate alligators. Fort Lauderdale had the Jungle Queen taking visitors up to a "jungle compound" to watch Indians wrestling alligators and sailing down river doing sing-alongs of old American favorites. In California, most marinas were big, classy, clean places with floating docks owned by the county or state tucked in behind breakwaters. There are almost no navigable rivers or canals in Southern California. Florida, however, has hundreds of miles of waterways with fabulous little marinas and hideaways. The first Florida marina where we lived aboard for six years was along the waterway down in Hollywood and it was owned by a character who frequently had afternoon visits from Mafioso types in limos with bodyguard drivers. He was missing his thumbs on both hands and frequently unmarked cars would park across the street and watch our comings and goings for days. Then, for a couple of months Gene Hackman tied his boat up next to ours and we'd exchange "good mornings" over coffee. The juxtaposition of the big marinas here with their million-dollar megayachts and the tiny little backwaters populated by fishermen, con men, airboaters and frog giggers makes for a rich environment for crime.

I really like the way you expose hidden Fort Lauderdale and hidden South Florida as the stories proceed. While many of us may know about the Haitian boat people and the dangers they face to get to the States, many do not know much about the specifics of the dangers they face, nor do they know much about the religion or culture. You gradually expose all of that as each story continues. Can you comment on that feature of your writing?

When I decided to write about the water and South Florida, it was at the tail end of the *Miami Vice* era. I told myself I didn't ever want to write about a drug smuggler as the central character because that had become such a cliché about the Florida crime scene. When you listen to the VHF radio here, and when you live down on the beach, you tend to be much more aware of the number of people who are smuggled in here. On January 1, 2000, I went down to Hallandale Beach, just south of Hollywood, Florida, at sunrise to toast the new millennium with a friend. We came upon a wooden boat in the surf line filled with the trash of people who had carried food and water for their voyage. In the middle of the boat was a compass covered in barnacles that had been salvaged from a wreck. There were literally footprints going up the sand away from the boat. That is the boat I later described in the opening chapter of my second novel, *Cross Current*. Smuggling human cargo is much more interesting than smuggling drugs to me. And then when it comes to boat people, Cubans are the Florida cliché, so I decided to write about the forgotten boat people. I had already made my decision to write about Haitians based on the "what if" postulation, "What if Elian had been Haitian?" That question got me thinking and researching all things Haitian. When I discovered the facts about restaveks, that changed the direction of the book.

Are there other personal incidents that get translated into your writing or those that changed the direction of a novel?

Almost everything that I write about is based on personal incidents. I think a good metaphor for the writer's imagination is a blender. Our stories are like smoothies and the ingredients are personal incidents, news stories, and other books we've read. It all gets whirled around in there and comes out in a different form. My state of mind has really impacted the direction of my fourth book. I wrote my first three books while working as a teacher and later as a coordinator for magnet programs at the school-district office. I had come to really hate my job—I felt that people at the district were completely out of touch with the reality of the classroom. I wanted to quit and write full-time. So, in my latest book, Seychelle is disgusted with her job, with the way things are changing in the world of towing and salvage. Everybody has jumped into the business and there is not enough business to go around. Guys who care more about profit than people are tainting the salvage business, making them all look like crooks. She has always painted—like her mother—and she now wants to quit the marine business and become a full-time artist. Will she quit? I won't know until I finish the book, but I can say that while I have been on a year's leave of absence and teaching only part-time, I am looking for a full-time job for next year.

The geography of your stories takes place on the waterways of Fort Lauderdale and the surrounding area, as well as a variety of land locations, for example, the Haitian neighborhood in Pompano, one of the "new" mansions that line the waterways, the Downtowner, etc. Many readers in Florida who are not associated with the waterways or have not seen the mansions from the perspective of the water might see their own home town or area from a completely new perspective. You expose that which is hidden in plain sight. Are you aware of this unique point of view that you bring to your readers?

I am aware that Fort Lauderdale is a different place when seen from the water. When I first arrived here over 20 years ago, my husband had a truck to go to work, and I had a dinghy for my transportation. I got to know this place by water first. I like the idea of giving readers a different perspective, and not only in terms of the physical geography, but also the social geography. Florida is unique in that there are totally different sorts of neighborhoods that abut one another. You can easily have million-dollar homes on one side of the street and public housing on the other. You can go from a commercial business district into a miniature little Haiti. Rather than being big neighborhoods like you might find in California, here, the geography is made up of pockets of like homes. And then twisting throughout it all is a river or a canal and any homes fronting that water are automatically in another category in terms of price and status. The only place that isn't true is where the North Fork of the New River goes through the poorer parts of northwest Lauderdale and that only goes to show that there are no rules when it comes to housing here.

You seem to know about Florida history and expose that in places. Did you know your history from early on, as Seychelle seems to, or did you have to do research and find ways to incorporate that information into the stories? In fact, why include it at all? What does the local history bring to the novel or add to the experience of the reader?

I guess I would have to say here that I have been heavily influenced by other Florida writers. First in that line would be John D. MacDonald. I first read him in the 1970s when I was sailing in the South Pacific and from then on I grabbed up every McGee novel that he published. When we left chartering in the Virgin Islands and sailed up to Florida in 1984, it was because of my reading of those books. I learned my first Florida history from the pages of those novels, and I really loved that voice that often went off on these philosophical riffs about developers and the past and future of this state. Throughout my first ten to fifteen years here I discovered other Florida writers like James W. Hall, Randy Wayne White, Barbara Parker, and Tom Corcoran who also included history as a backdrop to their stories. So yes, I began to do research through reading and visiting lots of Florida historical sites. You cannot really understand crime in this state without looking at the history of the scalawags and con artists and characters who've been killing and stealing on this peninsula for years. I think there is something about warmer climates that attracts people who like to do things the easy way, often the illegal way. It is one thing to look at a single instance of crime in a book. I think it's more interesting to look at it in the context of the history and lives of the people involved.

Do you plan to add maps or drawings of the waterways to help the reader visualize the locations, invented or otherwise?

No. A book is different each time it is read by a different reader. The reader brings his life experiences to the page and interprets the words there in his or her own way. That's how it should work. It's not important that they imagine Fort Lauderdale as it really is. Better that they create their own mental image.

How do you develop your novels? What is the relationship between characterization and plot in your novels? Is one more important than the other? Do you develop one more first or emphasize it more than the other?

Since I am writing a series, I have a core group of characters who grew out of the first novel. I then look for a milieu of crime—like immigrant smuggling or casino gambling boats. Then I think about Seychelle and I wonder how she could get involved in this world. At the same time, I think about what personal issue Seychelle is going to deal with in this book. I always have a subplot of a personal issue that tends to cross over into the world of the crime. As I outline the story, I invent new characters.

What about the main characters, especially Seychelle's family? They have a particular history. Seychelle is approaching middle age; she has recently lost her father, has struggled to change and then maintain her identity as a salvage operator and all-around business boater, fits into the middle between the extremes of the brothers, struggles with her own sense of guilt about her mother's suicide, etc. While all of these traits make here complex and believable, why did you choose these particular traits about Seychelle?

Oh boy, you are touching on my soapbox topic here. And your recent email question asked about my feminist tendencies in the gender of certain characters.

Indeed, I do consider myself a feminist and it has pained me to see men's books treated as more serious or significant than women's. After doing tons of reading in both novels and short stories, I have come up with an opinion about this. The flawed hero is a much more interesting character. The typical P.I. story is about a flawed man who knows he has done wrong things in his past and he now seeks justice in order to find some measure of personal redemption. Too many books by women have their main characters as essentially good people in the beginning and they are good at the end. They are driven mostly by a need for recognition because the world doesn't see how smart or effective they are. The problem is that redemption is a much more fascinating motivation and creates more compelling stories.

Can you elaborate on this theme a bit? What makes redemption more interesting? Did you pattern Seychelle after any flawed character in particular? Were you inspired by other flawed figures as heroes? Are there any personal experiences that drew you to this kind of hero?

Redemption is the desire to be a better human being and it is certainly nobler than to merely want others to notice that you are already a good person. I can't say that I patterned Seychelle after any particular character, but I did examine the possibility of writing about a cop or a P.I. and I decided I didn't want to do either. There is this term in the genre, "amateur sleuth," that evokes a certain type of traditional mystery, and I knew I didn't want to write that, either. I wanted to write action/adventure/suspense books with a strong dose of the outdoors. So, I looked at the books I liked to read and I realized that most of them had main characters with jobs other than detecting jobs, though no one would really call them amateur sleuths. I'm talking about James W. Hall's Thorn who ties flies and Randy Wayne White's Doc Ford who runs his biological supply company. And then, of course, there was MacDonald's Travis McGee who was in the "salvage" business in a different way, but still not a detective. I even looked at many of Hemingway's characters, and I found that these men had been in war or in Thorn's case committed a crime, and they carried a load of guilt. I realized that this is a sort of American archetype that goes back to our Wild West heritage where man existed out in the lawless plains and had to ignore laws to survive. Then he came into the city and he wound up being made Marshall and had to try to make justice while knowing he was made of the same wild stuff as the men he was putting behind bars. In this archetypal story, women are not the savages who need to be civilized, they are the civilizers; they are Aunt Polly, not Huck. This concept of seeking redemption is the basic knowledge that one is a flawed human being and trying to become a better human being. I wanted to write about a woman who felt driven to do good to make up for past sins and yet I didn't want to make her a real criminal. I thought it would be much more interesting if it was a sin that only she really recognized, hence Seychelle feels guilt for not being able to prevent her mother's suicide.

Do you include Seychelle's self-doubts to counterbalance her determination and heroic qualities? Can you speak to why you chose those particular self-doubts?

I wanted to make a character who felt guilty and was seeking redemption through saving others. I didn't want to write about a P.I. or a cop or anything like that. I wanted someone who is driven to save people and I had to give her a job that was about that. Salvaging boats is often about salvaging lives. The metaphor was built in. I didn't want to make her solving murders so much as trying to salvage the lives of the living.

Seychelle's mother ends her life by filling her pockets and walking into the ocean. Did you have in mind other female artists who have died in a similar manner, or was it simply fitting for her to pass on this way?

As an English teacher, I've taught Kate Chopin's *The Awakening* many times. Edna left behind her husband and children when she swam out to sea. She was the model for Annie, Seychelle's mother. Someday I would like to tell her story. I think she is a fascinating character, but since she has been dead since the start of the series, that would be a whole different sort of book—not a crime story.

All of your main characters seem a bit larger than life—at times the stereotype can be seen through the flesh and bones you place around them. Is this inevitable because the genre of crime fiction places these constraints on any action-oriented, crime-fighting narrative? I am thinking of the reluctant hero; the handsome and mysterious sidekick/love interest; the handsome, charming, but slightly sinister bad guy; the protective, outspoken, motherly lawyer—all charming characters to be sure.

Yes, I think the choice to write in a genre is a bit like choosing to write a structured poem. A sonnet makes certain demands in terms of structure and the artistry of the poet is to create within those bounds. Likewise, reluctant sleuths and brainy sidekicks are common building blocks of this genre, but I'm trying to flesh out my characters and make them unique. I'm never quite sure whether Jeannie or BJ would qualify as her sidekick and in terms of love interests, I'm trying to make BJ the opposite of the manly alpha male.

You are developing a changing family and personal life for the main character. Do you eventually see any radically different changes for Seychelle? Will she ever move from Fort Lauderdale, for example? Will her newly found grandmother become a thorn in her side or a new ally? How do you see your characters changing over time?

I'm currently finishing book four and it begins in Key West. While Seychelle has not moved there, I felt like taking her out of Fort Lauderdale for a while. The tentative title for this book is *Wreckers' Key*. I intend to take my boat over to the west coast of Florida this spring, so it's very possible that Seychelle may be making a trip over there in an upcoming book. As for changing the characters over time, I am aging them and in the new book, Seychelle is considering quitting the salvage business. I'm not sure where that is going to take her. And something happens at the end of *Wreckers' Key* that has the potential to change radically the life Sechelle has known.

In the process of telling the story, some light falls on the nature of a particular social problem, whether it be illegal immigration, runaway teens, or other problems. Is the exposure intentional? Why these social problems and not others? Are these problems particular to Florida and to South Florida? Are any of these problems you or someone you know faced?

If I am going to spend all the hours writing a crime novel, it has to be about something about which I am passionate. I can't write about murder in general. That's not me. Runaway teens and sexual predators—now that's something I care deeply about and it's worth spending time with that. Though my third book seems not to be that much of a social issue, I found myself intrigued by people who turn their backs on loved ones. My father and his sister fought and then never spoke again for the last twenty years they were both alive. In that book I was also writing about a 13-year-old boy who loses his father. My own son's father died at that age and I wanted to put Seychelle in a somewhat motherly position with this boy trying to help him cope—as I had to. All my books have had children in them. As a mother and teacher, I think protecting children is of utmost importance. But I've found that while I thought I was only writing about children, I've also been writing about the change in the concept of family. The traditional nuclear family is no longer the model for most of the families I know, and I want to show that in my fiction. Seychelle will never marry and go that traditional route, but her family is constantly growing.

Do you see present or future local Florida issues that are developing now or in the future that you want to write about?

No. Usually by this time I have started thinking about the next Seychelle book I will write after the one I am currently writing. That hasn't happened yet. I am thinking about the possibility of writing something different. I might take a break from Seychelle when I finish this book and write something totally different.

Is there any social issue you don't or won't write about?

No. I can't think of anything I would shy away from.

Who do you write for? Who do you keep in mind as a person when you write? Does this person have a particular age or gender?

I don't really have an individual audience in mind. For me, writing is a bit like doing improv. Sometimes I even talk out loud and then hit the keys to transcribe it. In a general sense, not a day to day sense, I'm writing words I hope will be appreciated by a more literary audience. I put in literary allusions and things that no one ever finds. Towards the end of *Cross Current*, for example, I thought I made an incredibly obvious allusion to Stephen Crane's story, "The Open Boat," when Seychelle is on the boat with the Haitians and they are sailing up the coastline trying to find someplace to land. Nobody ever even noticed it.

Do you outline, then write? Do you work out details in your head first, do you focus on plot or on assembling characters around a situation and letting them speak? Do you have a good idea about where the story will end before you begin? Do your expec-

tations change as you write and does the plot change or do the characters change as you continue to write?

Yes, I do outline. However, as the book is written and new ideas occur to me, I don't hesitate to veer off the outline. Sometimes characters just say stuff that you didn't anticipate and it's good and you've got to go with it. In fact, in most of my books, the guy who I first thought would be the major bad guy turns out not to be the one.

How long did it take you to write your first novel in this series? How about now?

Surface Tension took me seven years. Now it takes me about a year and a half.

You are writing short stories as well as novels. Do you write in different genres? Do you plan to?

I have written a few short stories over the last year. The next one will come out in the collection, *Miami Noir*, edited by Les Standiford from Akashic Books in November.

You seem to get stronger as a writer the more you write (sounds trite, I know, but it's true). I know that many writers sort-of tell the same story over and over with different situations, but not only do you advance the human issues of your main characters, but the added complexity of the personal lives of these characters makes the writing stronger and more complex. Is that a trait that you intentionally developed from the beginning? Does this mean that some of the stereotypes you are forced to begin with will fade as the characters' lives progress and change? How far are you willing to take these characters? Are those changes away from stereotypes a sign of your willingness to explore the more serious side of fiction writing? Can you go too far in that direction and lose the sense of even writing an exciting crime fiction story?

I believe that stories must put the protagonist through an arc. It's just classic English stuff, but I believe it is true. When I read a book—and this is true of lots of mystery fiction—and the character is the same at the end as she was at the beginning, then I know I don't really want to read anything more by that author. Miss Marple never changes, neither does Spenser. The problem with writing a series character who has to have some kind of life-changing, exciting epiphany in every book is one of believability. How many times can I put her through hell and make her come to some kind of an ah-ha as a result? I don't know the answer to that one.

If you weren't writing mysteries, would you still be writing? If so, what and why? Would you still be writing about Florida? Why?

I want to write a memoir someday about all the sailing I have done. I also want to write a stand-alone sailing thriller possibly set in the U.S. Virgin Islands. Don't know if there's enough time to do all I want to do. I'm so slow.

Thank you, Christine. It has been a pleasure reading your work and listening to your comments about it. I am looking forward to reading about Seychelle and all that might happen to her in the future.

Bibliography

Kling, Christine. *Bitter End.* New York: Ballantine Books, 2005.
_____. *Cross Current.* New York: Ballantine Books, 2004.
_____. *Surface Tension.* New York: Ballantine Books, 2002.
_____. *Wreckers' Key.* New York: Ballantine Books, 2007.

Paul Levine, Attorney, Novelist, and Television Mystery Writer

by Cal Branche

Paul Levine's mystery writing include seven books in the Jake Lassiter series, each of which was very well-received by the critics and especially readers. Those titles include *To Speak for the Dead, Night Vision, False Dawn, Fool Me Twice,* and *Flesh & Bones; 9 Scorpions* was a standalone mystery novel involving the Supreme Court. A versatile writer, Levine wrote for the television series, *JAG,* and was creator of the television series *First Monday in October.*

CAL BRANCHE: *Why do you set your works in Florida?*

PAUL LEVINE: I lived in Miami for 30 years (1969–1999); the place fascinated me from day one—that being three days after graduating from Penn State. With my tassel hanging from the rearview mirror, I drove my Chevy Super Sport to Florida with all my belongings and started working as a general assignment reporter for *The Miami Herald.* That's how I learned the basics of Mia-muh. I went to law school at the University of Miami, where I was on the national moot court championship team and the Law Review. So it looked as if I should practice law, if only because I had a knack for it. And practice I did, for 17 years in downtown Miami in the shadow of the courthouse. I lived in Coral Gables and Coconut Grove, so... Man, that's my area.

I've now lived in Los Angeles for the past seven years, but I still consider Miami home; I still think I know it better than the West Coast. And I still think it's fascinating. It's hard to say why without resorting to the clichés. It's the capital of Latin America. It's South Beach with all that weirdness and trendiness and club scene. Hey, I remember Ocean Drive and Lincoln Road when the place was God's waiting-room. So, even though I'm amused by the phoniness and pseudo-hipness of the place, it's still fun.

Then there's the crime. Weird crimes. Edna Buchanan has documented those better than most, both in her fiction and nonfiction. And because I write courtroom novels, the legal system sucks me in. Three judges who were friends of mine all went to federal prison for bribery. A lawyer I knew was killed, apparently by one of his clients. Lawyers and doctors conspire to manufacture phony cases. The courts are as weird as the streets. Moon over Miami? You're as phony as a movie set.

Which other Florida writers really "capture" the state?

If we're not limiting the question to living writers, I'd start with John D. MacDonald, who was a huge influence on me. The Travis McGee novels stand up pretty well 40 years later. *Condominium* does, too, especially in the light of all the recent hurricanes and the problems with construction. Charles Willeford's *Miami Blues* is one of my favorites. He captured some of the weirdness before it was in vogue. Carl Hiaasen's *Tourist Season* had a big impact on me. Carl makes it all look easy, when it's not! I was practicing law when I read that book, and it truly inspired me to try and write fiction.

I think different writers capture their own slices of Florida. I've read and enjoyed Les Standiford, James W. Hall, Randy Wayne White, Tim Dorsey, Bob Morris, Edna Buchanan, Jon King, Chris Kling, Jim Born, Carolina Garcia-Aguilera, Jimmy Buffett, Vickie Hendricks, Dave Barry. I know I'm leaving people out; there are so damn many!

Whom do you read, and why? Not just mystery writers, but I hope they are on your list.

Besides the people I just mentioned, I admit to being a huge fan of Tom Wolfe. It's probably because our styles are so different. His powers of description just knock me out. His ability to do the set piece: the stud horse sequence in *A Man in Full*, the fraternity party in *I Am Charlotte Simmons*, a courtroom scene in *Bonfire of the Vanities*—well, they just knock me out.

Alan Zweibel is one of the funniest writers alive. He's written for television (Larry David) and for Billy Crystal's outstanding one-man show ("700 Sundays"), but his recent novel (*The Other Shulman*) really blew me away. If you remember Woody Allen's short stories and maybe mix in some James Thurber, well, that's *Zweibel*. (He's also nominated for the 2006 Thurber Prize for American Humor for *The Other Shulman*. I add, somewhat immodestly, that *Solomon vs. Lord* is also nominated.)

On Scott Turow's suggestion, I've started reading the now-neglected James Gould Cozzens. Terrific. The short story, "Clerical Error," is one of my favorites. And speaking of short stories, has there ever been a better first line than Jack Ritchie's in *A New Leaf* (later made into a movie with Walter Matthau and Elaine May)? There are so many others, we're talking dozens here, I admire so much. Really too many to name.

How did you get into the business of writing mysteries?

We had been married three months and I rather thought it was time to get rid of my wife. It was my therapy. I'm not joking. I was burned out practicing law; I felt my life had very little social utility. It was either see a shrink or write fiction. That's how I created Jake Lassiter, the protagonist of my first mystery series. He's a lawyer who didn't take all the crap I did. He'd punch out a witness or lawyer, or more frequently, get punched out himself.

What was your preparation for being a writer? And when did you first know you were a novelist?

No preparation that I'm aware of. When I sold the first book, *To Speak for the Dead*, I was hoping that meant I was a real novelist. When I was out of book writing for seven years (as I was writing for TV: *JAG* and *First Monday*), sitting down to write a new novel on spec was pretty damn terrifying. But that was *Solomon vs. Lord*, and that pretty much convinced me I could do this.

Were you aware of the history of the form? Has that awareness affected your ideas of plot, character, theme?

I'm still not very well versed in the history of the craft.

When you began to form your main characters how did you go about doing it? What are the characteristics of your main characters?

Steve Solomon and Victoria Lord both represent sides of my personality. Steve's the reckless one who circumvents the rules. Victoria plays the game by the book; Steve burns the book. He thinks a crooked path is the shortest path between two points. She would never think of getting off the well-groomed path. He believes in justice; she believes in law.

Has there been a gradual development of your protagonist(s)? How careful are you in preparing for character change/development?

I'm actually unable to answer, except changes happen without my planning or sometimes even knowing. Often, events in my life with my wife Renee will lead to similar events in the Steve/Victoria relationship.

How do you prepare for writing? How do you do research? What are your "writing" work habits?

I start with an outline. Research as I go. Start writing with a 1st act outline done, then stop and outline some more.

Publishers and reviewers invariably categorize crime/mystery/detective fiction as a genre. Are those qualifications limiting? Should we distinguish these works from "novels"? How do you classify your work so far?

Classifications make it easier for readers. Bantam calls *Solomon vs. Lord* a legal thriller. But it's nominated for the Thurber humor award (and for the Macavity as best mystery of 2005). I think crime fiction is a nice tag that overlaps genres.

Writers—knowingly or not—reflect personal philosophies in their work. Now that you have spent many years writing novels, what is your philosophy in terms of crime and punishment and good vs. evil? How did your law career affect your work?

I think that practicing law should give anyone a healthy cynicism about the so-called justice system. A sense of humor helps, too.

What makes a good, or great storyteller?

When I learn the answer to this one, I'll l keep it to myself!

Can you comment on the differences between novel and television writing?

It's really simple. Three points. (1) A novel is your own. Every word. In TV, you are working for the executive producers, the producing partners (usually a studio) and the network. You're dealing with characters and an initial story (the pilot) created by others. It is no way your own. Speaking for myself and no one else, writing novels is more fulfilling. I suspect it is different for those rare birds who have created many successful shows and have enormous clout with the networks, à la David Kelley, Steve Bochco, Dick Wolf, Don Bellisario, etc. (2) Novels can be any length and in any form. Otherwise, how could Mickey Spillane and Thomas Pynchon both be novelists? TV writing is strictly structured. In network TV, you're writing four (or sometimes five) acts separated by commercials. Time constraints are everything. Hence, you must use the camera, i.e., visuals, to tell much of the story, and you must keep the dialogue brisk. I believe TV writing helped me write crisper dialogue in the "Solomon vs. Lord" novels. (3) Thanks to a strong union (Writers Guild of America), TV writers are very well paid and have a health insurance program funded 100 percent by the industry. Income for novelists varies from the pitiful to the plentiful, but the mean is quite low. There is no health insurance provided by publishers.

Many readers of this book on Florida mystery writers may want to try their hand at writing as well, but feel uneasy about starting. Nicolas Freeling once wrote to me that a writer usually has a compulsion to tell a story, and often they begin at an early age, but as in Freeling's case, he was well into his thirties before writing his first. Do you have a compulsion to tell a story?

Writers write for a variety of reasons, some of them even logical. But yes, I think there's a burning need in some of us (a flu-like fever) that makes us believe we have stories to tell, stories that will entertain or enlighten. So, "compulsion" is a good word, as it implies illness. After a while, a writer who quits his/her day job also has a "compulsion" to pay the mortgage, and that fuels storytelling, too.

I wonder if you could comment more on "outlining." Is it very important and necessary? How does one do an outline?

I outline, but not all writers do. Elmore Leonard doesn't. He once said that if he knew how the story would turn out, he wouldn't write the damn thing. On the other hand, Stephen J. Cannell writes a full outline, 75–80 pages or so, and he feels he speeds up his writing.

I outline less than I used to, now usually just the first act, then I write it, stop and outline the second act, and do the same with the third. For beginning writers, I strongly urge writing a complete outline.

How do you approach trying to create an interesting character, one whom the reader will care about?

I base characters on composites of people I've known, and because I write with humor (when it's working), I figure if I'm entertained by the character, the reader will be, too.

Do you think that tv mysteries and thrillers promote an interest in reading mysteries?

I'm not sure. Certainly, hit films prompt people to go out and buy the book that's the underlying material. *Seabiscuit. Cold Mountain. The Devil Wears Prada.* TV is different. You basically don't pay for it, so it's not taken as seriously. TV is the background noise of our lives. My guess is that watching TV only makes you want to watch more TV... Or go to sleep.

Bibliography

Levine, Paul. *The Deep Blue Alibi*. (Solomon vs. Lord series). New York: Random House, 2006.
____. *False Dawn*. New York: Bantam, 1993 (rpt. Crimeline, 1994).
____. *Flesh & Bones*. New York: Avon, 1998.
____. *Fool Me Twice*. New York: William Morrow, 1996.
____. *Kill All The Lawyers*. New York: Bantam, 2006.
____. *Mortal Sin*. New York: William Morrow, 1994.
____. *Night Vision*. New York: Bantam, 1991.
____. *9 Scorpions*. New York: Pocket Books, 1998.
____. *Slashback*. New York: William Morrow, 1995.
____. *Solomon vs. Lord*. New York, Random House, 2005.
____. *To Speak For the Dead*. New York: Bantam, 1990.

Michael Lister, Prison Chaplain and Novelist

by Matthew McLendon

Michael Lister was the youngest prison chaplain in the history of the Florida Department of Corrections. His seven years occupying this job gave him unparalleled access to the world which forms the basis for many of his novels: the North Florida prison system. Lister's true-life experience brings validity to his writing and infuses his stories with a reality that could only be achieved by someone with his intimate knowledge of the world of crime and its characters.

His series based upon the ex-cop turned prison chaplain, John Jordan, draws heavily upon these personal experiences. The third book of the series, *Flesh and Blood*, was published in the fall of 2006. The fourth, *The Body and the Blood*, will be out soon thereafter. Lister retired from the prison service in 2000 in order to write full-time. Michael's latest project is *The Big Goodbye*, a noir novel set in 1940s Panama City, featuring P.I. Jimmy "Soldier" Riley, who according to Lister is "a young, wounded, woman-haunted knight errant who walks the mean streets of wartime Panama City alone."

MATTHEW MCLENDON: *Michael, every writer seems to have his or her own particular writing process. What is the process—if any—you go through in writing? For example, do you use outlines, or do you just sit down and "start"?*

MICHAEL LISTER: I used outlines when I first started writing, but only for my first few novels. Now, I spend a lot of time with the characters and story before I ever start a book, getting to know them and their stories. Then, as I write, I'm always thinking about the characters and their stories until I finish the book, and each day as I finish that day's writing, I make a few notes on how and where to start the next day.

That's interesting. So then, when writing, which do you feel is more important, plot development or character development, or, do you feel they are equally important? How much attention do you pay to each?

I think both are critical, but character comes first, and plot grows out of it. Character is destiny. What characters do, how they react, determines the plot. To me, the worst writing is plot-driven, where characters are forced to fill a role that serves the plot. They become cardboard cutouts instead of multidimensional, living, breathing beings. That said, you've got to have a good plot—especially in the mystery genre, so I pay a lot of attention to it as well.

How do you go about developing the elements of the story? Do you "know" where the elements come from—that is, what is your inspiration?

This is a real mystery. I know that life, observations, reading, and experiences are the raw materials of my fiction, but how exactly I'm not sure, and I honestly don't think I want to know. I know that what emerges from the process is as nearly unrecognizable as what went in. It's like the paint smeared on a painter's pallet compared to one of her paintings. You can identify the individual elements, but you can't completely explain how they became what they did.

I think many artists in whatever genre feel that way. Have you ever had a problem with writer's block?

I've never experienced writer's block. In fact, just the opposite. I usually have more ideas than I know what to do with, and occasionally it takes me a few days to figure out what to write next.

Lucky you! It sounds as if you might have the problem all writers wish for: too many good ideas. So with your lack of writer's block, do you find the actual act of writing enjoyable or difficult?

It's both—a lot of work and a ton of fun. It's not easy, but there's nothing I find more fulfilling.

Let's talk a bit about the "scholarly" or "critical" aspects of mystery literature. Critics and scholars are insistent on classifying writing into strict genres such as mystery, detective, crime fiction, etc. Do you find such classifications limiting?

Not really. Though most of what I write can be classified in the broad category of crime fiction, I also write literary fiction, essays, screenplays, and short stories. Genre classifications help readers find what they're looking for and also let them know what to expect. They give writers a framework and conventions—both of which can be followed or played against.

As a writer, do you feel there is a difference between mystery novels, detective novels, and crime fiction?

I see crime fiction as the broad umbrella under which everything else falls. The noir novels and stories I write may or may not have a detective, they may or may not be a mystery in the classic sense, but they all involve crime.

Then, do you think these classifications are subgenres of the broader genre "novel," or should mystery and crime fiction be considered its own genre?

I think they are subgenres of the novel. And I think you can go even further. My John Jordan novels are clerical detective stories, a subgenre of mystery, which is a subgenre of crime, which is a subgenre of the novel.

I think that's a really good point; we can further extrapolate this process. How do you classify your own work?

In different ways depending on the work. My John Jordan novels are mysteries. My Jimmy Riley stories are noir novels. But in both cases they are first and foremost novels, meant to be unique, original, the opposite of formulaic—which to me is the lowest form of genre.

Yes, I think most readers would agree with you that formulaic stories are fundamentally unsatisfying. Why do you think the "mystery" or "crime" genres remain among the most popular today?

For many reasons, but chief among them is because of the way they explore human nature—the very best and worst we are capable of.

I think that one could argue all great writing ultimately explores human nature. Do you consciously approach writing as an exploratory or revelatory tool?

I see writing as more exploratory than revelatory, though there are certainly many revelations for writer and reader throughout the experience. I think all writing is in some sense autobiographical, but it's often far more subtle than readers realize.

So do you think your novels and stories reveal more about you or your readers?

I hope what I write reveals more about human nature than about me. However, the more specific the experience, the more likely readers are to identify with it. The hope is that the individual voice can become the universal. But to answer your question, it's not conscious. I don't have an agenda—something I'm trying to convey or reveal, just characters, plots, and themes I want to explore.

Interesting; that really leads me to one of the first questions I had when I started reading your work. In the John Jordan mysteries, the eponymous protagonist is a prison chaplain in rural North Florida just as you were. Not to be overly superficial, but is John Jordan a representation of you, is he a "persona"? If so, then what do you think you are working through in your own life with this character?

There is certainly a link or a connection between us, but we probably have as many differences as we do similarities. Sometimes I think of him as a kind of doppelganger, but I wouldn't call him a persona. I might have been him had I been born into a different family, so in some ways, he is me in a darker, alternate reality.

Your life experience certainly informs your work. In addition to these experiences, what authors would you cite as major influences on you and your work?

Robert B. Parker, who led me to Chandler and Hammett, who led me to Hemingway. Andrew Greeley, who led me to Graham Greene and G.K. Chesterton. Also, James Lee Burke, Frederick Buechner, the Bible, and Shakespeare.

That's a great list, but I must say Buechner, the Bible, and Shakespeare are not at the top of my list of what I would guess a 21st century mystery/crime writer would name as major influences. Why have you included them and in what ways have they influenced you?

One of the reasons I most like crime fiction—both as a writer and as a reader— is because when it's good, it deals with ultimate issues: mortality, morality, sin, redemption, truth, justice, hate, compassion, obsession, etc. For me, the Bible, Shakespeare, and Buechner have been great influences when it comes to humanity and our exploration of ultimate issues.

You've been speaking a great deal about the ultimate issues of life which I imagine you certainly would have addressed in your work as a prison chaplain. How did you come to leave this work?

In one sense, I never left. I continue to volunteer in the prison system: teaching classes, counseling, and organizing various charity projects. This not only gives me the opportunity to make a small contribution for the least and lowest, but keeps me immersed in the environment I write about. I left full-time chaplaincy for full-time writing because I felt it was time. I was given the opportunity to spend most of my time writing (books, screenplays, articles, and columns—by doing all of these I could scratch out a sort of living), and I took it because I believe writing is at the center of everything I was created to do. I took "early parole" so that I could focus far more of my time and energy on my obsession with writing, but I did so knowing I would never fully leave my prison parish.

Did you start out writing in the mystery/crime genre, or did you write other types of work before?

The most oft-given writing advice is to write what you know, but I say write what you love. I write crime fiction because I love it. I was a fan first. I did write in other genres or no genre at all and still do, but mystery is my first love.

So then as a fan you did have some awareness of the genre, but were you aware of the long history of the form? How does this history influence you?

Before I ever wrote my first word of crime fiction, I had some awareness of the genre's history just from being a reader. However, it was after my first book came out that I became a student of crime fiction, and I have a much broader and better understanding of the form today. The more I study it, the more I love it, and my appreciation of it certainly influences my writing of it.

Yes, that always seems to be the way. How did you prepare for a career as an author?

I was a storyteller long before I became a writer. As a teacher, I've always used story. My background and education is in theology, which all comes down to story. Religion is the story of humanity and our search for meaning. It's filled with stories of human triumph and failure, and I've been highly influenced by it—particularly the stories of the Hebrew Bible and the parables of Jesus.

*Because of your background as a prison chaplain, themes of religion run through your work, especially the John Jordan mysteries. There are a number of mysteries which incorporate religious themes or persons (*The Name of the Rose, The Father Dowling Mysteries, *and* Cadfael *come to mind). How have these influenced you, if at all?*

They have. I'm a fan of the subgenre, and though what I'm doing is quite different from other clerical detectives, I have enjoyed studying about and reading them. Father Brown is a favorite, as is *The Name of the Rose*.

How do you see your work as different from others' work in this subgenre?

I'm the first (and only so far as I know) to put a clerical sleuth in hard-boiled detective novels. John Jordan is far more human than most of the other clerical detectives I've read about, and he's the only one in a prison environment.

Reading your work, you seem to have very definite ideas about organized religion. In Blood of the Lamb *you have John Jordan think to himself, "Ironically, those with the least to say usually say the most and the most outwardly religious were often the most theologically unsophisticated." Do you consciously (or conscientiously) consider John Jordan as a tool to disseminate your personal beliefs? Is there really any way to avoid this and remain objective in the writing process, or is there no need for such objectivity in fiction writing?*

John and I share certain views, but I don't think I use him as a tool for expressing them any more than I would stop him or others from expressing views that I disagree with. In the case of organized religion, I like the dramatic tension of having a person of faith who is functioning inside organized religion who is not comfortable in it. To me, it's very similar to the tension between mercy and justice or compassion and violence in John's life and work. Fiction isn't the place for an author's soapbox, and I try never to rant or to have any kind of agenda. However, if a character wants to—whether it's something I agree with or not—I'm happy for him or her to do so.

The recent furor over The Da Vinci Code *seems particularly relevant to the mystery genre and there are certainly religious themes in it. Have you read* The Da Vinci Code?

I resisted reading it for a long time, but I had so many people wanting to talk to me about it, that I finally read it.

What do you think about it in relation to what you're doing?

I was familiar with the material in it from the many nonfiction books I had read on the subject, but I was really impressed with how Brown was able to weave so much into a fast-paced thriller. As a feminist, I'm partial to the Divine Feminine, and I appreciate what he has done to spread the concept. I wish people wouldn't get bogged down in the details and just appreciate the myths and metaphors. For me religion is best and most profound when it's experienced as story and poetry, not adhered to as doctrine and dogma.

We seem to have had an almost identical experience and reaction to this cultural phenomenon. However, with my background in art history I am troubled by Brown's admonition at the beginning of the book that the details he has brought together are "facts" when it has been argued that the book is riddled with historical, theological, and art historical errors. Increasingly I feel that the lines between fact and fiction, especially in terms of history or historical narrative, are being blurred. In my own experience as a reader, this "blurring" seems to be occurring the fastest in quasi-historical crime fiction. Do you see this as a problem? Is it something that worries you as a novelist?

I completely agree. In fact, I've led a few discussion groups on the book and said the very same thing. These are not facts. There is much that is inaccurate. I'm for an author doing anything he or she wants to in fiction, but make sure the readers know it's fiction (even when you do, many readers will still believe it to be fact). Don't call it facts or say it's based on facts— even when it is. Brown is an easy target, and I try to avoid being critical of other writers, but I have to say I find his research as weak as his writing.

Obviously your life experience has greatly informed your work, and as you live in Florida, it makes sense that you've set your work here. Has living in Florida been a great influence in your life and writing?

I'm a Floridian as much as I'm anything. I've lived here most of my life, and genuinely love the place.

As a native Floridian (a seemingly dying breed) I can definitely understand that. Are there certain aspects of the state that you feel are conducive to this genre of writing?

There must be. Our gun-shaped state produces some great crime fiction. I think South Florida is obvious—from John D. McDonald to *Miami Vice* to James Hall, Les Standiford, and the writers their program at Miami International University is producing. I think North Florida is less obvious, which is why I like writing about it.

Good point, there is a great difference between North and South Florida. It's really almost like two completely different states. Miami Vice among other popular examples has really focused the popular attention on the south. Do you feel an affinity with urban or rural Florida, or both?

Both, but urban only as a fascinated and attracted visitor. I've lived in rural North Florida most of my life. It's my beat. That said, I often feel like a foreigner here, but this is my home. I have a love-hate relationship with it and try to infuse my fiction with both. The Florida I write about is like L.A.—

Lower Alabama—and is unlike most of the state. North Florida has more in common with the South and Southern Lit than Florida.

Florida definitely has its own character. What do you feel sets Florida writers apart from other writers, that is, why are they distinct?

I think all good fiction is regional, so the Florida writers who really let Florida permeate their works are truly distinct. This is something I try to do with North Florida. To me, it comes down to careful observation and being honest and open about your environment and the people in it. When it comes to capturing the rural Southern Gulf Coast region, no one does it better than James Lee Burke. I identify and have more in common with him than any Florida writer I can think of.

You seem to be making the point that Florida is really two separate worlds: North and South. I think your point that all good fiction is regional is excellent; however, if Florida is two distinct regions, are we wrong to be talking about "Florida writers" or "Florida fiction"?

Though it is two very distinct regions, it's one state. We are bound together, which is what makes Florida so interesting to me. Joining two opposite or opposing people, places, or forces creates a cauldron, out of which comes drama. It's what happens in prison. So I think Florida fiction writers are one group, but one with a lot of diversity based on the region we're writing about.

Being a Florida writer you must have strong ideas about what you think are the major issues or changes, other than the diversity issues you've already mentioned, affecting Florida today. Do these impact your work?

The transition of North Florida from rural mill towns into a destination spot for tourists and second homes for the wealthy of the world is having a huge impact on our area and it is finding its way into all my books, but especially *Blood Sacrifice*, the fourth John Jordan novel. I have learned a good bit about Florida history, and some of it finds its way into my fiction. This is especially true of my Jimmy Riley series, which takes place in Panama City of the 1940s.

Then do you think Florida is headed in a positive or negative direction?

We're growing faster than any other state in the country and will soon be third in population. We're destroying the natural beauty of this amazing place of ours for a few bucks (quite a few), killing wildlife that will not come back, and overdeveloping. I don't see a whole lot of positives. I find myself writing about some of the same issues John D. MacDonald wrote about thirty years ago.

With all of these negatives, have you considered setting your work outside of Florida?

I really haven't. I mean, I have scenes here and there set in Atlanta, New Orleans, etc., but not entire books. I might one day. Atlanta is a likely place since I've lived there and visit often. New Orleans is also a possibility just because of how much I love it. A different setting would alter my work greatly because of how regionally specific I try to write.

In addition to your interests in the South and Florida, you obviously have a great love for mystery/crime fiction. Have you ever thought about writing in another genre? Can you envision yourself as a non-crime or mystery writer?

I write a good bit of literary fiction, and I've always thought I'd write a Western one day. The Western is the mother of the detective novel. But I can't see myself writing science fiction or romance.

Yes, I definitely see parallels between the Western and the detective novel. A brief perusal of your biography reveals that you are quite a prolific writer. What other genres have you worked in, screenwriting, theatre, nonfiction, etc.?

I write scripts, short stories, and essays, and enjoy them—especially short stories and essays.

Do you find this work more, less, or equally satisfying as the crime/mystery genre?

Nothing is as fulfilling to me as narrative fiction, particularly the novel.

Michael, thanks so much for your time. I look forward to reading your new work.

Thank you.

Bibliography

Lister, Michael. *Blood of the Lamb: A John Jordan Mystery*. Madison: Bleak House Books, Inc., 2004.
    _____. *The Blood-Red Rec Yard Ruse*. Panama City: Pottersville Press, 2003.
    _____. *Flesh and Blood: John Jordan Stories*. Panama City: Pottersville Press, 2006.
    _____. *North Florida Noir* (editor and contributor). Panama City: Pottersville Press, 2006.
    _____. *Power in the Blood: A John Jordan Mystery*. Sarasota: Pineapple Press, 1997.

John Lutz, Sometime Florida Crime Writer

by Anna Lillios

In John Lutz's novel, *Tropical Heat*, his private-eye hero, Fred Carver, reveals how easy it is to solve a crime: "It didn't take Sherlock Holmes, just someone with the proper slant."

Carver and Alo Nudger, who is another one of Lutz's private eyes, are ordinary men who acquire the necessary "slant," perhaps, because they are characters with disabilities and must sharpen their powers of observation to survive. Carver is lame and Nudger suffers from debilitating fears. The worlds they inhabit—Nudger in St. Louis and Carver in Florida—blear the line between good and evil. Carver describes Florida as a surreal juxtaposition of the "Ku Klux Klan and Mickey Mouse and drugs and the Bible and sunshine and murder and palm trees." Both Nudger and Carver do not hesitate to cross the line to combat the corruption they see all around them. Frederic Svoboda in "The Snub-Nosed Mystique: Observations of the American Detective Hero" defines the detective hero in terms of this uphill struggle: "The detective hero must acknowledge with the cynicism of a disappointed romantic that established civilization is no more than a veneer, that an unwinnable frontier still divides the civilized and savage elements of modern life."

Since his first short story appeared in *Alfred Hitchcock's Mystery Magazine* in 1966, John Lutz has published more than 40 novels and 250 short stories and articles. According to him, his work includes the following types of writing: political suspense, private eye novels, urban suspense, humor, occult, crime caper, police procedural, espionage, historical, futuristic, amateur detective—virtually every mystery subgenre. For his efforts, he has won many awards, such as MWA Edgar, the PWA Shamus, the Trophee 813 Award for best mystery short story collection translated to the French language, the PWA Lifetime Achievement Award, and the Short Mystery Fiction Society's Golden Derringer Lifetime Achievement Award. He's also been honored in the past by his peers who elected him president of the Mystery Writers of America and president of the Private Eye Writers of America. His work has been translated into many languages and adapted for almost every medium. His novel *SWF Seeks Same* became the hit movie *Single White Female*, starring Bridget Fonda and Jennifer Jason Leigh. He co-authored the screenplay of another novel, *The Ex*, which became an HBO movie. His latest novel, published in 2006, is *Chill of Night*, which elicited the following comment by a *Publishers Weekly* reviewer: "Lutz breathes fresh life into this genre piece by keeping the suspense high and populating his story with a collection of unique characters that resonate with the reader."

ANNA LILLIOS: *What inspired you to become a writer?*

JOHN LUTZ: In a nebulous sort of way, going back as far as I can remember. I think writers are born with, or develop early, a special relationship with the language. Around age thirteen, after reading Ray Bradbury's *A Sound of Thunder*, I realized that words could be used for much more than simply conveying information, and my course was set.

How did your original inspiration turn to writing mystery and private-eye novels? In an interview you say that your "original motivation is gone" and that you continue writing for "selfish reasons." Do you still feel this way?

I suppose so. I greatly enjoy writing, and the fact that I actually am paid to do it delights me. I don't have some special message or agony to relate or exorcise; I love to rearrange the randomness of life in ways that allow me to concoct and tell stories. Ten thousand years ago I probably would have been sitting in a cave at a campfire, using basic words and hand gestures, entertaining or boring the hell out of people. Where could they go?

Storytelling has certainly evolved in the past ten thousand years so that now we have many different specialized ways of telling a story. How do the stories you tell fit into this ancient tradition? Do you feel that crime fiction or mystery writing is a separate genre—apart from novels?

A novel is a novel, whatever the genre. The form, the story, the beginning, middle, end, and meaning, are what attracted me, second only to the pleasure of rolling one word off another for effect. Virtually all novels are mysteries. Add criminality and that's where they fit on the library or bookstore shelf.

In your opinion, how do your own private-eye novels fit into the mystery category?

Mystery is a very broad genre, subcategorized for convenience. There's no reason a private eye novel can't resonate with the reader in the same way as a novel published as "literature." So sure, mysteries are "novels." It doesn't really make much difference if your protagonist is chasing a murderer or a white whale.

What differences do you see between these categories?

Only the obvious. Private eye, amateur sleuth, police procedural, espionage, suspense, romantic suspense, historical mystery, etc. Each requires pretty much the same skills, those necessary to write a good novel—period. And of course there's quite a bit of overlapping. Categorizing novels does provide a way for the reader to narrow the search for the sort of book desired.

Do you structure your novels in any way to correspond to the genre?

Only up to a point. Readers, and editors, are looking for something familiar yet different.

What is the different quality, in your opinion, that you think readers seek out?

Ah, that's the big question. Writers and editors are constantly trying to answer that one. A fresh twist on a familiar concept seems to work well. But it has to be the right fresh twist, and the right familiar concept. A new and unfamiliar concept can also work, but of course...

What is your writing process?

I compose in the morning, revising as I go. In the afternoon I read what I've done, am sometimes appalled, and do more revision. When the novel is completed, I revise again. And again. I like to revise.

William Faulkner wrote that what inspired him to write The Sound and the Fury *was the image of little Caddie climbing the pear tree in order to look into the house at her grandmother's funeral. How do your stories begin?*

That depends on the concept. Be it inspired by character, plot, or setting, I do think that to be at its best the tale has to be character-driven.

How do your stories develop from this initial inspiration? Do you know how the stories will end before you begin writing?

I start with the germ of an idea. A hook. Then I ask myself what if, then what if, then what if… Always I know how the book is going to end before I begin writing, then I usually change it at least somewhat.

What makes you change your plan?

Usually slight changes in the body of the work early on alter its course at least a few degrees, which are magnified by book's end so that adjustments need to be made. Not major adjustments, just revisions to compensate for drift.

Has your writing undergone an evolution through the years?

Oh, I'm much more skillful. It might be that the human activity most closely related to writing is dancing. I used to think it was perfecting a golf swing, until I took some dance lessons in order to write a suspense novel set in the world of ballroom dancing. In dance and in writing, the learning is primarily in the doing; the skills have to be mastered and then applied subconsciously. The nice thing about writing is that you don't have to worry about turning your ankle, though you might step on some toes.

Why have you created several series?

In order to provide variety and challenge. My two private eyes are in many ways opposites, and the detectives in the New York thrillers I'm presently writing are like neither of them. And of course, several series provide several checks.

What do you mean by "checks"?

I meant cashable checks. Sorry; thinking like a commercial writer.

Have you enjoyed your experience working on Hollywood films? Were you happy with the transformation of SWF Seeks Same *into* Single White Female?

I was on the set of *SWF* for a while in New York and considered my job to be avoiding tripping over a cable. However, my wife and I appear in the movie, though you have to look fast to find us. My experience with everyone connected to the film was positive, and I found filmmaking a fascinating process to observe. But I'll stick to writing novels and short stories. By the way, I think the movie is great.

Can you tell me where you and your wife appear?

We're on television in the movie, when the Bridget Fonda character looks at a TV in her apartment kitchen. Being on TV in a movie makes for a small image, and it goes fast. Look for the woman in the dark blouse with a rose pattern, alongside a man wearing brown slacks, a shirt with rolled up sleeves.

In The Simple Art of Murder, *Raymond Chandler, defining the typical detective as a hard-boiled man, says: "Down these mean streets a man must go who is not himself mean...." In your novel* Tropical Heat, *one of Fred Carver's former colleagues describes Carver in the same vein: "You were tough, skeptical, had principles, and would surprise me, and you, with your compassion." Tell me about your typical hero.*

Seems to me that compassion in the hero is very important in order to make the hero likable and to involve the reader. Writing fiction is mostly about evoking at least some level of emotion. Once you do that, you have plausibility and reader identification. When readers are feeling, they forget to disbelieve.

Why do you give a few of your heroes physical flaws, such as Nudger's nervous stomach and Carver's lame leg?

They are underdogs from the get-go and gain reader sympathy. Emotion again. Also, while not many readers will share the characters' physical shortcomings, most people have shortcomings of one sort or another, and so identify with the hero.

Your heroes seem to have no problem crossing the line between law and lawlessness. How do they feel about "stepping outside the rules," as Alo Nudger puts it?

They will definitely step outside the rules. And in special circumstances step outside the law. Readers seem to accept this much more in fiction than in reality. They do know the difference.

What happens to your characters beyond the boundaries of the law? What do they learn?

Generally they learn, or have again confirmed, that the world is complicated beyond their understanding, and one can only do the best one can and then live with the results.

Are you implying that, in the settings you create, corruption is rampant everywhere, including in the legal system?

Not rampant, but certainly there, and sometimes in unexpected places.

What is the world view that you present in your novels?

I think it might differ with each novel. I suppose if there's a recurring theme, it is that we should all go easier on ourselves and on each other.

How can we go "easier on ourselves" in the competitive world in which we live? Do you think this type of compassionate state exists anywhere in the world?

Not in a perfect way. I suspect the state of being human makes that impossible.

What about here in Florida? Where is your favorite Florida setting?

My favorite Florida setting for fiction is the east coast, with Miami, a more diverse population, and wilder surf than on the west coast. Which is not to say that's where I prefer to live. After traveling around in Florida for years, my wife and I settled on Sarasota, where we now spend most of our time. The area is growing fast and has a thriving arts community, including excellent live theater. It's stimulating to live in a place that is experiencing growing pains, and of course has all the interesting aspects of many parts of Florida—great weather (most of the time), people from somewhere else, the ocean, beach, and, for some reason, bizarre crimes. Overall, as a fertile field for fiction, Florida seems to have everything California has, plus alligators.

How would you describe the essence of Florida?

The essence of Florida is stunning beauty as a counterpoint to primal danger. Despite the sun-washed lushness of the landscape, not very far off the road, or beyond the fence delineating where we lounge with our margaritas, live things with claws and sharp teeth. Some perhaps inside the fence.

What is it about Florida that makes it a good setting for crime fiction?

Here again we are like California. If everyone isn't from elsewhere, you don't have to go back very far in people's ancestry to find origins outside the state. The pioneer spirit lives on here, as does that of the carpetbagger. As the state is exploding with population, opportunities abound and attract all sorts. It makes for an interesting mix, and so interesting detective fiction, which at its best is an investigation not only of a crime, but of the society in which it was committed.

Which Florida writers do you read and admire?

I'm going to tiptoe around this trap. As a setting and a place to spend time, Florida in recent years has attracted some wonderful writers. I enjoy their work, but if I were to name them I would inevitably leave someone out, and they can be dangerous.

With which writers would you place your work?

When it comes to detective fiction, I'm more of the Chandler school than the John D. MacDonald, though I very much admire the work of both writers. I'm not sure exactly where I would fit in. I'm one of those Floridians from somewhere else.

When you use a Florida setting in your novels, do you think of its historical context?

Florida's history is always lurking in the back of my mind as I write fiction set in the state. Remnants of that history are all around us; the various races and cultures persist; and to find the environmental crisis and developers rushing to transform the state, all one has to do is open the door.

How much has Florida nature captured your imagination?

Florida nature is great as a means of intensifying characterization, and of giving it complexity and texture. The heat and humidity contribute to pressure and suspense, and the swamp provides a great metaphor for the primal part of the human mind. And of course there is the ocean, where beneath the postcard-blue surface, sharks are circling.

A New York Times reviewer claims that your novel, Torch, *is "[an]other savage entertainment set in that surreal hell Lutz calls Florida." How do you respond to this description of Florida?*

I do agree that Florida is a surreal mix of bizarre elements. The *New York Times* reviewer was on the mark when he described the setting of my Carver novel *Torch* as a "surreal hell." But Florida can also be a surreal paradise.

The frostline crosses Florida just north of Orlando at around the 29th parallel. Wallace Stevens, in his poem "Farewell to Florida," sets up a juxtaposition between his "North [which] is leafless and lies in wintry slime" and Florida which has "pine and coral and coralline sea." Do you consider the frostline as a symbolic dividing line between mainstream America and the subtropics?

Oh, yes, Florida is outside the boundaries of mainstream America, and the farther south of the frost line you travel the more that applies. I think citizens of Key West would agree.

In his essay "America in Extremis," Michael Paterniti claims that in Florida "the dots do not connect." In his view, the state has become "a bellwether and bane, the national headline and tabloid heart" of the nation, because of all the "bizarro" events that occur here. It is a state in which "everything now seems to happen first—

or somehow in the extreme, that as a microcosm of America, has come to reflect the psyche of America itself." He even speaks of a Florida "curse," as he questions: "Why here? Why psychopaths and terrorists, upside-down elections and general weirdness? Is it the unrootedness of people, the extraordinariness of the landscape, the lack of seasons that untether you from the past? You do begin to wonder, is it something in the air?"

People can live out their fantasies, for better or worse, just about anywhere, but Florida offers them extremes. Which brings us back to Hiassen and Paterniti's "surreal mix of elements." Which is just the mix for a fiction writer.

Bibliography

Lutz, John. *Bloodfire*. New York: Holt, 1991.
____. *Bonegrinder*. New York: Putnam, 1976.
____. *Burn*. New York: Holt, 1995.
____. *Buyer Beware*. New York: Putnam, 1976.
____. *Chill of Night*. New York: Pinnacle Books, 2006.
____. *Darker Than Night*. New York: Pinnacle Books, 2004.
____. *Dancer's Debt*. New York: St. Martin's, 1988.
____. *Dancing with the Dead*. New York: St. Martin's, 1992.
____. *Death by Jury*. New York: St. Martin's, 1995.
____. *Diamond Eyes*. New York: St. Martin's, 1990.
____. *The Ex*. San Diego, CA: Kensington, 1996.
____. *The Eye*. Co-authored with Bill Pronzini. New York: Mysterious Press, 1984.
____. *Fear the Night*. New York: Pinnacle Books, 2005.
____. *Final Seconds*. Collaboration with other authors. San Diego, CA: Kensington, 1998.
____. *Flame*. New York: Holt, 1989.
____. *Hot*. New York: Holt, 1992.
____. *Jericho Man*. New York: Morrow, 1980.
____. *Kiss*. New York: Holt, 1990.
____. *Lazarus Man*. New York: Morrow, 1979.
____. *Lightning*. New York: Holt, 1996.
____. *The Night Caller*. New York: Pinnacle Books, 2001.
____. *The Night Spider*. New York: Pinnacle Books, 2003.
____. *The Night Watcher*. New York: Pinnacle Books, 2002.
____. *Nightlines*. New York: St. Martin's, 1984.
____. *Oops! A Nudger Mystery*. New York: St. Martin's, 1998.
____. *Ride the Lightning*. New York: St. Martin's, 1987.
____. *The Right to Sing the Blues*. New York: St. Martin's, 1986.
____. *Scorcher*. New York: Holt, 1987.
____. *The Shadow Man*. New York: Morrow, 1981.
____. *Shadowtown*. New York: Mysterious Press, 1988.
____. *Spark*. New York: Holt, 1993.
____. *SWF Seeks Same*. New York: St. Martin's, 1990.
____. *Thicker Than Blood*. New York: St. Martin's, 1993.

_____. *Time Exposure.* New York: St. Martin's, 1989.
_____. *Torch.* New York: Holt, 1994.
_____. *Tropical Heat.* New York: Holt, 1986.
_____. *The Truth of the Matter.* New York: Pocket Books, 1971.

Short Story Collections

_____. *Better Mousetraps.* New York: St. Martin's, 1988.
_____. *The Nudger Dilemmas.* Unity, ME: Five Star, 2001.
_____. *Shadows Everywhere.* Eugene, OR: Mystery Scene Press, 1994.
_____. *Until You Are Dead.* Unity, ME: Five Star, 1998.

Bob Morris, Central Florida Journalist and Mystery Novelist

by Hank Raulerson

"*I understand that you are a horticulturist, Mr. Chasteen.*"
"*Nope, I just raise palm trees.*"
—from *Bermuda Schwartz* by Bob Morris

Bob Morris gets around. The Winter Park–based author has been variously a newspaperman for the *Fort Myers News-Press* and the *Orlando Sentinel*, a travel writer for magazines like *National Geographic Traveler* and *Outside*, an editor of travel magazines including *Caribbean Travel & Life*, and a food writer for *Bon Appetit*. It seems near-inevitable that Morris would turn his talents to fiction, and of course he has. Morris is the author of a series of mystery novels set in the Caribbean, the titles of which are geographically instructive: *Bahamarama* (2004), *Jamaica Me Dead* (2005), and *Bermuda Schwartz* (2007).

The hero of these novels is Zack Chasteen, a former University of Florida football star and current palm tree grower and unlikely solver of mysteries. When he's not in prison (he was framed!), Chasteen lives in LaDonna, Florida, a lovingly mythologized town on the Mosquito Lagoon, where he maintains a nursery of the aforementioned exotic palms. Chasteen doesn't spend a lot of time at LaDonna, being called out to the islands on errands of mercy or rescue, frequently accompanied by his elegantly British soul-mate Barbara Pickering or his enigmatic sidekick Boggy, the last living Taino Indian. Morris manages the seemingly fantastic with aplomb, grounding his novels in the closely observed particularities of place and anchoring them in the hardheaded pragmatism of his protagonist. Zack Chasteen doesn't carry a gun but he comes well-armed, like his author, with a fine-tuned version of Hemingway's bullshit detector, wary of the worldly and the mystical alike. Beyond that ever-present irony, though, is an abiding love of place, especially Florida, for Morris a land both beautiful and doomed.

HANK RAULERSON: *You're a fourth-generation Floridian—a rare creature in a state where twenty years' tenure makes one a "native." You grew up in Florida and have seen it from both the inside and the outside. Does Florida have a "culture" that is definable? What is it about Florida that so fires the literary, or at least the writerly, imagination?*

BOB MORRIS: Man, that's a lot to chew on for an opening question. Florida certainly has a culture that is definable, even if it's not always desirable. Having said that, I'm not sure that I can define Florida culture except to say that it is a definite function of place. Meaning, because Floridians nowadays come from so many different places, our culture is a great festering stew of stuff. It ain't Utah or Minnesota, baby. No easy appellations here. It's constantly defining itself, from the high to the low, and that's why some might think it non-existent. But we've got them fooled.

As for firing the writerly imagination, I come at it from both a native and a former newspaper perspective. Used to be that California was the State of Weird. But Florida has long since outweirded California. Anything can happen here at any time. It's dangerous and bizarre and wonderful.

It has been noted of Florida that its history is compressed, sort of history in fast-forward. Consider that much of at least Central and South Florida was more or less frontier at the turn of the last century. Some folks confuse this foreshortened history as no history at all. Are you a student of Florida history? How has this history shaped your writing?

I take the cafeteria approach to Florida history. I'm hungry for all of it, but I typically only sample it in small tasty bites. My favorite Florida history book is the *WPA Guide to Florida*, published, I think, in 1934 and reissued since. A wonderful compendium of folklore and scholarship. It's in my car whenever I drive the backroads and byways.

Beyond that, I benefit from my "bone history." My people first came to Central Florida in the 1880s. My grandmother and my great-aunt lived in Leesburg and Yalaha after they got married. And since they had no telephones, they corresponded with daily postcards, talking about everyday events, rites of passage and the humdrum. I have several hundred of those postcards and visit them regularly. This is what makes bone history about a place. And it is inconceivable that it would not shape my writing.

I couldn't help but laugh when, in Jamaica Me Dead, *Zack Chasteen quotes his grandfather saying that "Florida had been on a slow slide to ruin ever since the invention of air-conditioning," what the grandfather calls "Dr. Gorrie's goddamn ice machine." My own grandfather used to say something almost identical. I can only imagine what Zack's grandfather (or my own) would say about his native state now. Do you share this concern about the state of the state? Where is Florida headed? Is Florida's growth sustainable?*

Oh, Florida is doomed, no doubt about that. The road to hell is paved straight through our fair peninsula. Sustainable growth? Ha. There's no such animal, at least not as practiced in Florida. It's all about greed and sprawl. It's in our state genes. The best we can hope for is to slow down the inevitable, forestall ultimate collapse. That much said, I wouldn't live anywhere else.

Which Florida writers get Florida right? Which writers do you admire? Envy?

Well, Marjorie Rawlings got it right. My great-aunt Dessie Prescott, who died a few years ago, was one of Marjorie's dear friends (Dessie is mentioned often in *Cross Creek*, especially in the fine, fine story "Hyacinth Float," about their trip up the St. Johns River.)

John D. MacDonald, of course, is the progenitor of all who would presume to write Florida-based mysteries. He got it right about ravages against the environment, developer greed and all the usual Florida bugaboos before anyone else did. And the fact that he set a social agenda, of sorts, in the confines of a mystery series is indicative that the so-called genre defies any limits that might be put upon it. For the record, my younger son—Dashiell MacDonald Morris—is named after John D. and Mr. Hammett of *Maltese Falcon* fame.

On the nonfiction front, lots of writers check in from time to time to take a shot at Florida, but my pal Bill Belleville (*Losing It All to Sprawl, A River of Lakes: A Journey on Florida's St. Johns River,* and others) is around for the long haul and should be required reading for anyone who calls this spit of sand home.

What writers were your early influences? Whose work did you read and reread? Which writers would you consider indispensable?

Early influences—Charles Dickens (I remember reading *David Copperfield* when I was about 10 years old and our family was making a tedious drive to Oklahoma to visit relatives. Without the book, I'd have gone insane) and certainly, like everyone of my generation, J.D. Salinger, not just *Catcher in the Rye*, but the short stories and, particularly, "A Perfect Day for Bananafish." After that the usual suspects—Vonnegut, Hemingway and later John Barth, Tom McGuane, Jim Harrison.

Read and reread: Robert Parker and Elmore Leonard.

Indispensable: Robert Parker and Elmore Leonard.

When did you figure out you wanted to be a writer?

The easy answer: When I flunked two consecutive terms of organic chemistry and understood I was not meant to be a marine biologist. I went back to Leesburg, worked at a pre-stressed concrete plant, saved up some money and spent a couple of years traveling around the world. I was broke on the road and I spent a lot of time sitting in cafes and bars, writing these long letters home about what I'd seen and done.

When I returned to Florida, my parents asked me what I intended to do with my life. I told them I had no idea. My mom said: "Well, you wrote beautiful letters home. We had them laminated and passed them all around town. Why don't you go to journalism school?"

That was all the nudge I needed. I enrolled at UF and got a degree in journalism and the rest is sordid history.

But truth is, as a young boy, in love with words and books, I remember having a regular sequence of dreams in which I'd see a big book suspended in the air, its pages turning and all the pages were blank. I remember thinking: It's up to me to fill those pages. So I don't know if becoming a writer was dream fulfillment, but it seems as good a guess as anything.

You've been a newspaper columnist, a travel writer, a food writer. Why did you make the leap to writing fiction? Is it, in fact, a leap?

Not a leap at all, just a natural progression. I'd always wanted to write books, specifically mysteries, but I got married, had kids and needed the safety net of a job with direct deposit and health insurance. I'm a chronic traveler. Any money I've ever made has mostly gone toward financing the next trip rather than doing something stupid like investing in stocks or real estate. Ultimately, this led me from newspapers to travel magazines. I was editor of a couple of them and still write regularly for the likes of *National Geographic Traveler*, *Outside* and others.

The downside of travel writing is that you visit a place and, if you are any good at all as a storyteller and a gatherer of tales, then you come home with so much more stuff than you can ever hope to squeeze into a 2,500-word magazine article. When I visit a new place I'm a vacuum cleaner. I suck up everything, from bizarre food to local sayings to the nameplates on the front of taxicabs to the type of pots and pans they have on the shelves in hardware stores. It's just all so rich and telling. But what to do with it? It's not the kind of material you incorporate into a magazine story, especially not the kind of story that magazines want nowadays, which are increasingly more about luxury experience than gritty travel.

So the only venue left, for me anyway, is fiction. Typically, I might visit a place while on a magazine assignment, but all the while I am trying to invent a story about the place based on all the foraging I do. In this sense, journalism lays the ideal groundwork for the fiction that follows. Same tools, same skill set...

Is there any tension between Bob Morris the travel writer and Bob Morris the novelist? Do you have to make a deliberate and conscious effort to take off one hat, put on the other? Is one more satisfying than the other?

Yes, Bob Morris the travel writer currently has a restraining order against Bob Morris the novelist but my attorneys tell both of me that I can't talk about it.

No, as I said above, the two complement each other, at least in my case. I'd have to say that the fiction is more satisfying, much more satisfying, since I don't suffer the constraint of space. If I were writing nonfiction books, which I intend to, I might feel differently, but this is yet to come.

Where I really have to take off my hat and get into a totally different mindset is with all the venal, under-the-radar writing that I do in order to pay the bills. While my books are doing well and on the ascendant, I am not yet at the point where I can depend on them alone to help me live with a certain degree of comfort. So, in addition to the books and the magazine articles, I often hire out to do quickie pieces for advertising agencies or p.r. companies. I even write advertorials for a number of magazines. None of this stuff has my name on it, and for that I am thankful.

Many writers wouldn't admit to doing this since they see it as below their station. But that's bullshit. It's honorable enough work, done for a good wage, even though I often have to put more gloss on a subject that I might typically employ. I'm a writer. I'll take any writing project that comes my way. And until I get to the point where I've got enough money in the bank that I can afford to be picky, then that's just the way it is.

How did you come to write mysteries? Do you see yourself as a "mystery" writer? Are the genre fiction labels—mystery, detective, crime—limiting? Should we make distinctions between genre fiction and so-called straight novels?

The best books are mysteries whether or not they suffer the mantle of genre. I mean, the Bible is a mystery, only the writers left us hanging, the bastards, because we still don't know—after all that murder and deceit and chaos—how it is going to end.

As a writer, the thing you are striving for the most is to get a reader to hang in there with you all the way to the end. In this day and age, that is asking for quite a commitment. And if the best way to achieve this is by wrapping your story in the cloak of a mystery—killing someone on the first page and then making the reader stick around for 80,000 words to find out whodunit—then so be it. Mysteries are merely palettes for telling the larger timeless stories—love, death, loss, redemption. Those are the basics. And if they afford you the opportunity to sneak in some sly commentary on social issues and culture and politics, then all the better.

I certainly see myself as a mystery writer. Proud of it. When people ask me what I do, I tell them: I write mystery novels. I don't have a problem with putting the genre label on it. Why should I? My books sell more copies than most of the literary stuff. What is there to be embarrassed about?

Do you see distinctions among mystery, crime, and detective fiction? Which genre does your work fall in?

Sure, there are mighty distinctions within the genre. All authors like to think their work is altogether different from any other, but that doesn't hold water. We all have to fall somewhere. The Zack Chasteen/Caribbean series falls into the amateur sleuth category. It's not hard crime, it's not noir, it's not straight-on detective and it's not a cozy—although it has some elements of all of those. Zack is just an everyday guy who steps into more than his fair share of shit. And sure, it is inconceivable that a normal everyday guy could come across such an abundance of death and double-crossing, but hey, that's the beauty of fiction.

The plots of your novels are pretty intricate, elaborate. At the same time you've created a number of memorable characters. Which is more important in mystery fiction, plot or character? Do you pay more attention to one or the other?

I'd like to think my work is both plot-driven and character-driven although there are those who maintain you can't be both. I like to create intricate plots because it keeps me engaged, and if I can keep myself engaged then there's a slight chance it might glue the reader, too. I come up with a barebones plot first, then let interesting characters drive it home. Plot and character serve each other.

That said, I strive not to let the story become too plot-heavy. And at the same time, I try not to sprinkle the story with too many interesting characters. Typically, when starting a new book, I create way too many characters, and I fall in love with all of them. So I have to backtrack and turn some of them into composites or save them for another day for the sake of simplicity. In *Jamaica Me Dead*, I originally had a smart-mouthed black woman detective from Fort Lauderdale teaming up with Zack to track down the bad guys. Her name was Dennie Pancake ("What? You got a problem with my name, bitch?") and I truly loved her. But she started to take over things so I got rid of her. I hope to revive her in the future, maybe even spin her off into something of her own. You can't be afraid to kill your loved ones, eh?

You've been called a natural storyteller. What does this mean? Where does this facility for storytelling come from?

I've also been called a facile liar, which might be the same thing. Beats me where it comes from. Maybe genetic. I grew up in a house where we all sat down to dinner every evening, around the table in the dining room, and made talk with one another whether we liked it or not. Arguing was a big part of it, holding your own, and that meant telling a good story, or at least being able to out-talk anyone else who tried to wedge in.

Also, I can't overlook the fact that when I was 15, I came down with a weird and awful disease—Guillain-Barré syndrome—that came on suddenly, overnight actually, and left me paralyzed for six months. I was flat on my back in a hospital, went from 160 pounds to 90 pounds and couldn't even close my eyes, totally cognizant throughout. I had a lot of what you might call "interior time." So I became fairly comfortable with just letting my mind wander where it would and entertaining myself. Then, almost as suddenly, the disease just went away. The only residual effect is in some of my face muscles. I can't, for instance, blow up a balloon. And sometimes I think I'm smiling but I'm not. Maybe this explains why I still like to lie flat on my back in bed and write stories on my laptop.

Do you work from an outline? Do you know where the story is going before you begin?

It's not so much an outline as it is a bunch of notecards that I am constantly writing down ideas on and then sticking up on a bulletin board in my office.

Each notecard is a potential mini-scene in a book or a snatch of dialogue that I envision one of the characters saying or something idiotic like: "Zack eats a rotten mango." Eventually, all the notecards are shuffled around and begin to take on a form. And then I start writing.

Also, very early on in the process, I have to write a synopsis of the book for my agent and my editor. This might just be a hundred words or so. For instance, here is the synopsis I wrote just yesterday for an upcoming Zack book, Trinidaddy-O.

> It's the week of the Caribbean's wildest street party, Trinidad's Carnival, a freewheeling spectacle of loud music, outlandish costumes and endless rivers of rum. And since *Tropics*, the travel magazine owned by Barbara Pickering, Zack Chasteen's wife, is sponsoring one of the gala Carnival events, Barbara is determined to be there, with Zack and their month-old son, Nathan, at her side. Also along for the ride is Zack's inscrutable Taino associate, Boggy, who has been recruited by an old girlfriend, a curator with Miami's Fairchild Botanical Gardens, to help her find a rare species of palm tree thought to be growing in the isolated rain forests of Trinidad's rugged northern range.
>
> The highlight of the Tropics gala is a performance by Clarence Swenson, aka Mighty Lord Daddy-O, the king of calypso and a musician known for biting political lyrics that have made him the scourge of Trinidad's high and mighty, from rich and greedy businessmen to corrupt officeholders and bureaucrats. But no sooner has Mighty Lord Daddy-O left the stage than a gang of gunmen shoots its way onto the scene and hauls him away. The island is immediately abuzz: Where is Mighty Lord Daddy-O? Who took him? And why?
>
> Displaying his chronic knack for stumbling into the stickiest of predicaments, Zack Chasteen is soon on the trail of the abductors with the many excesses of Carnival providing a raucous backdrop.

Now, I can tell you honestly that the book might not unfold like that at all. Lots of things are gonna change. But it makes my agent and my editor happy. The publisher will send me a nice advance. And I have something to hang a story on while I mess with it.

Typically though, before I can do any real writing—the 1,500 words a day, straight-ahead stuff—I have to know *exactly* how the book is gonna end. I also must have the title. Otherwise, I'm lost.

What is your daily work schedule like? Do you set daily goals? Do you follow a specific work regimen?

I get up early, fiveish, and I write something every day. It might not always be good and it might not always advance the book-at-hand, but I write something. And I mean every single day, seven days a week, no matter what. At home, on the road, hungover, sick, whatever. Also, because I am constantly juggling numerous freelance writing assignments, speaking engagements, promotional events (there is a massive amount of promotion involved with selling your books, simply massive) my ideal schedule is often shot to hell.

But when it gets down to the bitter end of a book—the last 25,000 words or so—I'm a demon. I put on the blinders and forget everything else. My wife begins giving me those long pointed looks that say: "You better damn well hurry up and finish because you are hell to live with." I'm in the zone and it's a good time, one that I love, because I am buried in the book and the characters. Writing *Bermuda Schwartz*, I piddled along at the beginning and was lucky to salvage 750 words a day. Then when it caught fire I was on the flume ride, ya know? I had one day, at the end, when I wrote 8,000 words and they were 8,000 pretty good words. That's a great day.

Nabokov's pencils famously outlasted his erasers. How much rewriting/revising do you do?

I rewrite as I go along, especially the first 50 pages or so. The first 50 pages might take me a month. Then I do less revising as it progresses because everything, hopefully, is in place and the story pulls me along. My first draft is generally a good, clean draft (my magazine editor background). I would be embarrassed to submit anything to my editor that had holes in it. The first draft of *Bermuda Schwartz* came back from my editor with just a very few notes and suggested revisions and that's the way I like it.

Some writers seem to have a love affair with language, a lyric facility, a playfulness; others feel they have to bludgeon language into submission (this is a gross simplification, I know). Do you lean in one direction or another?

I enjoy playing with language, but only if it doesn't get in the way of the story. I try to write as clean and as simply as possible (my books rank real low on the Fog Scale), while at the same time trying to add as much style as I can without muddying up the water. Just because you can turn a phrase doesn't mean you have to show off before the reader.

Your work is set both in Florida and in the Caribbean. How much research goes into preparing to write novels set in the Bahamas, Jamaica, Bermuda?

Well, I certainly travel to all those places and spend as much time as I can soaking up as much gristle as I can. I like to arrive in a place with no particular story in mind and then see what presents itself. The blank slate approach...

For *Bahamarama* and *Jamaica Me Dead*, I'd visited those places numerous times and so there were layers to draw from. Plus, I read a lot of folklore and fiction and history from the islands to give me some texture. For *Bermuda Schwartz*, well, I didn't really intend to write a mystery set in Bermuda. I went there on a magazine assignment, thinking the next book would be set in Mexico—*Cancun Kills*. But then things just happened. I went scuba diving on some old shipwrecks and I met a couple of shady folks involved with offshore banking and, bingo, a story unfolded. I spent only five days in Bermuda and came away with the nugget for a book. It obviously wasn't heavy mining. I didn't have to dig deep. But that was good because, while place is important, I don't want place to overwhelm story. The secret of any good book is conflict. And in my books, conflict is created when character (that's Zack) meets place.

Speaking of place, your work has been hailed as having a strong sense of place, especially the island settings, where even natives have been impressed with its verisimilitude.

I want people to read my books and come away thinking that they have vicariously visited the place. I love the Caribbean. It is a rich, rich place. But one thing that grieves me is the cruise-ship mentality that too many people apply to the Caribbean. They think all the islands are pretty much the same—umbrella drinks, pretty beaches and good shopping. But they are so wonderfully and enchantingly different—from the folklore to the food to the local patois. The books are my attempt to set each island apart. So if I get a little bit of it right, then I'm happy. As a fourth-generation Floridian, I bristle at the idea of outsiders writing about my turf... Except when they get it right. So I try to apply that same ethos to writing about places where I am a foreigner. I strive for authenticity, but know full well that I can't write about a place like a native.

It's been said that Florida writers tend to make protagonists who are outsiders, who dwell on the fringes, usually by choice. Does your protagonist Zack Chasteen fit this mold?

I think many Florida writers, myself included, create protagonists who cling to a long-gone vision of Florida, an ideal. Randy White's Doc Ford lives in a Tarpon Bay that is no longer like the old Tarpon Bay. Carl Hiaasen has characters who live in Stilt City. Jon King puts his guy in the Everglades. And Zack Chasteen is the last resident of LaDonna, which is a fictionalized version of Eldora, a ghost town on Mosquito Lagoon. So yes, they are automatic outsiders, which is pretty much the way you feel if you are a fourth-generation Floridian vastly outnumbered by all the newcomers.

He may be an outsider but Zack Chasteen puts himself into some pretty tight spots. Why does he refuse to carry a gun?

A couple of reasons for that, the main one being that it is just too easy to get out of a scrape when you have a gun. My stories would be a whole lot shorter if Zack carried a gun. Most of his problems could be instantly solved, and where is the fun in that?

Most people don't carry guns, certainly not with the frequency that they appear in most mysteries. I'd rather that my guy use his wits to save his ass.

The other reason—I'm lazy. I don't really know a lot about guns—I own a shotgun for occasional skeet shooting and bird hunting, but that's it—and I don't want to do all the research that would allow me to talk knowledgably about them. Other writers are much better at it. Lee Child, for instance, can go on and on about muzzle velocity and the exact number of nanoseconds it takes a bullet to reach its target, and it is fascinating. I enjoy reading it, but I don't need to know it and if I tried to write as if I knew it then I would just show my ass. And my ignorance.

There's quite a lot of violence in your novels—hand-to-hand scrapes, shoot-outs, bombings—but the violence is not graphically rendered. That is, while the body counts are pretty high, the blood spatter/gore quotient is fairly low. Is this an attempt to balance realism with commercial palatability?

Huh? It's not really a conscious attempt to do anything except not ruin someone's breakfast. I read too many books that bog down with the gore. If you say that someone gets shot then it doesn't take a whole lot of imagination to figure out what it might look like. Plus, I see no reason to burden myself with the chore of coming up with wonderfully descriptive ways to describe the sight of blood. It's red, lose too much and you're dead. What more to say? I'd rather get on with the story.

A lot of Florida fiction has a political bent—I'm thinking of Hiaasen's eco-villains or Randy Wayne White's do-gooding conservationists. Your fiction seems less overtly political, even when it's set in Jamaica, where "everything is political." For example, both political candidates in Jamaica Me Dead, *Alan Whitehall and Kenya Oompong, are relatively well-meaning and sympathetic. Do you see your fiction as apolitical? Is this a deliberate stance? Is there room for politics in a crime novel?*

Again, it's not deliberate. I'll reference politics, or take a few pot shots at something that irks me, but these are mysteries, not political platforms. I know what I like and dislike—I'm a liberal Democrat, dammit—but I don't want to add excess baggage for the reader. This is not to say that I wouldn't employ a stronger political line, but only if the story warranted it. No hidden agendas...

Funny that you should mention Kenya Oompong in *Jamaica Me Dead*. She was a pure creation of my imagination—someone who had worked the ghettoes of Kingston and formed a political base. About a month after the book came out, Jamaica held its elections. The surprising result—the first woman prime minister in the country's history, Portia Simpson Miller, an activist who formed her political base by working the Kingston ghettoes. Far be it from me to mention life imitating art...

Boggy is an interesting study. How difficult was (is) it to create a character who is the last Taino Indian alive? Boggy seems to represent the nativist mystical impulse as against Chasteen's hard-headed pragmatism. Is that a fair reading?

Well, you give it much more academic implication than I might, but yeah, that's it, pretty much. I wanted a character who was more than just a handy goofball sidekick. I wanted someone with real roots in the Caribbean, someone who knew the legends and the folklore. And someone who, at the same time, was just enigmatic enough to dwell in the shadows and know things that Zack could not possibly know. This gives Boggy the ability to save Zack's butt on a regular basis, often in mystifying ways that might be just a tad out of step with reality.

I'm fascinated by the Taino culture and have studied it at some length so Boggy just sprung from all that. The fact that he is the last living full-blooded Taino does stretch the imagination, but that's a healthy thing. Together, I like to think that Boggy and Zack are the total package—a man of bullish action and a man of mystical incline.

How was the writing of the second novel different from the first? Was it easier? More difficult? Do you have a favorite?

Nope, the second one was harder. And so was the third. And the next one will be just as hard. The first one, *Bahamarama*, was easy because there were no expectations. Now I have to build on that, hearkening a bit to the backstory, while allowing each book to stand on its own. That's one reason why my next book, tentatively called *The Good Scout*, is a stand-alone thriller set in Costa Rica. No Zack or Boggy in it. Just need to step away and refresh for awhile.

No favorites, except for the one I'm working on and can't wait to finish. I love all my children equally. So far.

What would do for a living if you couldn't be a writer?

I'd do something with food, either be a chef or run a restaurant or grow good stuff to eat. I do all the grocery shopping and cooking in our house. And it is the way I relax after a day of writing. Beyond that, I'd be worthless at anything else.

Is writing fun, or is it a job?

It's a fun job. There are days of utter misery, just like any job. But they are vastly outweighed by the end results—knowing that people read and enjoy my books. I mean, I get to travel as a tax write-off and then sit around my house working in my boxer shorts. What's not fun about that?

Bibliography

Morris, Bob. *Bahamarama*. New York: St. Martin's Press, 2004.
____. *Bermuda Schwartz*. New York: St. Martins Press, 2007.
____. *Jamaica Me Dead*. New York: St. Martin's Press, 2005.

Barbara Parker, Mistress of Crime Writing

by Claudia Slate

Since Barbara Parker was fourteen years old, she has been a resident of Florida, the setting for all but the last in her *Suspicion* series, novels featuring Miami lawyers Gail Connor and Anthony Quintana. Parker used to be a lawyer herself, first a prosecutor and then in private practice, specializing in real estate and family law.

Parker's first mystery novel, *Suspicion of Innocence* (1994), was nominated for an Edgar Allan Poe award by Mystery Writers of America. Others in the series are *Suspicion of Guilt* (1995), *Suspicion of Deceit* (1998), *Suspicion of Betrayal* (1999), *Suspicion of Malice* (2000), *Suspicion of Vengeance* (2001), *Suspicion of Madness* (2003), and *Suspicion of Rage* (2005). She has also written three novels not in the series: *Blood Relations* (1996), *Criminal Justice* (1997), and her latest, *The Perfect Fake*.

Parker holds a B.A. from the University of South Florida, a law degree from the University of Miami, and an M.F.A. in creative writing from Florida International University. Parker has two grown children and lives in Lauderdale by the Sea, Florida, with her pug, Maximilian von Mango (Max).

CLAUDIA SLATE: *Why have you set most of your novels in Florida?*

BARBARA PARKER: I set my work in Florida because it's the place I'm most familiar with. I learned the hard way why that's important. Before my first mystery, *Suspicion of Innocence*, there was a paperback (don't ask me the title) that I set in Connecticut, a state I knew nothing about. It seemed like a good idea at the time; I was afraid readers would be turned off by Miami's ethnic clashes. Big mistake. My ignorance of the setting led to a generic—and forgettable—story. The next time out, I decided to write in my own backyard. The book had an authenticity and excitement that the first one didn't.

Lucky for me, this was around 1990, just when Florida mystery/crime fiction was getting noticed. I rode the wave.

When you open a novel, you step into another world. It's the job of the novelist to make that world credible, even when writing about life on the Planet Zog. Not only must the setting be "real," it must fit the story. Imagine a Travis McGee novel set in Arizona. The plot and the characters would have to change, too. My *Suspicion* series could not have been placed anywhere but Miami because the tension between the Anglo and Cuban exile communities is part of the story. I didn't pick Miami at random; having lived in the area for thirty years, I knew the terrain and the people.

Why did you set some of your subsequent novels outside of Miami?

Each story demands its own setting. In *Suspicion of Vengeance*, I put a man on Death Row. My main characters, sophisticated lawyers in Miami, must travel to a small town where everyone "knows" that the defendant is guilty, and my protagonists are the outsiders. Setting the story in Miami would have robbed it of this essential conflict. I chose a small town (Stuart, Florida) that was a fairly easy drive from home, and I spent several days researching. I took dozens of photographs, rode with a police officer, explored the historical museum, and talked to people who knew the town a lot better than I did. Through their help, I was able to create a convincing world for my readers.

Venturing out of South Florida with *Vengeance* gave me the confidence to go even farther. The next books were set in the Florida Keys and Havana. I finally jumped the Atlantic with *The Perfect Fake*, my new novel (to be published in 2007). Most of the book takes place in Italy. I wouldn't have written about Cuba or Italy without actually going there, but it's amazing what you can find on the Web. For a scene near the church of Santa Maria Novella in Florence, Italy, I found a site with a 360-degree panoramic view of the piazza.

What is it about Florida that speaks to you?

What I find most fascinating about Florida is the mix of people, who move here from all over the world. You can find urban sophistication, rural simplicity, and a wide variety of cultures, beliefs, and worldviews.

Can you tell me about your literary roots—your influences? For example, I see that you hail from North Carolina. Do you find the South or Southern literature as an influence?

Am I a Southerner? I think not; I'm a Floridian. My family moved to a small central Florida town (Inverness) when I was fourteen, then to Tampa two years later. I moved to Miami in 1974 and have been in South Florida ever since. This isn't a Southern place at all; it's a patchwork of cultures: New York, the Midwest, the Caribbean, Latin America, Europe—such a mix provides plenty of drama.

And yet, as I ponder your question, I have to say that the small-town South had its influence. We didn't have much money, so reading books was an acceptable entertainment. My father liked to recite poetry, and I had an aunt who had us convinced she was minor royalty. There was the town idiot who rode around on a three-wheeled bicycle, and nobody paid him any mind. We accept weirdness a little more easily than they do up North, I think. I grew up doubting there was any such thing as "normal." When you have a grandmother tell you a Bible story every night, or as soon as school is out for the summer you kick off your shoes and go play Indian in the woods, it naturally leads to the conclusion that life is a narrative, not a series of random events.

If you could live anywhere in Florida, where would it be? Why?

If I could afford it, I would live on the water in Miami, with a boat tied to the dock behind my house. Miami is the most vibrant city south of Washington, D.C. But I'm presently living a few blocks from the ocean, so I can't complain.

Why do you think so much crime fiction has come out of Florida?

There is a lot of crime fiction everywhere these days. If there's more of it in Florida, it may be that we writers are simply following a trend that exploded in the late 1980s with writers like Randy Wayne White, James W. Hall, Edna Buchanan, and Carl Hiaasen. Florida crime fiction was hot. Now I don't see any particular advantage to setting a book in Florida.

What kinds of books attract you as a reader? Do you have favorite authors?

I like books with delicious prose, memorable characters, and a story that pulls me in. This is basically what every reader wants.

By "memorable characters" so you mean creating characters by including specific details about a character's body positioning, as you do here in Suspicion of Rage, *for example? "Holding the mangled aluminum basketball-style, he flexed his knees and aimed at the rusting trash bin." And: "Sprawling on the sofa, Raul put his hands behind his head. He wore a sleeveless T-shirt, and the muscles bunched in his arms."*

I never thought of body positions as "memorable," but I suppose that's part of the recipe for a "memorable character." Without those small details, all you get is a generic human of no particular size, shape, ethnicity, or personality. "Memorable" also relates to what a character *does*—his reactions to situations and to other characters. Just as a reaction will be specific to that character, so will his speech pattern. One person will use slang and another will have a more educated vocabulary. If you listen closely, you will notice that the same man will speak differently depending on his mood. A writer must also consider what a character eats, drinks, wears, and drives.

Do you read other authors as you write?

When I'm on a deadline I have very little time to read, but if I'm reaching for a particular tone or technique, I might consult a particular author. For example, if I need a "tough-guy" voice, I might flip through a novel by Robert Crais or Lee Child.

What are some of the reference books on your shelf?

No writer should be without *Rodale's Synonym Finder*. I also have a very fat dictionary, which lies open on the shelf for easy access. Here are some others: *Bartlett's Familiar Quotations, The New Penguin Dictionary of Modern Quotations, The Concise Columbia Encyclopedia, Dictionary of Myth and Fable, The New York Public Library Desk Reference,* and *A Writer's Companion*. You will also want basic grammar books and dictionaries in Spanish, French, Italian—better still, find someone who speaks them fluently.

Do you use any unconventional sources?

As a mystery writer, I have handbooks on guns, poisons, and so on. I went to a used bookstore and browsed the outdated travel books. I snagged a 1920 guide to Miami that way. When I research a particular topic, I buy books and videos about it. To create "The Miami Grand Opera" for *Suspicion of Deceit*, I bought season tickets to the opera and interviewed singers. Over the years I've collected quite a few books on Cuba, both fiction and nonfiction, along with maps, travel handbooks, information downloaded from the Internet, and notes from interviews with people who know more than I do. Writers aren't as smart as you think; we rely heavily on our sources.

Why do you think mysteries have become increasingly mainstream and popular?

Mysteries have always been popular, but now they are given more respect because so many of them are not just good reads; they're well written.

Could you elaborate on what you mean by "well written"?

"Well written" means I enjoyed the book, learned something from it, and was sorry when it was over. This is obviously very subjective. Jose Saramago won the Nobel Prize for Literature, and I can't get past the first chapter of his novel *Blindness*. Yet I devoured *The Da Vinci Code*, which no one would seriously argue is "literature." But who cares? If you like it, read it… On the other hand, do try occasionally to step outside your usual reading habits. You'd be surprised how many people read only mysteries, or only romance, or only "literature." Try something different, like a graphic novel (*Sin City* or *Persephone*) or a travel guide (*1000 Places to See Before You Die*).

What do you see as the difference between crime novels, detective novels, and mystery novels?

A detective novel is a crime/mystery novel with a detective (a police officer, a private investigator, or the like). Otherwise, I see no difference.

How did you get into the business of writing mysteries? Were you aware of the history of the form?

I started writing mysteries because I wanted to write something that would sell. I was not aware of the history of the form at the time, nor did I care. I still don't.

What was your preparation or training? When did you first know you were a novelist?

I have an M.F.A. in creative writing from Florida International University (Miami). I first knew I was a novelist when I wrote a novel. Before that, I aspired to become a novelist.

What are the mechanics of your work?—i.e., outline or no outline? Do you finish one manuscript before beginning another?

I used to outline extensively. Now I have a basic idea that I fill in as I go along. I always finish one manuscript before starting another; it would be too confusing to do otherwise.

What are your work habits?

In the early stages of writing a book, I do a lot of research, traveling, and talking to people in the particular field I want to write about. I put my thoughts down on paper with a pen. As the story takes shape, I spend more and more time at the computer. During the last three months of writing, I am working about seven days a week, as many hours a day as I can stand it. The entire process takes about a year.

How do you develop your stories and/or story elements?

My stories develop from the research that I do on the subject matter. It's like going into the field and gathering wild flowers. You come home with a basket full, then you begin to arrange them. If you need to fill in some places, you do more research. My stories have never been autobiographical. My own life isn't nearly as interesting as the ones I create on the page.

Have some of your novels required more research than others? Do you enjoy that aspect of writing?

For me, research is the most enjoyable part of writing. And, yes, many of my novels required a great deal of research—*Suspicion of Vengeance* comes to mind. Not only did I study capital appellate law, I corresponded with two men on Death Row, toured Florida State Prison, and spent some time in Martin County, Florida, where the book was set. The book set in Havana required just as much study. I have learned about boat building, ballet, opera, rock-and-roll, grade-B horror films, map collecting, drug dealing…

Do you always know how your novels will end when you begin them? Does anything ever surprise you about the plot or characters as you proceed?

There are generally two basic plot lines unfolding simultaneously in a mystery. First, the crime. Who did it and why, and how does the bad guy get his (or her) just deserts in the end? Second, the hero's journey. (I'm stealing that phrase from Joseph Campbell.) The hero is on a quest to (a) help a friend; (b) save himself; (c) save or understand the society in which the action takes place; or (d) any combination of the above. The two major plot lines are the wheels that carry the story. They move forward at the same speed. They both propel the plot (quickly, we hope). They are metaphorically similar. They must work together so that neither the solving of the crime nor the resolution of the hero's journey can happen without the other.

The "crime" plot is usually resolved before the "journey" plot, but not always. Yes, I know who the bad guy is. Sometimes I know in advance how he bites the dust, and sometimes in the revisions I might decide to throw him off a cliff instead of shoot him.

Do you ever run into plot difficulties?

Too often I get stuck halfway through the book and realize I have two "crime" plots—one in the past, one in the present. I have to figure out how each relates to the other, and how both affect the hero's journey. I go take a walk and try to think my way out of the woods. I swear that next time, I will write a simple plot, but I never do.

So this process doesn't always go smoothly?

It almost never does. The journey is clear only in retrospect. When someone asks me if I know how the novel ends before I begin, what can I say? It's like getting from here to Los Angeles without a map. You head west, but you don't know if you're going to go through El Paso or Albuquerque. You hope for a few adventures along the way, but if you take too many side trips, your reader will get tired and want to go home.

Are parts of your novels drawn from your own life experiences? For example, is there any of you in Gail Connor or vice versa? Are any of your other characters patterned after people you know or have known? Did familiarity with your own children help in your characterization of Gail's daughter, Karen?

I am not my characters; they are not me. But of course we share many traits, and to create them, I stole pieces of other people I've met, observed directly, or read about. I don't make anything up; no writer does. We might notice things more intently, or differently, than most people do, but in general, we're wizards at combining our observations into new combinations and patterns. And we know how to do research. If I want to create a believable girl of twelve (like Karen), I don't rely on my memory; my own daughter has been an adult too long. It's better to interview a person of the appropriate age. Sometimes, however, you don't know anyone like the character in your story. For example, in the new book, *The Perfect Fake*, I wanted to create a hit man from somewhere in Eastern Europe.

How do you find such a person?

I used the driver for my local Honda dealership who took me home after I'd left my car in the shop. He's Croatian, he has a huge mustache, and he has such interesting opinions about the Muslims in the former Yugoslavia. But every hit man needs a pistol. I Googled "assassin" and "pistol" in the same search phrase and came up with a Walther P99. I removed his left thumbnail, made him a chain-smoker, and bought him some shirts from the Tommy Bahama store on Miami Beach. I also made him a suspected war criminal. Don't worry. He won't get away with it.

When reading about Gail and Anthony's love affair, I was sometimes conflicted in my feelings about the character Anthony: as attractive, intelligent, and caring as he is, he is also a take-charge, possessive, macho Latino. Do you intend to create that tension when you characterize him? Is that tension something that you have experienced in your personal life?

Did I take inspiration for Anthony Quintana from experiences in my own life? I should be so lucky. Readers' responses to Anthony have been interesting. A few years ago at a book-and-author luncheon, a reader came up to me before the event and said she couldn't stand Anthony Quintana and hoped I killed him off in the next book. I mentioned this during my talk, and several of the women in the audience gasped and cried out, "No!" My editor once told me that if Anthony went, "There goes the franchise."

What about readers' responses to your independent female protagonist, Gail?

Gail has been overshadowed by Anthony, I'm afraid. What usually happens in a book with a male-female pair is that the female reader puts herself into the role of the female character. The reader's eyes are therefore focused outward, and the character who holds more interest for her is the man. The woman in the pair becomes less interesting and less admirable because that's not where the reader is looking. Female readers of my series do not usually have much to say about Gail, or they complain that she is too hard on Anthony. Male readers have nothing to say about Gail or Anthony; they are more interested in the action or in the setting.

An informal poll of my female readers put Anthony's approval rating at about 95%. It's Gail they don't like. "Why is she always complaining?" "What does Anthony see in her?" "Why doesn't she pay more attention to her daughter?" I hardly know what to think of this, but the truth is, female characters are more difficult to like. A bookseller told me that even among women readers, books with male protagonists sell better than books with female protagonists. Go figure. With the next book, I won't have to worry about it.

Why not?

I'm giving the Connor/Quintana series a rest. If anyone asks, I tell them Gail and Anthony ran off to Paris, and they aren't answering their cell phones.

If you were not writing mysteries, would you still be a writer? Of what? What else would you be?

If I couldn't write mysteries, I'd like to be a travel writer, but I don't know if I could make a living at it. There is no way I'd go back to being a lawyer.

That's interesting—your not wanting to be a lawyer again—since the protagonists of several of your novels are attorneys. Your protagonists lead such exciting lives, although exhausting! So are you saying that you would rather write about their lives than live them OR are you saying that most lawyers don't live the lives of your characters?

If I wrote the life of a lawyer *as it actually is*, nobody would buy the book. Same with the life of a detective, a trauma nurse, or a secret agent. Reality is not a story; reality is usually boring.

Most people would probably rather write novels than continue in their ordinary jobs. As a lawyer, I was doing one thing: practicing law. As a writer, I can do anything I want, and when I get tired of being a lawyer or a hit man, I can sing opera, catch tropical fish, forge a map, or drive into the Italian Alps.

How important are gender, ethnic, and political issues in your writing?

I don't set out *in advance* to make a statement about a particular issue. My goal at the beginning of the process is to put a character into a difficult situation and force him or her to get out of it. In Suspicion of Vengeance, for example, I thought it would be interesting to throw Gail Connor into a criminal case that was way over her head—a death penalty appeal would be just the thing. Would the client be guilty? No. It would be better if he were innocent, and Gail has to save him.

Then comes the research. Who is this person? Where is he from, and what is he like? He isn't an angel, of course, but how bad is he? What does the victim's family think of Gail's reopening the case? What is the position of the state's appellate lawyers? The police who investigated the murder? They must have had some evidence against him. Under what circumstances can innocence be proved, post-conviction? What procedural obstacles does the justice system put in our way?

Beginning the novel, I was ambivalent about capital punishment. The arguments on both sides seemed to have merit. After many months of research, including interviews with prosecutors, defense attorneys, and police, and correspondence with two men actually on Death Row, I began to hold the view that the death penalty is both morally and financially indefensible, except perhaps in a few extreme cases. I am not an absolutist on anything—rather, not on most things.

If I had been a die-hard opponent of capital punishment before starting the book, I don't think I could have examined the issues dispassionately, nor could I have created realistic and sympathetic characters who happen to hold different opinions.

As a writer—and I hope a conscientious writer—I shy away from gender, ethnic, and political issues. If the story leads me toward a certain conclusion, that's fine. I will have arrived at it honestly, not glibly, after a great deal of thought.

How is your philosophy, your overall view of mankind, reflected in your writing?

Looking over my novels, I see a bias against people who misuse their power and/or money; gated communities; conspicuous consumption; politicians, and bureaucrats. Actually, I leave it to others to say how my overall view of mankind is reflected in my writing. It is hard enough just to get the book written, and as soon as it's done, I have to throw myself into another one.

If you really want to know about my philosophy, you can probably look at the final scene of Chapter Two of *Suspicion of Innocence*, or the very last chapter of *Blood Relations*.

How so?

This is very odd—I am not particularly religious, but both of those scenes involve older men who are spiritual guides. One is a priest, the other a Torah scribe. Come to think of it, the protagonist of *Criminal Justice*, Dan Galindo, undergoes three (a significant number in the Christian church) instances of immersion and revelation. And in the chapter of *Suspicion of Vengeance* in which Gail's client is executed, take a look at the symbols of renewal and rebirth, especially in the last few paragraphs.

Interesting. I'll have to think about this.

How have readers responded to your work?

You can't please everyone, but I generally receive a very positive reaction. I treasure letters from readers who say they have learned something, or that they keep my novels on their shelves to reread or share with friends. That's the kind of thing that keeps a writer going.

Bibliography

Parker, Barbara. *Blood Relations*. New York: Penguin, 1996.
____. *Criminal Justice*. New York: Penguin, 1997.
____. *The Perfect Fake*. New York: Dutton, 2006.
____. *Suspicion of Betrayal*. New York: Penguin, 1999.

_____. *Suspicion of Deceit.* New York: Penguin, 1998.
_____. *Suspicion of Guilt.* New York: Penguin, 1995.
_____. *Suspicion of Innocence.* New York: Penguin, 1994.
_____. *Suspicion of Madness.* New York: Penguin, 2003.
_____. *Suspicion of Malice.* New York: Penguin, 2000.
_____. *Suspicion of Rage.* New York: Dutton, 2005.
_____. *Suspicion of Vengeance.* New York: Penguin, 2001.

Nancy Pickard, Socially Conscious Crime Writer

by Nancy M. Shelton

Although prize-winning author Nancy Pickard resides in Merriam, Kansas, her visits to Florida often add up to more than a month per year spent in the Sunshine State. The author of seventeen books, as well as short stories, essays, and nonfiction, Pickard vacationed in Florida during her childhood, but says the area made no lasting impression on her as a youngster. In later years, she found herself captivated by the sultry environment. Perhaps the name of Pickard's home state, which derives from the Sioux word meaning "people of the south wind," has a special application for the writer, who now gravitates to South Florida and says she's grown to love and feel more at home in the Lauderdale area than any other place on earth.

After earning a bachelor's degree in journalism from the University of Missouri at Columbia in 1967, Pickard worked as a newspaper reporter and editor for three years, for three more years as a corporate training writer, and another seven as a commercial copywriter before being overtaken by the desire to write mystery novels for the rest of her life. Pickard is the first writer to win the Agatha, Anthony, Macavity and Shamus awards for her fiction. The *San Diego Union* declared: "Nancy Pickard is acclaimed as one of today's best mystery writers. Mounting evidence suggests that this description is too limited ... Pickard [is] one of today's best writers, period." A three-time Edgar Allan Poe award nominee, a Mary Higgins Clark award finalist, and a recipient of a Lifetime Achievement award for suspense fiction from *Romantic Times*, Pickard was awarded the prestigious Thorpe Menn Award in 2001 for excellence in a Kansas City–area author. In 1997, the Friends of the Library in Kansas City presented Pickard with the Edgar Wolfe Literary Award.

On her Web site, Nancy Pickard Mysteries, http://www.nancypickard mysteries.com/, in a refreshing departure from writers' standard deprecations about the subject, Pickard says, "I don't care what anybody says—awards are nice. It's encouraging to get one; it's a happy, satisfying moment after the long trudge of writing. Awards have helped my career, and lifted my spirits, and given me courage to go on." A founding member and former president of Sisters In Crime, the international organization dedicated to the advancement of women mystery writers, Pickard has served on the national board of directors for the Mystery Writers of America. Her works have been published in England, Canada, Australia, France, Italy, Spain, Holland, Japan, Finland, Sweden, and Germany.

In 1993, Pickard was chosen to complete Virginia Rich's unfinished Eugenia Potter story, *The 27-Ingredient Chile Con Carne Murders*. Rich, who died in 1984, had written three popular culinary mysteries and was working on a fourth at the time of her death. Pickard has added two more books to the series: *The Blue Corn Murders* and *The Secret Ingredient Murders* (with Sally Goldenbaum). She has published an anthology of short pieces, *Storm Warnings*, stories too numerous to mention in several collections, and a nonfiction book with Lynn Lott, *Seven Steps on the Writer's Path*.

Pickard's most recently published works of fiction are *The Virgin of Small Plains*, released to critical acclaim and readers' raves in April of 2006 and since optioned for television, and the three hugely popular mysteries in her Marie Lightfoot series: *The Whole Truth*, *Ring of Truth*, and *The Truth Hurts*. This series' heroine is a best-selling crime fiction writer living in the fictional town of Bahia Beach, Florida, between Pompano and Lauderdale.

NANCY SHELTON: *Was your motivation for the Marie Lightfoot concept to make the shift to a Florida locale?*

NANCY PICKARD: In leaving Jenny Cain, my first need was to create a new series, but I didn't get excited about it until it occurred to me to set it in Florida. So the egg may have come slightly before the chicken, but I don't think it would have hatched without it.

In a 2001 interview, when Susan McBride asked if Marie Lightfoot is anything like Nancy Pickard, you responded, "Marie doesn't think of herself as a journalist, but as more of a storyteller who happens to deal in fact. In not thinking of herself as a journalist, she is certainly like me, because even though I have a degree in that field, it was obvious to me early on that I wasn't that crazy about facts. I preferred to make things up ... but what the Marie series allows me to do is branch out more into suspense as well as mystery." She was also the heroine who allowed you to situate those books in Florida. Will we be hearing more from Marie?

The truth is there may never be another Marie book now that I'm doing stand-alones set in Kansas. But then again, you never know. The fact that I can't seem to leave her behind, and am doing short stories about her, may suggest that she's not finished with me yet.

In Ring of Truth, *you say, "Natives will tell you this state isn't what it seems. What it looks like is recent and skin deep; what it really is goes deep to porous limestone." Your attraction to Florida certainly goes beyond the superficial.*

Here's a story that I think indicates the depth of my willingness to put up with just about anything to be in Florida. Some years back, an unknowing publicist scheduled me into a Miami Beach hotel for a book tour. That sounds fine, but the problem was she had me landing at Miami Airport at midnight, on a Saturday during Spring Break! My taxi waded through throngs of breakers to get to a crummy hotel with a surly receptionist who claimed not to have my reservation and I ended up paying with my own credit card. My porter was a security guard who, when we reached my room, changed my locks for safety's sake! I locked my new lock, slept like a baby, got up the next morning and found the closest Cuban restaurant, drank three cafés con leche in a row and happily sat and wrote a scene in which I used all the difficulties from the night before. That scene never made it into my work, but maybe it will one day in some form or another.

You've said you spend a great deal of time, maybe a month or more a year, in Florida. Are these trips vacations for you?

I don't count them as vacations, really, because I travel to Florida to work. It feels like "just life" moved to a different location. In fact, I never think of going to Florida as a holiday. It feels more like moving to another home, even though I don't have a home in the state. But I do go to the same places over and over—the home of some writer friends in Wellington, the home of another writer friend in Hollywood, and the home of friends in Lauderdale.

If you could live anywhere in Florida, where would it be?

I'd love to live in Lauderdale, on a canal with boat access to the Intracoastal and the Port of the Everglades.

What is it about Florida that most interests you as a writer?

The dramatic contrasts of cultures, languages, geography, and geology, the crime, and the way South Florida is a glimpse of America's future, in my opinion. It is simply one of the most interesting states in the Union. The state possesses such dramatic contrasts between light and dark in both the literal and metaphorical senses. Florida, California, and Alabama are said to be the three most interesting states in the country geographically. Florida's like several different countries all crammed into one odd meandering shape. From the tall pines in the north around Tallahassee to the mangrove swamps down south, I love all of it. Sometimes I think that hardly anything is as it seems on the surface in Florida, that it's all illusion, and what better setting for fiction could there be than that?

What parts of the state hold the greatest appeal for you?

I'm most interested in the south urban coastal areas, possibly because of Cuban coffee and empanadas.

So you're a fan of Cuban cuisine. Have you ever visited the country? Is it the Cuban influence that draws you to South Florida?

I've never been to Cuba. I can't really pry apart the various strands of my strong attraction to southeast Florida and name the one that makes the most difference to me, but I do love the Cuban influence. I also enjoy the heavy New York-Northeast Coast influence, the retired population, the Haitian presence, and the whole cosmopolitan mix. When I stroll down the Boardwalk in Hollywood and hear all those accents and languages, I'm happy.

In Ring of Truth, *you describe "the real Florida," with obvious relish: "Right in the middle of the most populous areas, there are hidden acres of snakes and Spanish moss, of gigantic looping ropes of vine. Poisonous frogs feast on insects that don't even have names. Tropical lizards disappear into the cracks of trees whose branches spread out as wide as their trunks climb high. This is the real Florida, as it was before people, and probably will be after us, too." So you're not put off by the tropical wildness of the place?*

One night on the porch of a friend's house in Florida, I turned out the lights to improve my view of the moon's reflection on the canal. Within moments, I heard strange, scurrying sounds, so I flicked the lamp back on to investigate the source of the noise, and saw several palmetto bugs scuttling around on the cement at my feet. Even the sight of these gargantuan insects, like nothing I'd ever seen in Kansas, failed to dampen my enthusiasm for what has become my acknowledged second home. I must truly love the place!

Do you know much about Florida's history? Does that knowledge play a part in your books?

I have studied Florida from just about every angle, including the historical. The history hasn't played any big role in my books thus far, but it's there, undergirding my sense of confidence in my "grasp" of the state, as I write.

What do you see as the important influences shaping Florida today? In what direction are they taking the state?

I suspect the important influences are, alas, the corporate ones, and that they are taking the state in the same direction they are taking the nation and the world. When I think of the coral reef off the Keys, and the manatees, and the panthers, and the Everglades, and the beaches, and the birds, I shudder for them and for us. So much about Florida is precious, and so delicately interrelated, and vulnerable. On the other hand, Florida is also home to many people who care deeply about its natural wonders and who work their tails off to protect it. I hope they don't get discouraged and give up.

In your estimation, which Florida writers really capture the state's essence?

Archie Carr wrote my Florida Bible, A *Naturalist in Florida*. I have reread parts of that book until they're crumbling. I just love the whole book. It relaxes me, and it's chock full of THE most interesting true stuff. Enchanting.

What is distinctive about Florida writers? How do you see yourself as fitting in?

It sometimes seems to me as if there's more sheer outrageousness in Florida fiction than other states can boast—also a lot of outrage, from writers who hate what's happening around them. There's a lot of humor, too, but I have no idea how I fit in. Maybe somebody else does!

Which Florida writers do you most admire?

Besides Carr, I especially love the work of T.J. MacGregor and I read everything she writes. But the truth is that although Florida boasts an unusual number of terrific writers, I usually avoid reading them, because I don't want to be influenced by their styles. A lot of Florida writers are strong stylists with really distinctive voices. I don't want to mimic them.

Publishers and reviewers invariably categorize mystery/detective fiction as a genre. Do you find the classification limiting?

No, not at all, neither creatively nor in terms of sales.

Should mystery/detective fiction be distinguished from "novels"?

I'm always startled when I hear somebody say, "I love mysteries, but I read novels, too." Excuse me, people, a mystery is a novel. I know what they mean, but I do wonder if they do! Do I think mysteries should be distinguished from other kinds of novels? It's okay with me. Anyway, they will be, no matter what I think, because they usually are distinguishable from other kinds of novels.

How is that?

It's pretty simple. You can tell a mystery, because it's a mystery. Dead body—check. Detective work of some kind—check. Puzzle—check. Solution—check. We can dress them up in literary language, we can drape them with deep characters, but they will still be identifiable by their basic plot elements, I'm glad to say.

Why do you think mystery/detective fiction is so popular?

It's comforting, in a strange way. There's justice, a rare commodity. And there's plot, another rare commodity.

What do you see as the difference between crime novels, detective novels, and mystery novels?

Money. Call a book a crime novel instead of a detective story or a mystery and you'll probably get a bigger advance, more promotion, and better placement in the bookstores. Possibly "crime novel" sounds bigger and more important.

How did you get into the business of writing mysteries?

One day I was overcome by a desire to write mystery novels for the rest of my life, and so I began.

Did the history of the form play any part in your decision?

Only in the sense that I was aware of that history, having read voluminously in the field.

In your preface to By a Woman's Hand, *an anthology of mystery writing by female authors, you call yourself one of the "early adventurers ... who traversed this terrain without a map."*

I was referring to the early days of my career, when the great influx of American women writers, writing about American women, moved into the mystery field.

Which mystery writer has had the greatest influence on you?

It's impossible to say; the list is endless!

Do you see yourself as a writer who patterned your work after Agatha Christie's formidable example or someone who intentionally avoided her influence?

There was some of her influence, along with the influence of everybody from James M. Cain to Robert B. Parker to Margaret Millar to Mickey Spillane to Dorothy Sayers to Earl Stanley Gardner to Mary Stuart to—

When did you first know you were a novelist?

When I sold my third one.

You are most celebrated for the Jenny Cain books. What can you say about the series?

The Jenny Cain series is known for certain qualities that were considered new at the time the books were written. One was that several of them dealt with important social issues in a more direct way than was usual, up until then, in mysteries. For instance, racism and the treatment of the mentally ill were two of the topics I raised. As a result, I began to be labeled a "social issue" writer, so I purposely steered away from that for a few books, because I didn't want to get typecast. My other departure from the norm was that the books within the series differed fairly dramatically from one another in their tone. They ranged from lighthearted and funny to somber and serious, which was unusual. Readers were long accustomed to every book in a series feeling like every other book in it. I threw in some unpredictability. I can't say it was a very good idea in terms of overall sales-people do like to be able to trust that when they pick up book four in a series, it will feel like book three. I understand that desire and share some of it, but creatively, it was essential for me to vary my books. If I hadn't been able to do that, I couldn't have kept writing the series. It was a method of keeping myself interested and creatively alive.

Do you work from an outline, with most of a book mapped out before you begin? Do you ever experience surprises along the way?

I have worked with an outline and without. I have mapped out entire books and plunged in without knowing anything in advance. But even when I work things out in advance, I meet surprises along the way—one of which usually is that none of my careful planning means diddly-squat to the book. It will be what it will be, and I can either like it or quit writing.

Is writing fun and rewarding for you?

Sometimes. Sometimes it sucks.

Which element is more important: plot or character?

The character's response to the plot.

Have you ever thought about becoming a traditional novelist?

I have thought about it, but not very seriously. I mean, really, what do you do in the middle of a book if there's no dead body?

Have you ever been interested in, or actually worked in, an alternative career?

Except for summer jobs that taught me that I'm a terrible waitress, I've never been anything but a writer.

Bibliography

Stand-Alone Novel

Pickard, Nancy. *The Virgin of Small Plains: A Novel of Suspense*. New York: Ballantine Books, 2006.

Jenny Cain Series

_____. *Bum Steer: A Jenny Cain Mystery*. New York: Delacorte Press, 1998.
_____. *But I Wouldn't Want to Die There: A Jenny Cain Mystery*. New York: Delacorte Press, 1993.
_____. *Confession: A Jenny Cain Mystery*. New York: Pocket Books, 1994.
_____. *Dead Crazy*. New York: Scribner, 1988.
_____. *Generous Death: A Jenny Cain Mystery*. New York: Dark Harvest, 1992.
_____. *I.O.U.* New York: Pocket Books, 1991.
_____. *Marriage Is Murder: A Jenny Cain Mystery*. New York: Scribner, 1987.
_____. *No Body: A Jenny Cain Mystery*. New York: Scribner, 1986.
_____. *Say No to Murder: A Jenny Cain Mystery*. New York: Pocket Books, 1985.
_____. *Twilight: A Jenny Cain Mystery*. New York: Pocket Books, 1995.

Marie Lightfoot Series

_____. *Ring of Truth*. New York: Random House, 2001.
_____. *The Truth Hurts*. New York: Random House, 2002.
_____. *The Whole Truth*. New York: Random House, 2000.

Contributions to the Eugenia Potter Series, based on a character originally created by Virginia Rich

———. *The Blue Corn Murders*. New York: Delacorte Press, 1998.
———. *The 27-Ingredient Chili Con Carne Murders*. New York: Delacorte Press, 1993.
Pickard, Nancy, and Sally Goldenbaum. *The Secret Ingredient Murders*. New York: Random House, 2002.

Short Story Collection

Pickard, Nancy. *Storm Warnings*. New York: Five Star Mystery, 1999.

Non-Fiction

Pickard, Nancy, and Lynn Lott. *Seven Steps on the Writer's Path*. New York: Random House, 2004.

Aileen Schumacher, Author of Historical Crime Fiction

by Amy Gottfried

A Florida resident for twenty-three years, Aileen Schumacher also has a strong link to the Southwest locale of her first three mysteries: she grew up in El Paso, Texas, and then went on to New Mexico State University, where she earned two degrees, one in biology and one in engineering. With her husband, she has run an engineering firm for the past twenty-one years, and is the author of the Tory Travers David Alvarez mystery series: *Engineered for Murder*, *Framework for Death* (nominated for the Anthony Award for Best Novel of 1998), *Affirmative Reaction*, and *Rosewood's Ashes*, which was awarded the "Damn Good Book Award" at the 2002 convention, "Florida: The Mystery Connection."

AMY GOTTFRIED: *How do you see* Rosewood's Ashes *as connected to Florida writing generally?*

AILEEN SCHUMACHER: Actually, I feel a bit of a charlatan in this collection. I'll just go ahead and say it: there are really very few Florida writers I read. Overall, I feel as though Florida is on its way to becoming caricatured. There's a genre now of Florida writing, which is great even though it doesn't appeal to me. But one author I do read is Barbara Parker. She does an excellent job portraying South Florida as it really is. I also think she has grown incredibly as a writer; some of her past work has blown me away, and I've read her from the beginning. Another writer I really enjoy is Les Standiford, who really appeals to me because he writes from the contracting community, about someone who is a contractor.

As for my own writing, I always try to write the kind of book that I would like to read. I got sucked into writing this Florida story by researching it, but it was very much the human-interest elements that attracted me, not the setting. We live about an hour from Cedar Key, in the vicinity of Rosewood, and whenever people would visit, we'd take them to the coast. It wasn't until we'd lived here for about ten years that someone mentioned to me the story of Rosewood because they'd heard about it on a PBS newscast. This was right before the issue got picked up by the legislature here and it became a bona fide controversial issue. So for me, it was the story of Rosewood that was so fascinating to me; it encompassed all the elements of family, betrayal, racial prejudice, money, our concepts of justice, our efforts to redress what cannot really be redressed. Researching Rosewood and talking to people about it, and learning just who you don't talk to about Rosewood, really gave me a stronger sense of Florida history and belonging than anything prior had.

Can I ask whom you don't talk to about Rosewood?

You don't talk to people who are missing teeth, and live in certain geographic areas, because they are the descendants of the people who truly believe that their ancestors died in Rosewood, that they were ambushed. There are areas where you are very careful—what you'd call the backwoods of Florida. Florida has forgotten about Rosewood because it's no longer in the news, but the descendants of the people who fought and died there have not forgotten. They very much believe that they have been taught the truth. Of course, we would all like to believe that what we were taught as our family history was the truth. There were white people in Cedar Key who lost relatives in Rosewood and believe not only that their family members were ambushed, but that seventy years later, people got paid for it. It's a very, very touchy subject for both sides.

Yes, and it's the kind of subject that you don't seem to fear. For example, Affirmative Reaction *tackles the issue of affirmative action, and* Rosewood's Ashes *has a character that plays the race card. Have you thought deliberately about the roles of race and ethnicity in your work?*

I think that what comes naturally to me first is the idea of gender, because it's something that I've always dealt with. The idea of race has been an echoing issue with me because—being transplanted from Texas and New Mexico to the South—we'd never (to make a horrible pun) dealt with race issues in such a black and white fashion. Part of the inner city movement that I was in as a high school student had to do with racial issues. I went to an inner-city school in a district that was something of an octopus: it took in very poor areas of town, and a few miles from us, the new high school in an affluent part of town had computers. Being involved in science and math, and being sixteen or seventeen and quite idealistic, I had great difficulty understanding why you could drive two miles and go to a school that had computers while my school did not.

I also had the advantage of being involved with people who, even at that age, were very idealistic and committed to what they were doing. We were going to change the world. One of the students who worked for me on the underground high school newspaper I edited has gone on to become a liaison with the Zapatista movement out of Chiapas. There were Brown Berets at that time (1969–1971) in El Paso; Chicano pride was a very new and abhorrent thing to what I perceived as the white middle class. It was not something discussed in my family or my neighborhoods, yet I went to a school that changed its character between the time that my brother attended and I did. The El Paso technical high school closed down and almost overnight, this school I went to became an inner-city Hispanic school. It was an experience that my parents and brother were unfamiliar with; I was going everyday to this place where we had switchblades, and we had two people who were hired full-time to patrol the halls with walkie-talkies. It was like being in a prison, but it was really interesting and exciting.

What fascinated me was the difference between the reality that I lived in, and the reality that my parents and family lived in. I lived in a white neighborhood and we went to a church where most people were white, but I attended a school that was probably 80 percent Hispanic and maybe 5 percent black.

So perhaps your early experiences in high school journalism helped to shape your later work. After about fifteen years of running your own engineering firm, your first Travers Alvarez mystery came out. Was this a long-simmering project for you, or a recent interest?

I got seduced into being a mystery fan when I was in college by reading P.D. James. The things I like best about mysteries appeal to the whole part of me that really likes engineering: finding an answer and having closure. I had gotten into a fair amount of difficulty in high school, being one of the radicals during the Vietnam War. The word *expulsion* did come up in my senior year, so I went off to college and decided that I was going to do quantitative studies, where you could get the right answer. And if you got the right answer, it didn't make people angry. After that, I spent a lot of time getting degrees in quantitative sciences, and then being a consulting engineer, and then starting a business and a family. It took that time and energy to make me feel secure enough to be willing to do something that is so personal. I'm still struck by the difference between laying out a set of plans and having the client say, "I don't really like that; I want the entrance somewhere else," or "This isn't what I had in mind," and laying out something that you've really put your heart and soul into and having someone say, "The dialogue really sounds stilted," or "That's just stupid." In retrospect, it took a lot of time for me to get to a place where I was willing to risk writing fiction. When I sat down to write my first book, it was with no more exciting impetus than wanting to see if I could do it.

There's a progression in your books; you're moving toward someplace new in each book. Rosewood's Ashes is certainly a mystery—many mysteries, in fact—but it also seems to be a work that's aiming for redemption, as well as questioning what redemption means or whether it's even possible in certain instances. I wondered whether, with this book, you were starting to move into new territory.

I definitely would not want to think that I was limited only to mysteries. Mysteries really appeal to me because of the elements of closure and problem-solving in the genre, but I have some ideas for other books out there. I'm very taken with Sara Smith's trilogy that started with *The Vanished Child*, and I'm not sure that I would consider her books mysteries, although they were initially marketed as that. She's accomplished something amazing with them. The whole spectrum of the three books really covers redemption. Good literature concerns itself with issues of life and death, with—for example—what pushes someone in war or peacetime to take someone else's life.

I'm hoping to incorporate the Chiapas Zapatista movement into something I'm working on right now. Their leader is an unidentified person fighting the battle of the oppressed against global urbanization and capitalism: a battle that cannot be won. I'm trying to figure out how I feel about portraying it. As for *Rosewood's Ashes*, if I was trying to achieve anything, I was trying to say that there are no easy answers. When I was researching the white supremacy movement, the sites that had profanity and horrible cartoons were easy to dismiss. But the white supremacy movement has also some very sophisticated sites with some things to say about what many people believe the civil rights movement has done to the white lower and middle class of America. Some of the stuff really does make sense; the idea I had in *Rosewood's Ashes* is that there is certainly injustice and evil in the world, but when we start to believe we are immune from it, and that we can recognize what's evil and unjust inherently, that's when we have problems. When I speak about *Rosewood's Ashes*, I ask people to think about themselves: if they'd been in that area in 1923, what would they have been doing? Would they have been joining the mob, or would they have stood by and watched, or would they have been one of the few who were actually trying to do something about it? That's the question we all hope never to have to ask ourselves. It's very easy to dismiss what is politically incorrect, as well as lynchings and white supremacist groups that burn crosses, but it's very uncomfortable to ask ourselves, "If I were in this situation, what do I think I would do?" That's more the purpose of the book than anything else.

There's also more literary expansion in Rosewood's Ashes. This is your first novel to use multiple voices as well as multiple storylines; for example, the light dialect you give Lissy Hodden Garner and Sylvester Carrier is something new for you. Were you thinking about experimenting with voice in this novel?

Every time I start a book, it scares the hell out of me. It was extreme arrogance to think that a middle-aged woman from Texas could write in the voice of a 1920s black Floridian. I agonized over that before I ever started. But once I sat down and started writing *Rosewood's Ashes*, the voice of Lissy Hodden Garner was just given to me. More than any character I've ever created, she just stood up and had her story to tell. That was truly something I was given; I don't take great credit for it. It is so hard as a writer not to get caught up in writing dialect and not to overdo it. I didn't want the dialect to sound condescending, but it was necessary in order to get across a sense of difference textually. Vernacular must change in order to have any character of its own. Still, this probably was one of the most difficult things that I ever did from a technical standpoint. Lissy was someone who stood apart. She was someone who watched. That enabled her to be who she was, and to be the one person who came out of Rosewood and had no interest in sharing her story. Also, many battles were fought over where I could use the word *nigger*. I had to use it because it was the term that would have been used, but I was very uncomfortable with it.

Rosewood's Ashes was the most difficult book I've ever written; I found the research to be so incredibly depressing. The good part was that once I sat down to write it, writing was not as painful as doing the research. But, in writing a historical novel, I realized I was no longer God. In a contemporary novel, you can decide who lives and who dies. But there was no way I could go back to save the people who died in Rosewood. I was stuck with this story. The one thing I did that kept my sanity was to save the dog. One of the first things that happened back in 1923 was that all the dogs were shot. So I decided I could be God enough in this book to save one dog. I held onto that because this was really grim stuff to wade through, no matter whose perspective you were hearing. Something horrible happened because of horrible things simmering for generations.

But about that dialect and the battles we fought over it: editors are the ones who are going to put the book out, and they're concerned, too, about the backlash over something that might be seen to be socially unacceptable.

Speaking of backlash of a different sort: how has parenthood affected your writing?

Having children is one of the most wonderful things in the world. At the same time, I never tell my childless friends that they've made a mistake. As a proponent of writing, I spent a lot of time before I started the first book thinking that, if only I had an hour to myself, I could do such amazing things. Then I realized that I could keep thinking that for the next ten years, or I could take the ten or fifteen minutes and write. You hear so many people say, "I'm going to write a book when…" Anyone can write a book, so long as it's important enough to them. My kids have been integrally involved in my writing. Very early on, my kids and husband were involved in reading anything I've ever written. Everything gets read aloud. My children have always gotten 10% of my royalties and that certainly made them support my writing. Then they grew to be teenagers, and if you read something aloud to a teenager that something doesn't flow—it's stilted or it's padded—they pick it up immediately. My kids were very helpful in giving a sense of immediacy to dialogue and to narrative. And if they got bored they'd show it. If a story couldn't keep their attention, then what was the point of it?

What kind of reader are you, that is, what kinds of books attract you (and more importantly, will you stay with) as a reader?

Well, if I don't care about the protagonist, I won't care about the book. This segues into the familiar question about plotting versus characterization, doesn't it? I will go along with a ludicrous plot if I care about the characters. So as long as I can believe in them, I'll wade through almost anything—graphic situations, bizarre happenings. If there's a wonderful plot involving people I am not interested in—one bizarre thing heaped on another, just for the sake of bizarreness—I'll put the book down. I suppose, if I had to choose one over the other (which I would hope not to have to do), the characterization is what hooks me in. But Barbara Parker has created a protagonist I didn't initially care for all that much; then she suckered me into wondering what happened to her anyhow, and my interest in this character has really grown. So that's my personal taste for characterization.

And so much good detective fiction revolves around just that: strong characters. I've been thinking about P.D. James since you mentioned her earlier, and her creation of Adam Dalgliesh and Cordelia Gray. James is also somebody who has long been acclaimed as a "novelist" as opposed to a mystery writer, a distinction she herself has challenged, asking what distinguishes popular works of fiction from literary works of fiction and noting that "many of the latter are not particularly well-written." Do you find those qualifications "mystery" or "detective" fiction limiting?

No, I really don't. That phrase "transcending the genre" translates into sales numbers in today's publishing world. That's the phrase used to herald the moment that a writer starts being reviewed as a fiction writer, as opposed to a genre author. As much as we all like to say, "Oh it's so limiting; I hate to be seen as simply a mystery writer," as a reader, I really like the fact that all the mystery books are put together in the same section. So I think there's a reason for genre classifications. It doesn't bother me to be a mystery writer; I find it helpful to distinguish for my own taste between what I consider to be suspense and "cozys." No one likes to be categorized, but there are very practical reasons for such classifications.

About cozys: I know they are immensely popular. I've heard the cozy genre attacked as presenting crime and death in a highly minimized way. That is, the genre has come under fire for making violence acceptable. I'm not sure I'd go that far, but I do understand the argument: in a cozy, violence is presented just as a necessary part of the puzzle. I don't tend to be a cozy reader. The characterization is so emphasized that, to me, the stories are not realistic. Because I read mainly contemporary authors, I don't have a great deal of expertise in the area of the "classical" mystery authors who might be called "cozys"—say, Agatha Christie. But what I term to be a "cozy" has little emphasis on the actual impact of violence on people's lives: the sense of having one's life torn apart by losing a loved one, or by becoming a suspect or a witness.

So who are the authors you like to read?

The two I will not read while I'm writing because I feel as though I'll never be as good as they are—so it's too depressing—are Carol O'Connell and James Lee Burke. Someone I've rediscovered recently is Martin Cruz Smith.

And how do you develop your stories and story elements?

Well, they're not autobiographical. Once, during a television interview with a woman who hadn't even read the book—and my husband right there in the studio—I was asked, "Are you in love with your police detective?" I couldn't think of a thing to say. But the engineering does come from my own experiences. And in *Affirmative Reaction*, there were things I did want to say about affirmative action; I do wish more people were involved in that debate. When I begin a book, though, I always have a good idea as to who got killed, who did it, and why. The challenge from then on is to surround that story with enough relevant information that there are other possibilities: I don't write the book to find out who did it. For me, the only reason to write a book—besides the story—is that there's a theme I'm examining. Every one of my books has a theme, though I hope as an author, I'm not putting across an agenda. My hope is to have people reexamine certain matters—say, child abuse, abortion, or racial issues—from a slightly different perspective. If, as an author, I can catalyze someone into thinking about something in a different way, or think about it at all, then I'll have succeeded. That's my reason for writing a book. For example, in *Framework for Death* I worked from my fascination of people who work outside of the law in custody issues, "rescuing" children from terrible parents. I began wondering: if you work outside the law as a vigilante, who checks what *you* do? I don't have the answers for any of the subjects I raise. But I would hope that, if we all thought about them a little bit more, we'd come up with some better answers.

So, even though what attracted you to mystery writing is the promise of closure, as an author you veer away from imposing that closure. That's something I see as a positive quality in your work, and something that moves beyond our usual expectations from a mystery, wherein everything is nicely wrapped up. It seems to me that you work hard in these books not to wrap everything up.

And boy, did I get creamed for that in a lot of reviews for *Rosewood's Ashes*. There's a murderer who's never tracked down, but more than that, the racial implications of Tory Travers's heritage were never fully answered. I can quote the reviews verbatim. For example: "And by the end, only Schumacher knows the answers; no one else does." But I wrote the book the way I did because that's how it had to be. I probably got more negative portions of reviews for *Rosewood's Ashes* than for any other book.

I can understand the criticism from the mystery and hard-core genre. But in *Rosewood's Ashes*, my characters visited an area and had the advantage of leaving that area, leaving things behind that are never solved. I still don't know who killed one of my minor characters in that book. Similarly, we don't yet know what happened in Rosewood.

Did you pick up a lot of flak just for tackling the history of Rosewood?

No, I did not. People who are willing to read a book like this are not going to be upset by the kinds of questions I raise. I was concerned because there's definitely a difference of opinion here. I interviewed a black descendant of one of the survivors, and was trying to walk carefully around the topics of lynchings and burnings, but none of that bothered her at all. When I asked her about the money, though, *that* bothered her. But what really surprised me was that she was just adamant that there are mass graves out there that have not been discovered. I thought she was talking about scores of black people who'd been killed, but no: she said her grandfather had gone there and buried scores and scores of white people, and that's been covered up. So there's a whole spectrum of perspectives as to what actually occurred, and everybody believes his own version to be absolute truth.

And what was your experience in interviewing black survivors?

The closest I could get was a descendant of one survivor. Other research came from previously done interviews and studies. When the book came out, the survivors were quite elderly, and there were arguments as to who has the "real" Rosewood story. I had the opportunity to interview a niece of someone who was killed at Rosewood. I was very low-key about asking certain questions. I didn't want to make anybody uncomfortable: I want to hear what someone has to say, but not something I've cornered her into saying. I was trying to dance around the question of lynchings and mass murders, but this woman spoke freely about it: she told me about her granduncle who was lynched, and the story that the paper ran. But then you ask about the money! The issue of money made her close up immediately; she was not willing to discuss any disbursements to her family. In fact, what most interested me in the history of Rosewood was that, in spite of these black survivors' having been through such a horrible experience, once the legislature pushed through the reimbursement bill and provided actual money, the survivors' group very much splintered. People were saying, "Your family got more money than mine," and "My family had worse things done to them." There've been charges of fraud in the disbursement of the money. In fact, there have been allegations (never investigated) that when a person who was quite active in getting this bill passed took the checks to these elderly survivors, he charged a finder's fee. If you really want to break up the solidarity of any group, no matter what binds them together, disburse money to them.

Researching this book on Rosewood was your first experience of having Florida influence your work, and you've mentioned that it made you feel as though you truly belonged to the state. Where in Florida would you live, if you could live anywhere else?

Fernandina Beach, by Jacksonville. It's one of those areas that is still like St. Augustine that hasn't been overdeveloped.

Would you say that Florida is rapidly being overdeveloped?

To me, as a scientist and an engineer, until we're willing to look at our population issues, there's no real answer to this question. Florida is a wonderful place to come to, a wonderful place to raise your children and start your business. But it's human nature to believe that, as soon as you are there the next people who want to come and raise *their* children are impinging on your view of the beach, and contributing to the traffic that you have to deal with. We have several problems with allocations of resources in this country, problems that are not limited to Florida: what we do with our water supply, what we do with our tax money. We're coming to a crisis of not being able to support what we see as the American way of life: if you work really hard, you can have anything that anybody else has. There are not enough resources to go around.

And in terms of the environment, we need to take an unsentimental view of what resources we have and how to best use them: is it really in our best interest to spend $350,000 to clean up a water supply that has barely detectable levels of petrochemicals? Of course, I hate seeing pictures of seals covered in oil, but the environmental movement will only be of lasting value if we look at it from a cost-benefit perspective, not idealism.

Population drives everything. I can't help thinking that, as an engineer, if we had fewer people, we'd have fewer—or different—problems.

Thinking of engineering: there's a link between the profession of engineering and the mystery itself, don't you think? That is, both are concerned with trying to discover what lies underneath the exterior. Your works sustain an ongoing focus upon structure, upon stabilizing and destabilizing forces that underlie our daily lives—and how easily they can go awry. What Tory Travers does as an inspections engineer is what any detective does: they both go beneath the surface.

In all honesty, many realizations about my work have been raised by other people. But yes, if I were trying to quantify what the two are doing, and where the conflict between them is, I'd say they're really doing the same thing in trying to find answers to puzzles. As an engineer, Tory Travers is wedded to the belief that if one has the information and runs the equations and does what one's supposed to do procedurally, one will find the answers. A detective, though, who works more with people and has to become a chameleon to get what information he wants, has much more of an intuitive approach. Really, my idea from the very beginning is that the two would have very different approaches to getting the same answers. Of course, Tory also thinks that being an engineer and problem-solver gives her the right to step into any arena to get her answers, whereas, from a law-enforcement perspective, Alvarez has seen the consequences of being involved with crime. He doesn't believe that people who are unqualified, who don't have the credentials, should go wading into certain areas.

How have readers responded to your work? Do you have an ideal reader?

Not at all. I want to write the kind of book that I would like to read. I can't hope to do anything else for me. Like any series writer, though, I have a group of fans who read my books because of what's in them. The choice a series writer faces is whether to do the same thing over and over, or to do something different. When you do something different, you run the risk of losing that fan base.

Overall, the kind and amazing things that readers have said are worth more than any royalties or trips. After I wrote *Affirmative Reaction*, someone wrote to me about Krohn's Disease; she'd suffered from it for years and had never before seen in a contemporary book any character with this disease. Then there are readers who tell me they'd never realized something about engineering until they'd read one of my books; or on the other side of the coin, engineers and architects who tell me they hadn't picked up a work of fiction in twenty-five years, but that they really liked my book. That really makes it all worth it. My guideline is that the book has to please me. If I can't write the book I want to read, I'm not interested in writing. I'm the reader I'm trying to please.

Bibliography

Schumacher, Aileen. *Affirmative Reaction*. Aurora, CO: Write Way Publishing, 1999.
———. *Engineered for Murder*. Aurora, CO: Write Way Publishing, 1996.
———. *Framework for Death*. Aurora, CO: Write Way Publishing, 1998.
———. *Rosewood's Ashes*. Philadelphia: Intrigue Press, 2001.

Les Standiford, Florida Crime Novelist and Nonfiction Writer

by Steve Glassman

Les Standiford is the originator of the Deal books, one of Florida's best-known series of crime novels. Altogether he has published ten novels, including *Havana Run* and *Deal with the Dead*, and the nonfiction *Last Train to Paradise* and *Meet You in Hell*. He holds a Ph.D. in English and creative writing from the University of Utah. Les Standiford is the founding director of the M.F.A. program at Florida International University in Miami, which has been called one of the ten best writing programs in the country by *The Dictionary of Literary Biography*. The most recent of his many honors is the lifetime achievement award granted by the Fort Myers annual books festival. Previous winners include Connie May Fowler, Peter Mathisen, Ben Bova, and James W. Hall.

STEVE GLASSMAN: *Les, how do you see yourself?*

LES STANDIFORD: I'm a kid who grew up in the coal-mining and manufacturing region of southeastern Ohio, and I have often said my whole life's mission has been to devise a way to stay off working on the assembly line. I was a smart kid though (I was what they used to call "salutatorian" or 2nd in a class of 200) and it was pretty clear that I was going to get to go to college, the first in my family ever to do so. I was a voracious reader as a kid, but of the sorts of things you might imagine: comics, especially the lurid EC horror, super-hero, and battleground types; Hardy Boys and Nancy Drew; and every Oz book in the series. "Literature" in school was a mixture of Henry Wadsworth Longfellow (seemed ridiculous) and Shakespeare (impressive, if imponderable as presented by the teachers we had). There was a county

A version of this interview was originally published in the AWP Chronicle, May/Summer 2002.

librarian, however, Helen Sunnafrank (to whom *Deal with the Dead* is dedicated), who steered me toward adult reading that was somewhat more elevated: she got me onto Bradbury, for instance, and from there to Dickens. In college, I was a psychology major, but dabbled in writing on the side.

There were no creative writing courses at the time, so it was pretty much a coffee-house, self-perpetuating little clutch of us who shared our stuff. At the time, I thought I was going to go on to law school and become a lawyer who wrote the occasional story on the back of a legal brief after hours. It never crossed my mind that writing would (or could) be a career. But then, in the last semester of my senior year, I stumbled into a contemporary literature class where I discovered for the first time that there were novels about life as it seemed to exist around me, written, furthermore, by people who were still living. Cheever, Kesey, J.R. Salamanca, Heller. Egad! I went to law school but couldn't bear it, and to graduate school in social psychology (had nothing to do with social matters, everything to do with rats and stats), but I was reading all these contemporary novels to keep sane (William Goldman's early stuff, every coming-of-age book I could get my hands on, out-there things by Terry Southern, Charles Webb, Charles Simmons), and discovered there at Ohio State a creative writing course being taught by a Mississippian, Robert Canzoneri. I talked my way into the course, he encouraged me, and I asked what to take for the upcoming summer term as a follow-up. There were no courses, he informed me, but why not go to a "summer writers conference," which he had to explain, of course. I looked at a bunch of brochures on a bulletin board outside Canzoneri's office, took one look at the sweep of the Wasatch Range on the poster for the University of Utah's confab, and said that's the one. I sent them a story I'd worked on for Canzoneri and they wrote back not only admitting me but offering me a fellowship to the thing. I packed up and left Ohio for good, as it turns out.

At the conference (the staff included Bill Eastlake, John Frederick Nims and Harry Mark Petrakis), I ambled into a seminar being taught by a man named George Garrett. I suppose I listened for an hour before I realized: I not only loved this man, I wanted to BE him. I wanted to have his life. Garrett was, I suppose, amused by my fervor, but affable and supportive and appeared to like my work. The die was cast. Utah offered me admission to their M.F.A. program and a teaching assistantship: "You mean my tuition is forgiven AND I get a paycheck for going to school?" At Utah, I ended up getting a Ph.D., and in the course of that process, came to study literature in a systematic way for the first time. I was able, by the time I graduated, to trace the history of the novel all the way from Sumerian tablet scratchings to the work (?) of Richard Brautigan. I studied under Pulitzer-Prize–winning poet Henry Taylor. My first published works were POEMS, for God's sake, in the *Beloit Poetry Journal*, and the *Kansas Quarterly*, and my stories were the type that ended up in the same sorts of journals. I won something called the Frank O'Connor Award for Fiction given by the Texas Christian University Press. I published a comprehensive monograph on Native American literature with the Modern Language Association, for heaven's sake. So when I talk about literature, it is NOT from the point of view of some fellow who only knows academia from the outside in and is dismayed/intimidated by what he sees. That sort of thing is as tiresome and self-promoting as the academic who thinks he is accomplishing something by waggling his finger at Stephen King.

I've got a foot in both worlds. I've had serious jobs outside the academic world (in addition to the knock-about stuff that all writers claim—forest ranger, bartender, fire lookout and carpenter, in my case—I have managed a 100-bed extended care nursing facility and an exclusive French restaurant across the street from the Capitol Building in Columbus, Ohio). I built one 3,000-square-foot home from scratch on a piece of raw cotton land in El Paso, Texas, and have just finished a stint as general contractor renovating my place here in Miami. But the greatest thing that ever happened to me was having the door opened to me into the literary life. And nearly as grand is the chance to write and publish novels. They turn out to be of a certain sort, but how could they be otherwise, given what I have told you?

Wow, Les, when you answer a question, you really answer a question. Let me ask Les the academic as well as Les the writer a question—why is Florida literature so intertwined with crime writing? Think of Florida writers, and after you mention Hemingway, Marjorie K. Rawlings and Zora, what is left but crime writing?

Well, Florida was founded upon a scam (Ponce de Leon and his fountain of youth), and hustlers have been selling snake oil down here ever since. Not too much happened in Florida between the time of the *conquistadores* and the arrival of Henry Flagler at the turn of the 20th century, but once the development of paradise began in earnest, the underwater-lot salesmen and associated con artists were sure to follow. We are still basically a frontier state, with massive change and influx the order of the day (think Australia of a former era), so cultural and political fractiousness is part of life here. With nothing settled, with no one firmly in charge, with the wildest political landscape this side of Italy, what would any good writer immersed in such a culture write about? Drawing room manners? Besides that, there is a basic contradiction between the unparalleled natural beauty of the place and the actions of the people drawn to it. When evil occurs in a gruesome place, it seems somehow expected. When it arrives with a grin in paradise, particularly South Florida, there's a particular resonance and fascination for a readership. All this is not to say that we don't have our fine poets (Campbell McGrath, Richard Blanco, Denise Duhamel) and our more literary practitioners of fiction and nonfiction (Dan Wakefield, Peter Meinke, Joy Williams), but like Boswell, crime writing speaks particularly to who and what we are about just now.

You didn't go to graduate school to be a mystery writer. In fact, you didn't come to Florida until quite a few hash marks were chalked up on your sleeve—and after sojourns in the Midwest and West. How about telling us about the evolution of Les Standiford, geographically, artistically?

Well, I always wanted to write books that people were going to want to read. I just wasn't sure at the outset how to accomplish that feat. I grew up in Ohio, but had always been fascinated by the West, maybe because cowboy movies were so popular when I was growing up. In any case, after I graduated from Muskingum College, I lit out for the territories, living in California for a while, and ending up in graduate school at the University of Utah, where I earned a Ph.D. in Literature and Creative Writing. My writing teachers were a fairly down-to-earth bunch, though it being the late '60s, we didn't talk a whole lot about plot or anything that smacked of a conventional form. I wrote a couple of novels that found good agents but no publishers while I was in graduate school and ended up teaching and writing little by little on the side until I had finally cobbled together a manuscript about a germ warfare spill in Yellowstone National Park, which seemed to combine my interest in the environment with a story line I thought might get a publisher interested. A well-known agent in New York agreed, but struck out at all 35 publishing houses he sent it to. He was still resubmitting it (some of those guys I sent it to are dead now, he told me once) when I took a hiatus from teaching to attend the American Film Institute in Los Angeles as a screenwriting fellow. That in fact is where the light bulb went on for me, where I really learned how to tell a story. I came back to the University of Texas at El Paso, where I was teaching at the time, and rewrote that manuscript from stem to stern. Six weeks after I sent it off to my agent, *Spill* was picked up by Atlantic Monthly Press and I was the happiest man alive. I sat down and went to work on another story I'd originally conceived of as a screenplay while I was out in Los Angeles, and my agent sold it to HarperCollins as

Done Deal, a story about a building contractor who inadvertently gets crosswise with the mob while simply trying to get his car fixed. To me it wasn't a mystery, or even a crime novel, more of a Hitchcock kind of tale about an ordinary guy who stumbles into huge trouble by accident and has to work his way out in a believable fashion. When Larry Ashmead at HarperCollins told me he thought I ought to write a second book for him and make Deal a series character, I was flabbergasted, but happy to give it a shot. Now there have been eight Deal novels and I have somehow become a crime writer.

If the Deal series had flopped, would you have happily gone into another field, genre?

As I say, I never intended to write a series to begin with. I think I would have continued to write stories about ordinary people who fall into big trouble, however, because that is a story which endlessly fascinates me; witness *Black Mountain*, another non–Deal novel I wrote about five years back, concerning a New York City subway cop who ends up trying to save himself and a bunch of city dwellers pursued by killers through the Montana wilderness. I think I am drawn to writing such stories because I like to read such stories.

If it's okay with you, let me ask Les the writing-program director a question. The students in your program who have done well, Barbara Parker, Dennis Lehane, among many others, write genre fiction. The same can be said of your better known faculty, James W. Hall, yourself.

I should say at the outset that I don't buy into the distinction between so-called genre fiction and any other "kind" of fiction. There are good books and bad books. That's all. Nonetheless, some of our most successful students have written mysteries. As we talk, Dennis Lehane's new book *Mystic River* appears on the *New York Times* best-seller list. Vicki Hendrick's *Miami Purity* was a veritable redo of *The Postman Always Rings Twice*. Barbara Parker continues to flourish, having made the *New York Times* list with her last, and James W. Hall and I have a score of thrillers between us.

Is the genre fiction spin on their work by design or accident?

Our students have gone off on these projects on their own volition, and out of their own interests. I try to steer the students toward short fiction early on in the process, then let them write a novel for a thesis if they've developed an idea for a novel. As to what sort of novel, that is up to them. If they've got it in them to do the kind of substantial mystery that combines character, style, place, theme, and story, then off we go. I just worked with Craig Miles Miller, who came over from the Iowa Workshop to us. He has written a lovely book called *Chester Stubbs* about a middle-aged loser trying to get his life back on track and nary a gunshot is fired within its pages. It has just been published by a small but respected publisher: Dennis McMillan, in Tucson.

So what did the study of literature at Utah teach you?

I cannot make a one-to-one correlation. I learned how to write well at Utah. I learned what I didn't know about structure at the American Film Institute. As my colleague James W. Hall says, if I hadn't gone to those screenwriting classes, he and I would STILL be running these failed novels through the word processor.

Why in your view have story and plot come to be terms almost of opprobrium?

The reason a lot of writers try to skirt the issue of story and plot is that it is the most difficult of all the writerly tasks. It is a pain in the ass, but a necessary one. I think of T.S. Eliot's lament: "Meaning is the bone you throw a reader while you do your real work upon him." Well, story and plot are the bones a serious fiction writer throws the reader while—et cetera. I learned what I know about this matter not at Utah (it was the late '60s—nobody dared discuss anything that smacked of structure), [but] in the 1980s when I left teaching at UTEP and went to the American Film Institute in Los Angeles as a screenwriting fellow. "Screenplays are structure," as William Goldman has said, and studying their writing is one very effective way to understanding how to do structure one's fiction. I made the mistake of trying to suck up to the then dean of American Film Institute, Anthony Vellani (worked with George Stevens on *Room at the Top, Shane, Giant*) by saying "I guess you're a big fan of your countryman, Federico Fellini?" Vellani went white. "Fellini?" he stared at me in disbelief. "Fellini does not know how to make a movie! You want to learn how to make a movie, you go watch *The Bicycle Thief*. Somebody steals a poor man's bicycle, he spends the rest of the film trying to get it back. Now THAT'S how you make a movie!" I didn't have a clue at the time, but I did go rent the film, and over the course of a couple years' study, it began to dawn on me how much I didn't know about storytelling. I was used to sitting in workshops listening to people talk to one another about their sentences. Sentences are important. Don't get me wrong. If I don't like a writer's sentences on page one, I never get to page two. But, beyond a certain level, good sentences are a given. It is like needing a good voice to go on and train as an opera singer. To succeed as an opera singer, you need to learn the form. To succeed as a writer, to make contact with most readers, you not only need good sentences (be able to carry a tune), you need to have a tune to sing, beginning, middle and end. Anyone who tells you different is shining you on. Unless you are a genius, of course. If you are a genius, you can do it any which way you like. And if you believe you are a genius, it doesn't matter what anybody says. George Garret gave me about the greatest compliment I ever received, after he'd read one of the Deal books: "Standiford is one of a handful of today's best writers who can bond all the excitement of a page-turning thriller with quality writing any novelist can envy."

Remind us who Garret is?

He is Henry Hoins Professor of English Literature at the University of Virginia. There is no more Literary gentleman (with a capital L) in the whole world. He ended up listing that thriller as one of his one hundred notable books of the year in *The Dictionary of Literary Biography*. And later, in a letter to me he said, "The problem with reading the books you and Jim Hall write is that everything else seems kind of boring." [*Laughs.*] Where does it say that to write a good book you have to also be a little dull or be uninteresting to most people? What a nutty idea. How did it get so backasswared that people would actually get points somehow for being sure not to be interesting when they sat down to write their story or their novel? As I tell my students, the only place students read books they aren't interested in is in college.

Should that be a test kept in the front of everyone in the literary business's mind?

Every time I say something like that in class you should see the look on my graduate students' faces. Oh, yeah, that's right, they will slowly come to realize. The only time I read a book I'm not interested in is because some teacher tells me I have to, that it will be good for me.

Where would Shakespeare be if he had not written for the audience?

He wouldn't be known.

To go back before that last aside—and to make sure I have this right—you are saying that in the workshop you have to get beyond how well the lines read?

Yes, the fiction workshop has to go beyond the "how good are your sentences" level, for my money. Let's get beyond talking about how to "write well" (fine to begin with, of course) and move forward to talk about aspiring to write a version of *Gatsby*. Lofty goal, sure, but "Ah, but a man's reach should exceed his grasp, or what's a heaven for?"—as Lord Byron said.

It's axiomatic that the British mystery revolves around plot, but the hard-boiled American detective story, of the kind you write, centers on character. In Raymond Chandler's case, character and tone. It would seem there should be a perfect match between MFA programs and detective fiction. So is there?

As for detective fiction in writing programs, I can't speak for many, but I suspect that few hold up the work of Hammett or Chandler or Burke or Crumley. Where they do, God bless them. Where they do not, well, I suspect it is simply due to the fact that in addition to being suspicious, individual teachers just don't read such models. By the way, the curator of Rowan Oak [Faulkner's home in Oxford, MS, now a museum] once told me that Faulkner was an inveterate reader of mysteries. "We have hundreds of the ones he read packed away in the basement," she said. What I have reveled in (and what I think I am able to convey to my students, whatever genre they may aspire to) is that by learning the demands of the mystery thriller, I have come to understand how to manipulate plot, how to structure all those passages and character bits that so consume me into a story that will captivate a reader while, as T.S. Eliot said, I do my real work upon them. At the same time, I am the same writer, sentence by sentence, I was when I was publishing stories in the *Kansas Quarterly*, *Descant*, and the like. The opening chapters of *Spill* were what won an NEA fellowship in fiction, the opening chapters of *Raw Deal* a similar fellowship from the Florida Cultural Affairs Council. Do you think they will ask for their money back?

Structure is something novels have always had to have. Even the most experimental (at least of early 20th century authors), Faulkner, understood structure of the traditional type so well that most of his time in Hollywood was employed in writing plot treatments for other authors' novels. What is the moral of this observation?

Without a structure you just might as well build yourself a Corvette without an engine or a rhinoceros without any legs: impressive to look at, maybe, but neither one of those things is going anywhere. Faulkner made money in Hollywood because he understood these things. The structures he chose for many of his own novels might have been inimical to film structure, but he obviously knew the difference. And in *The Reivers*, he used his Hollywood know-how to build a different kind of novel.

Since we are on the topic of Hollywood, can we talk a bit about that great bastion of Philistinism? Gore Vidal and Vonnegut, among others, have cursed its influence on the contemporary novel. However, that hasn't stopped Vonnegut from allowing celluloid versions of his novels to appear on the silver screen, and Vidal cut his teeth in the industry. You have had one book, Spill, *made into a film and you probably don't know anyone who has turned down a film option.*

I heard Bruce Jay Friedman and my colleague Dan Wakefield talking about Hollywood in a seminar the other day. They were saying how it used to be you never wanted to admit you'd "lower" yourself to have a film done of one of your books. Now everyone wants a movie made. The world has turned. Publishing is more like filmmaking than ever before, no longer "a gentleperson's business" but a bottom-line operation run by those employed by conglomerates. Thinking changes. Books get harder and harder to publish, so maybe it's partly that writers fantasize making a "big score" and retreating to a little nicer version of a coldwater flat to write their "real" books, I don't know. My colleague John Dufresne is working on an adaptation of *Louisiana Power and Light*. That doesn't lessen him or his critically acclaimed book. Someone asked Elmore Leonard once if he was upset about what Hollywood had done to one of his books. Dutch pointed to a copy of the book in question on a nearby shelf. "They haven't done anything to my book," he said. "It's right over there, looking like it always has."

In your view, what are the pros and cons of Hollywood's influence on the novel in late 20th, early 21st century?

Modern readers (and writers) have been undeniably shaped by film. Most all of us grow up with a filmic sensibility now. I suspect that on the whole, novels are more lean and suggestive, more visual, more highly structured for the most part. But for all the similarities and all the things a writer can learn from film, movies and fiction are essentially different. The film is at heart about what happens, the external world. But any novel worth its salt is, in the final analysis, about the inner world of its characters. Things happen, but it is the meaning of events that is most important. Fiction is built to explore the inner world of a character, that is its stock in trade. It is far more difficult to do so in film. The greatest novels have always had it all, you know: theme, character, place, language and plot. Suggesting to a student that any one of those things doesn't matter so much—well, a student ought to get his money back.

What about your experience with Hollywood? Please answer the question I really want to know—did you make a lot of money? And was it worth it?

As to my own experience in Hollywood: not only are those the biggest checks I've ever cashed but I learned a great deal about how to make stories work.

What's not to like? The writing of a screenplay is a lot more intellectual than inspirational, more crossword puzzle than poem, but it is not without its own pleasures. It's just that unless a screenplay is produced, you don't have much when you're finished. Complete a novel manuscript and you have something.

You are now working in another genre altogether, nonfiction.

I wrote *Last Train to Paradise*, a nonfiction account of Florida developer Henry Flagler and his building of a 153-mile-long railroad from Miami to Key West, including the hurricane of 1935, the strongest in history, which blew it all away. As I sat looking at this mountain of notes I had taken in researching the story, I asked myself, "What on earth are you going to do with all this material, Les?" And then the answer came: "Tell the story." I ended up writing it as if it were a thriller, which it is, of course, with the only difference being that when I needed a fact, I couldn't just make it up. As it turns out, the book has been highly successful and I have also finished a second work nonfiction for Crown, called *Meet You in Hell*, about Andrew Carnegie and his partner Frick who crushed the infamous Homestead Steel Strike.

Who were your favorite authors? I don't mean the people you mention in the prefatory material; I mean the folks you really keyed on to the point of reading exclusively or almost exclusively for months or years.

Writers who have mattered greatly to me include Hemingway and Fitzgerald, of course. *Gatsby* is for me the perfect novel and *Deal with the Dead* has some little homages to *Gatsby* buried away in it. Later, I fell in love with the work of Bernard Malamud and have read everything he has written, many of the books several times. The first stories I wrote were imitations of Hemingway, but Malamud was the influence for the first success I had as a writer. I published seven or eight stories in literary magazines, all trying to tread that line between fabulism and realism that he walks so well. In fact, I brought out a novella with an online publisher called LiveReads (a print-on-demand version is available too), called *Opening Day*, based on one of those stories. This one is about an 80-year-old former Negro League player, now a groundskeeper for the worst team in the AA Mid-Florida league, who rather miraculously gets a chance to play again and thereby finally earns his rightful due. At any rate, I used to spend a lot of time bending reality toward the extreme edges of plausibility. Now, as a writer of crime thrillers, I find myself taking events from the extreme edge of experience and trying to make them seem plausible—thus my comparison of the Deal series to the Hitchcock films (the ordinary person caught up in extraordinary circumstances).

One last question, Les. Would you agree with Gore Vidal's claim that academe has ruined more writers than it has ever helped?

As to Vidal's claim, I am not so sure. I think that any writer who can be ruined by anything will be. Edward Abbey, the wonderful nature writer and a good friend of mine when he was still alive, for years split his time between a writing career and seasonal work (usually six months) for the U.S. Parks Service. Ed liked having two masters for as he said, it made him subject to none, gave him the sense he could always walk away from either if things got intolerable. I felt pretty much the same. For years, before I began to publish books, I saw myself as a teacher who wrote. Now the balance has shifted a bit the other way, so that I have become more of a writer who teaches. I think my students benefit from the change. And I feel very lucky indeed: what other profession would allow me the flexibility, would actually encourage the development of this parallel career? Would I have worked harder and published books sooner if I had locked myself in a garret somewhere and only wrote? Maybe. But I might just as well have gravitated out of financial necessity to a kind of writing meant primarily to pay the bills. My students are a great source of vitality in my life. The best of them are my peers and a number have become my friends. When it is all said and done, Steve, I count myself a lucky man.

Bibliography

Standiford, Les. *Black Mountain.* New York: G.P. Putnam's, 2000.
____. *Bone Key.* New York: G.P. Putnam's, 2002.
____. *Coral Gables: The City Beautiful Story* (nonfiction). Atlanta: Riverbend Books, 1998.
____. *Deal on Ice.* New York: HarperCollins, 1997.
____. *Deal to Die For.* New York: HarperCollins, 1995.
____. *Deal with the Dead.* New York: G.P. Putnam's, 2001.
____. *Done Deal.* New York: HarperCollins, 1993.
____. *Havana Run.* New York: G.P. Putnam's, 2003.
____. *Last Train to Paradise: Henry Flagler and the Spectacular Rise and Fall of the Railroad That Crossed an Ocean* (nonfiction). New York: Crown, 2002.
____. *Meet You in Hell: Andrew Carnegie, Henry Clay Frick, and the Bitter Partnership That Transformed America.* New York: Crown. 2005.
____. *Miami: City of Dreams* (with Alan Maltz). Key West: Light Flight Publications, 1997.
____. *Opening Day, or The Ghost of Satchel Paige.* New York: LiveReads, 2001.
____. *Presidential Deal.* New York: Harper Collins, 1998.
____. *Putt at the End of the World.* New York: Warner Books, 2000.
____. *Raw Deal.* New York: HarperCollins, 1994.
____. *Spill.* New York: 1991.

James Swain, Magical Mystery Writer

by Cal Branche

James Swain has a unique personal attribute: he is an accomplished magician, especially adept with cards. This skill, mated to a desire to write mysteries, has produced his protagonist, Tony Valentine, who has been an instant hit with fans. Swain's books have been published in Japan, Germany and France. Swain himself, a native of New York, is considered one of the world's foremost authorities on casino scams and swindles. His novels include *Grift Sense* (2001), *Funny Money* (2002), *Sucker Bet* (2003), *Loaded Dice* (2004), *Mr. Lucky* (2005), *Deadman's Poker* (2006), *Deadman's Bluff* (2006), and *Jackpot* (2007).

CAL BRANCHE: *Tony Valentine works one case set entirely in Florida. Was it time for him to go someplace else other than Las Vegas or Atlantic City?*

JAMES SWAIN: I'm not sure that was the basis of my decision when I started that particular book. At the core of the story, an old con man is trying to educate a young con man, and I could think of no better place to tell the story than South Florida.

Which Florida writers really "capture" the state in your opinion?

In my opinion, the writer who's depicted Florida accurately in terms of crime writing is Elmore Leonard.

Whom do you read, and why? Not just mystery writers, but I hope they are on your list.

I read all the classics growing up, Hemingway, Steinbeck, Faulkner, and later Bellow, Mailer and Malamud. I really loved those books. I got introduced to mystery writers later on. I read *La Brava* and Jim Hall's superb *Under Cover of Daylight* around the same time, and they blew me away. Since then, I've been addicted to reading mysteries. Michael Connelly is my favorite.

How did you get into the business of writing mysteries?

When I sold my first novel, I figured it was a one-shot deal. I went to New York and met my editor, who'd published Stephen King's *The Green Mile*. She told me there was a market for a whole series of these books. I left that lunch knowing I could do this.

What was your preparation for being a writer? And when did you first want to be a novelist?

I've wanted to be a novelist since I was fifteen. An English teacher in high school got me started.

Were you aware of the history of the form? Has that awareness affected your ideas of plot, character, theme?

Yes to both answers.

When you began to form your main characters how did you go about doing it? What are the characteristics of your main characters?

I have three leads in my novels. Tony Valentine, an ex-cop who catches casino cheats, his ne'er-do-well son Gerry, and his neighbor Mabel. They form the core of every story. In the first version of my first book, they were minor characters. My wife read the ms and thought they were the strongest characters in the book. I give her all the credit for finding them.

Has there been a gradual development of your protagonist(s)? How careful are you in preparing for character change/development?

There is a chronological development of my character, and his relationships, throughout the books. My readers seem to like it, and it makes the writing much more interesting for me.

How do you prepare for writing? How do you do research? What are your "writing" work habits?

I try to write every day. I gather research for several hours every week, and travel to Las Vegas about four times a year. When I'm deep into a book, I'm not the easiest person to be around.

Publishers and reviewers invariably categorize crime/mystery/detective fiction as a genre. Are those qualifications limiting? Should we distinguish these works from "novels"? How do you classify your work so far?

I would rather be called a mystery writer than a novelist any day of the week.

Writers—knowingly or not—reflect personal philosophies in their work. Now that you have spent many years writing novels, what is your philosophy in terms of crime and punishment and good vs. evil? How did your law career affect your work?

I think novels make lousy soapboxes, but I'm sure some of my opinions about crime and punishment have crept into my stories. But I think it's best to leave them out.

My perception of good and evil has changed since I started writing crime novels. Whenever I encounter a truly despicable person, I take a look at their upbringing and parents. Inevitably this is where the problem started.

What makes a good, or great storyteller?

For me, it's all about pacing and delivery.

Your website contains many cautions about gambling. Do you think your novels serve that kind of purpose as well, even though it may not be the main theme?

Yes. Many readers have told me they stopped gambling in casinos after reading my books. A TV producer I know credits me with saving him over $250,000 a year.

What makes a good, or great storyteller?

I think Mark Twain said it best. Twain was being interviewed, and the interviewer asked him why *The Adventures of Huckleberry Finn* was such a great book. Twain's reply was, "I didn't let my writing style get in the way of telling the story."

Bibliography

Swain, James. *Deadman's Bluff*. New York: Random House, 2006.
_____. *Deadman's Poker*. New York: Random House, 2006.
_____. *Funny Money*. New York: Random House, 2002.
_____. *Grift Sense*. New York: Random House, 2001.
_____. *Jackpot*. New York: Random House, 2007.
_____. *Loaded Dice*. New York: Random House, 2006.
_____. *Mr. Lucky*. New York: Random House, 2005.
_____. *Sucker Bet*. New York: Random House, 2003.

Elaine Viets, Classy Crime Writer

by Melanie Brown

Elaine Viets is the author of two national bestselling mystery series. Her Dead-End Job Series is set in South Florida and is a satiric look at a serious subject—the minimum-wage world. Elaine and her character, Helen Hawthorne, work a different low-paying job in each book, from telemarketer to hotel maid. *Publishers Weekly* called *Murder Unleashed*, her fifth novel in the series and her hardcover debut, "wry social commentary." Elaine's second series features Josie Marcus in the pink-collar world of mystery shopping. It debuted with *Dying in Style*, tying with Stephen King on the Independent Mystery Booksellers best-seller list.

Elaine's short stories have appeared in *Alfred Hitchcock Mystery Magazine*, the *Drop-Dead Blonde* anthology, *High Stakes*, the award-winning *Chesapeake Crimes Anthology*, the Mystery Writers of America's anthology *Blood on Their Hands* edited by Lawrence Block, the Mystery Writers of America's *Show Business Is Murder* anthology edited by Stuart Kaminsky, and *The World's Greatest Mystery and Crime Stories* edited by Ed Gorman and Martin H. Greenberg.

Elaine has appeared on national television, including the Discovery Channel and *The Sally Jesse Show*, and she has served on the national boards of the Mystery Writers of America and Sisters in Crime. She won the Agatha and the Anthony Awards. Elaine has called Florida home since 1997 and currently lives with her husband in Ft. Lauderdale, Florida, where she is actively observing the many characters of Florida and researching her next book.

MELANIE BROWN: *From hurricanes to hanging chads to shark and alligator attacks to criminals on the loose, the image portrayed of Florida and its residents often makes us look at best laughable and at worst insane for living here. As one Florida resident who is still willing to own the title to another, it's truly a pleasure to visit with you today, Elaine, and discuss not only your fiction but also the influence living in Florida has had on your works. Why have you chosen to set your work in Florida?*

ELAINE VIETS: My first series was set in my hometown of St. Louis. But after I moved to Florida in 1997, I realized my new home was the perfect setting for a mystery series. When you write about the Midwest, readers expect you to have standards, morals, and taste. Florida doesn't have any of those—no morals, no standards, and especially, no taste. When I lived on the beach in Hollywood, Florida, I saw a 70-year-old man wearing only a leopard-skin thong and gold chains. He had not looked in the mirror for many six packs. I had a lot more freedom when I wrote a Florida series.

Florida truly is inhabited by a cast of characters that would only be believable here. In the first novel of your Dead-End Job Series Shop Till You Drop, *you wrote "Almost no one was from here. No one you wanted to know anyway." Florida's residents—including you—are certainly chiefly transplants from other places. That said, although you aren't one of the true "born and bred" Florida "natives," you have been living here for nearly ten years. Does this make you a Floridian? And for that matter, is your Dead-End star, Helen Hawthorne, a Floridian?*

My definition of a Floridian is anyone who lives here all year long, especially during hurricane season. A Floridian appreciates the state's faults as well as its virtues. Yes, Helen and I are both Floridians.

Well, as a Floridian, are there certain aspects of the state that you feel are conducive to the mystery genre?

Although I'm now a Floridian, I'm originally from the Midwest, and to me, South Florida seems rootless and lawless. Both traits are conducive to mystery writing.

I can see how this opinion has made it into your novels. In fact, I recall Helen being greeted upon her arrival in Florida with the words, "Welcome to South Florida, land of deadbeats, drunks, and druggies…. Most of the single men down here are some other woman's mistake. The trick is not to make them your mistake" (79). I'm certainly not disagreeing with you, but what leads you to see Florida as so rootless and lawless?

I've never been in a place with less respect for the rules—and that includes several years of living on Capitol Hill. The problems start at the top. Cops and assorted lawmakers are always in trouble. Even the governor's wife felt she didn't need to pay duty on the clothes she brought into the country, and his kids need to be periodically bailed out of trouble.

Well, yes. From backwoods good ol' Southern boys to cigarette-boat-driving drug dealers, thanks to popular culture, we Floridians do have quite the reputation, don't we? Both geographically and in terms of its residents, Florida is quite diverse. Do you feel an affinity with urban Florida or rural Florida or both?

Urban Florida. I am a city person. Urban Florida is a fluid society and welcomes newcomers. It's easier to move about and meet people here. I've had family members who grew up on farms in various places around the country, and I know too much about rural life to sentimentalize its brutality, prejudice, poverty, and lack of opportunity.

Your characterization of rural life as having a lack of opportunity is interesting and makes me think about Helen and the demands she faces living, for all practical purposes, hand-to-mouth, just getting by. Do you see this is a major issue in Florida today?

One quarter of the state is working poor, according to a recent study. This has a tremendous impact on the work force, which lives in or on the edge of poverty. Also, this is a right-to-work state. Wages are unusually low, and without union intervention, the workers are less likely to have proper training or safe working conditions. There is a high percentage of illegal immigrants working jobs in this state. These people are forced to work for unnaturally low wages in unsafe conditions. The state is also overcrowded, public transportation is nearly nonexistent, money is cut for education, and developers are given free rein to destroy the environment. All these issues have an impact on my Dead-End Job Series.

Although your description is honest, that's a pretty bleak portrayal of our state. Given where we are now, where do you feel Florida is headed?

Unless we elect a more enlightened leadership, we are headed for chaos.

The working poor do in many ways live in a state of chaos in your novels. You've characterized this chaos for readers throughout the novels of your Dead-End Job Series as an inevitable consequence of the dead-end jobs themselves, first in Shop Till You Drop, *with the declaration: "Dead-end job workers were powerless. They were yelled at by customers and abused by cheap bosses. Their hours were changed without notice. They were fired for no reason. They had only one weapon, and Helen was about to use it.... 'I'm quitting,' Helen said" (270). In your most recent novel in the series,* Murder Unleashed, *you further clarified the lack of choices faced by those in these jobs: "That was the problem with a dead-end job: Helen had no protection. She couldn't complain.... Helen might find herself out of work." In the name of field research, you yourself have worked each of these jobs that has so tortured Helen. How accurately do Helen's dead-end job experiences represent your own?*

Fairly accurately. These dead-end jobs are often physically difficult, and Helen and I are both dead tired after a day at work. The customers can be demanding. The bosses can be thoughtless and sometimes downright cruel. I did meet some very good supervisors when I did the research for *Just Murdered, Murder Unleashed,* and *Murder Between the Covers*. But when I worked as a telemarketer in *Dying to Call You,* the employee abuse was horrendous. I put a lot of it into the book. Also, I wrote about the phenomenon I call "clerk abuse," where middle-class people take out their frustrations on the salespeople. That was true in most jobs, especially the bookstore one. Helen and I have taken our share of verbal abuse from customers.

While your Dead-End Job Series challenges readers to consider the world of the working poor, this isn't the only issue that is brought to the forefront. The novels are also commenting on the stereotypical South Florida lifestyle. In Shop Till You Drop, *Margery explains to Helen one of the traits that makes Florida Florida: the ability for someone to disappear into the background, living unnoticed. She explains, "Nobody has roots here. In the Midwest, if you don't know a guy, you can make a few phone calls and find out about him" (80). Did you consider setting your Dead-End Job Series outside of Florida? If so, how do you think a non–Florida setting would alter your work?*

This series could only take place in Florida, which has such a rootless society. In places such as St. Louis, Helen could not get all those low-paying jobs, and she would be too well-known.

In addition to our ever-changing population, there are many other quintessential characters representative of Florida. You are obviously well acquainted with one of them, the legacy of Key West's most famous resident, Ernest Hemingway, and his six-toed cats. Helen's cat Thumbs, rumored to be kin to Hemingway's felines, is a recurring character throughout the Dead-End Job Series. Other than Hemingway, do you know much about Florida history?

Florida has had rampant greed, murder, and poor environmental planning since the very beginning. The killer hurricane of 1928 was so destructive because of the problems with Lake Okeechobee. A recent report says the lake is once more a danger, as we head into hurricane season.

You've obviously enjoyed coming to know and writing about your adopted home state of Florida. Is writing easy and fun for you, or do you find it to be work?

Both. It's work I enjoy.

What was your preparation in becoming an author? What significant experiences did you have that you feel led you to this profession?

My degree is in journalism, and I spent more than 25 years writing for a newspaper and then as a syndicated columnist for United Media in New York. Journalism was terrific preparation for a novelist. It taught me to respect deadlines. I interviewed literally thousands of people from CEOs to the homeless, from bikers to nuns. I learned about writing dialogue, about research and preparation, which have all helped me to write novels.

What is the process you go through in writing? Do you use outlines, or do you just sit down and start?

I'm the sort of person who wrote the essay first in school, and then did the outline. So my "outlines" are 90 to 130 pages. They're done chapter by chapter, and contain blocks of dialogue and descriptions, as well as most of the characters.

It sounds like the writing process is a very detailed but relatively quick process for you. Have you ever had a problem with writer's block? If so, how did you get through it? If not, why do you think you have dodged this common problem?

I only had writer's block once, with my first series. I couldn't start the book. My agent told me I couldn't write anything for a whole month. Naturally, I disobeyed him, started the book, and finished it on time. Apparently, child psychology works well with me. I've dodged the problem most of the time because I worked so many years as a journalist. Reporters are not allowed the luxury of writer's block. We cannot wait for inspiration. We have to turn in our stories, and they must be on time. For us, writing is a job.

When writing fiction, which do you feel is more important: plot development or character development? How much attention do you pay to each?

Both are important, and I don't think you can choose one over the other. If your characters are not interesting and believable, then readers will not follow their adventures for a whole book. If your plot is lackluster, readers will be disappointed in the novel. A writer needs to keep readers entertained with both.

How do you go about developing the elements of the story? Where do the elements come from—that is, what is your inspiration?

The story, the murder, and even the murder weapon come out of my research. For instance, in *Murder Unleashed*, I worked at a high-priced dog boutique.

One of the things all dog boutiques fear is that someone's precious pet will be lost, stolen, or injured. A dognapping became an important element of the novel. Groomers are proud of their long scissors, and those became a murder weapon in the story. While I worked at the boutique, Fort Lauderdale was threatened by a hurricane, and that became part of the story, as well as the customers' reaction to the storm.

How did you come to write in the mystery/crime genre? Have you ever thought about writing in another genre? Can you envision yourself as a non-crime or mystery writer?

No. I'm not interested in writing anything but mysteries. Mainstream novels have become dull, academic, and divorced from society's real issues. Mystery novels seem to be tackling the problems: injustice, low-paying jobs, women's role in society, racial issues, etc.

What other genres have you worked in, screenwriting, theatre, nonfiction, etc.? Do you find this work more, less, or equally as satisfying as the crime/mystery genre?

I've written nonfiction. Fiction is far more satisfying. I like creating my own world.

Critics and scholars are insistent on classifying writing into strict genres such as mystery/detective, crime fiction, etc. Do you find such classifications limiting?

Absolutely. Mysteries are too varied to be pigeonholed.

Not to pigeonhole you further, but how do you classify your own work?

I write mysteries that are women's fiction. The lines between mysteries, crime fiction, and detective novels are too blurry to be defined.

Why do you think the mystery or crime genres remain among the most popular today?

Because they address issues that people are interested in, such as race and women's roles in society. Mysteries satisfy a need for justice, which people cannot get in real life. Good mysteries are about bringing order out of chaos and righting wrongs. People have a hunger for that, and it's not served by other genres.

Were you aware of the long history of the form? Does this history influence you?

Of course. It is a proud tradition, and I'm glad to be a small part of it. It's also important to be aware of the kinds of plot twists and characters that have been used in the past, so I'm not duplicating things that have already been done.

What authors would you cite as your major influences? Why?

Mark Twain, Carolyn Keene, Agatha Christie, and Sue Grafton. I'm from Missouri and was deeply influenced by Twain's vision of the world and his reporting of life in the Midwest, in the California gold camps and the excesses of the Gilded Age. He was a wonderful observer of people. Carolyn Keene was the name for several authors who did the Nancy Drew series. I had my mother's set of Nancy Drew mysteries from the late 1930s. I was fascinated by them, and by the adventures of this young (and for the time) liberated woman. Agatha Christie wrote traditional mysteries. Miss Marple was someone easily discounted and overlooked, who made a terrific sleuth. Sue Grafton was the mother of the soft-boiled mystery. Again, she had a strong, intelligent female detective.

Which Florida writers do you think really understand and capture the character of the state?

Carl Hiaasen. He perfectly captures the blend of greed, corruption, beauty, and wackiness that makes up Florida. John D. Macdonald wrote some lovely descriptions of Florida, and he was an early campaigner for the environment, but his attitude toward women is seriously dated. Barbara Parker's *Suspicion* series is a good description of life in Miami.

What do you feel sets Florida writers apart from other writers and makes them distinct? How do you fit into this view?

The sense of place in Florida is so strong that it's almost another character. Readers expect Florida books to have a weirdness not found in other places, except maybe California. My character Helen is only possible in a fluid society such as South Florida. There's also the state's extreme weather, which plays a part in so many books—the extreme heat and the hurricanes.

Elaine, it has been such a pleasure visiting with you today about your Dead-End Job Series and life in Florida. Best wishes to both you and Helen as you undoubtedly pursue yet another dead-end job—I, for one, am ready to read all about it!

Bibliography

Florida's Dead-End Job series with Helen Hawthorne

Viets, Elaine. *Dying to Call You.* New York: Signet, 2004.
_____. *Just Murdered.* New York: Signet, 2005.
_____. *Murder Between the Covers.* New York: Signet, 2003.

_____. *Murder Unleashed.* New York: New American Library, 2006.
_____. *Shop Till You Drop.* New York: Signet, 2003.

Josie Marcus, Mystery Shopper series

_____. *Dying in Style.* New York: Signet, 2005.
_____. *High Heels Are Murder.* New York: Signet, 2006.

Francesca Vierling series

_____. *Backstab.* New York: Dell, 1997.
_____. *Doc in the Box.* New York: Dell, 2000.
_____. *The Pink Flamingo Murders.* New York: Dell, 1999.
_____. *Rubout.* New York: Dell, 1998.

Nonfiction

_____. *How to Commit Monogamy: A Lighthearted Look at Long-term Love.* Kansas City, MO: Andrews McMeel Publishing, 1997.

M. Diane Vogt, Author of Florida Legal Mysteries

by Ellen Smith

M. Diane Vogt, an attorney by training and practice, has written the acclaimed Judge Wilhelmina Carson legal thrillers. The Chinese government was so impressed by the series that it has purchased and translated the novels into Chinese as an entertaining way of helping its people understand American life and this country's legal system. Diane is currently working on a new thriller series featuring Karen Brown, a "retrieval specialist" with a cover identity as a travel writer. Karen Brown debuted in the anthology *Thriller: Stories to Keep You Up All Night*, edited by James Patterson (Mira, 2006). Her short story, "Death's Deceit," appears in *North Florida Noir* (Pottersville Press, 2006). Diane is Vice-President of National Events of the International Thriller Writers, former member of the board of the Florida chapter of Mystery Writers of America, and active with Sisters in Crime. A lawyer in private practice for more than 25 years, she has represented the world's largest corporations as well as individuals and governments. Her fiction combines legal realism with characters readers care about to provide engrossing stories readers don't want to put down.

ELLEN SMITH: *Why detective fiction?*

M. DIANE VOGT: Life is a mystery. Learning about ourselves and trying to figure out how the world works is at least a part of the prime directive for a writer. In my case, interest in mystery fiction was a part of my genetic makeup. You see, my dad was a mystery fan and he instilled in me a love of the genre, the puzzle, the desire and the ability to figure things out. It would have been nice if he'd also contributed the math gene, because he was good at that, too, and I'm, well, not.

Legal thrillers have always provided high drama and intense conflict, inside or outside the courtroom. As a child, I was a devoted fan of Perry Mason. Every week, Dad and I would watch Erle Stanley Gardner's Mason outsmart the bad guys on television, matching wits with Mason in the process. Sometimes, Dad could guess who the real killer was before he was revealed. Dad smarter than Perry Mason! Imagine that! "Lawyers as heroes" shows on television then included *The Defenders, Ironsides,* and many more. Dad and I enjoyed them all. Later, he became a fan of *Matlock,* too. These television programs along with films such as *Twelve Angry Men* and *To Kill a Mockingbird* convinced me that lawyers were noble, caring, heroic and productive members of society who played a vital role in our country of laws. Those evenings were at least in part responsible for me becoming a lawyer and, many years later, writing fiction.

All types of fiction captivated me, but I also adored John D. MacDonald's Travis McGee and became enamored of Florida. While living in the Detroit suburbs and working in the city, Florida drew me like no other location has ever done. Tampa has been my home since 1992, at least in part because of McGee.

How has being a lawyer influenced your work?

Of course, fictionalization of the world is necessary to good stories. But like Erle Stanley Gardner, I take very little dramatic license with the lawyers I portray and the world they inhabit. Many of my stories are based on cases I worked on or learned about in my law practice. Unlike Gardner, my plots are more complicated and the solutions often lie in the ambiguities. And my characters don't always win, even though they are usually right.

One of my story goals is often to allow readers to experience the realities of our legal system. From an insider's perspective, I reveal what actually happens in lawsuits, courtrooms and lawyers' offices, not just in criminal matters, but in civil cases—where most people collide with the law. While the law works well, the reality of our legal system is that most people will never use it and those who do will be dissatisfied because the process consumes so much time and money. Like all things, the legal system is flawed and can never be perfect.

My stories reveal the law's anomalies or gaps in what the system can handle, where a real-life client would rightly exclaim at the outset, "You've got to be kidding!"

When did you become aware of the mystery genres—and which kinds (movies, novels, TV)?

Very early in life, I realized that mystery and crime fiction, very broadly defined to include all aspects of thriller and suspense, was the genre that intrigued me the most. While I read widely, watched movies and television in all genres, mystery was my favorite.

For a long time, I loved reading and watching mysteries without realizing there were subgenres to be aware of. Although I enjoyed the police procedural, the private investigator novels, legal and other thrillers, spy novels, and amateur sleuths, I didn't realize that they were distinctly different types of mysteries. But I knew that the kinds of stories I enjoyed the most, whether they were on television, in films, novels or short stories, were those where a distinct plot—usually a crime of some sort—was central to the tale.

Today, I read widely. I'm still not overly picky about the subgenres I enjoy. I adore noir, the anti-heroes, cyber crime, thrillers, and caper stories as much, or more, than the traditional cozy. The only real criterion for me is that the book must have a surprise, preferably at the end, that I didn't see coming. Maybe it's that old *Perry Mason* thing again. Remember how Perry's client was never guilty and part of the fun was to guess who the real perp was? The mystery in the story itself is still important to me. It's the unanswered questions facing characters I care about that keep me reading or watching.

Did anything influence your choice to become a mystery writer? If so, how and in what ways?

Once I entered law school and began reading those heavy case books, I realized that all legal cases are little mysteries, that perhaps every life is its own mystery. How did the client get him/herself into the situation that brought them to the court? Why did they behave the way they did? What motivated the other side? What is justice in each situation?

When I began to practice law, every client's problem presented a new set of questions and a need for solutions. The practice fed my hunger for mystery, but not my desire to know the answer to every question posed by each case. In real life, many questions remain unanswered. You see, in real life, things are messy. Criminal defendants are advised to say nothing and that's smart advice. Often, we never know whether the defendant is guilty or not. Civil cases revolve around disputes and different perspectives of the same facts and situations. Usually, each party is trying to divulge as little as possible while advancing his own claims or defenses. Crime fiction, on the other hand, must have a satisfying ending. With crime fiction, things can be resolved. We can know why and how and when and where. The genre satisfies our universal need for answers.

When I read *Presumed Innocent* by Scott Turow and *The Firm* by John Grisham, I finally said, "Okay. I can write books that interest me and there just might be an audience out there for books about lawyers and what they really do." While much legal fiction is dramatized beyond the constraints of reality, the types I enjoy the most are those that work within the realities of the law and provide a good story in that framework.

When did you first realize that you were a mystery/detective/crime writer?

My parents read to me from infancy and a regular weekly trip to the library was a part of our routine. But I didn't start reading just for fun on my own until I was about ten. The first book I remember reading was *Huckleberry Finn*, although I'm sure there were others before that. But something about the story fired my imagination and set me on a path that I was destined to follow: reading reading reading, and then, eventually, writing.

There was a time when I read absolutely everything that came my way. But I leaned toward stories with thrills, suspense and surprises, an element of mystery and wonder, right from the start. I mean, if *Huckleberry Finn* wasn't a mystery, then what was it? At least to a ten-year-old girl! Of course, I progressed from Nancy Drew through Agatha Christie, took several turns around Robert Ludlum and Helen MacInnes, spent many wonderful hours with Phyllis Whitney and Daphne DuMaurier, Doyle, of course. And Stephen King, Rex Stout, Laurence Sanders, Sue Grafton and Sarah Paretsky and many, many more. Eventually, I began to write what I loved, what I knew, and what I wanted to learn about. Maybe I was thirty-five by then. Okay, so I'm a late bloomer. Remember, Grandma Moses didn't start painting until after her ninetieth birthday!

What kind of preparation (formal education, career choices) has helped you with your writing? Have there been any dead ends or distractions?

After the usual liberal arts education, I became certified as a secondary education teacher. This was 1974 and there weren't that many teaching jobs out there. I didn't get one. Now, of course, I believe that early failure was one of the best things that ever happened to me. But then, I needed to find another way to make a living. I took a few different kinds of jobs, worked in retail, as a secretary, and finally decided that since I'd liked Perry Mason, perhaps I could be a lawyer. Before you laugh, you should know that Perry Mason influenced hundreds, if not thousands, of kids who ended up in law school. The more frightening thing is that students today go to law school because of television shows like *Ally McBeal* and *The Practice*, shows that don't present lawyers in an idealized fashion or focus on their commitment to truth. Contrary to some fiction out there, most lawyers are not liars.

Being a lawyer is mostly about writing well, communicating through the written word, persuading an audience by words on a page. The legal writing aspects of my law school experience were some of my most successful. I was invited to join Law Review and my first work, a casenote, was published in 1979. After that, I didn't publish again for almost twenty years.

What I came to realize was that lawyering was writing with a better paycheck. My writing skills carried me a long way as a lawyer, to some of the top honors in the country. But I longed to write fiction. Owning my own law firm made that possible because I didn't have anyone to please but myself. I could devote long hours to learning the craft of fiction without having to answer to an executive committee. Traveling to workshops and conferences, attending writers' retreats, participating in critique groups, and other necessary training rituals kept me busy for another ten years before my first novel was published. I was almost 45 years old by then.

Dead ends? There's been a few. But then again, too few to mention. No, wait, that's Sinatra. For me, once I finally decided that I needed to take the plunge and actually write and submit something, I met with modest success. But the writing life is full of pitfalls, rejections, delays, and disappointments. It's part of the business. The biggest dead end I've faced so far was when my publisher went into bankruptcy in May 2004. I had a four-book contract that evaporated into thin air. Not only that, but I had signed contracts that gave the publisher, now the bankruptcy trustee, ownership of my creations. It came as a big shock to me that something I had created, that didn't exist until I made it up, now belonged to someone else. I had to hire a lawyer and get my rights back. And then, figure out what to do next.

Why do you set your work in Florida? What is it about the state in general and Tampa in particular that provide workable material?

As I mentioned earlier, back in my constant reading days, I read John D. MacDonald. And loved everything he wrote. Through him, and Travis McGee, I fell in love with Florida. Of course, the warm weather helped, too. I was living in Michigan at the time and hated the winters. When I got a chance to move to Florida in 1992 to practice law here, I convinced my husband to give it a try. And when we moved to Tampa, we both fell it love with it.

Tampa isn't Ft. Lauderdale and the differences between my Florida and McGee's Florida continue to intrigue me. Tampa is an old city with history and charm. It's also a business center and has been called "the Midwest with palm trees," because of the number of Midwesterners who move here. The pirate legends and celebrations, Cuban cigar factories, the struggle to bring winning sports teams (including hockey, amazingly enough) to the area, all encouraged me to write about Tampa.

I've never regretted it. We're not wacky South Florida here, although some of my writing colleagues disagree with me on that point and write wacky stories about wacky people who live in Tampa. But I'm thinking those people moved here from California. (Kidding. I actually love California.)

Did any other Florida writers influence you?

I read everyone and love the work of most of my fellow Florida writers, so I guess all of them influence me in various ways.

Do you believe that Florida writers can affect what happens in the state?

I subscribe to Louis B. Mayer's view: "If you want to send a message, use Western Union." I don't write fiction or read it for the purpose of affecting public policy, economic development, environmental responsibility and so on. I realize other writers feel their muse leads them in that direction and I absolutely believe in the power of fiction to influence our world. The proliferation of Florida crime fiction definitely improves the image of the state and encourages others to visit or move here.

Can you account for the fact that Florida is producing so many excellent writers in the genre?

There's a lot of talent in Florida and a lot of material. We have a population of about 18 million now. And we live in paradise, a place more than fifty-million people visit every year. The combination, I think, is attracting talented writers and producing some killer fiction.

How do you go about writing a mystery novel? Do you spend much time outlining? Does plot or character control the progress of the story?

Writing is an organic process for me. Something begins the idea for a story and then I think about it, fool around with it, talk to myself as I exercise by walking four miles a day, until it develops into a plot with characters and setting and all the other elements of a good story. Although I didn't start out using outlines, I have, over the years, learned the value of a good outline. It helps to figure out the structure of the story and to keep me on track as I'm writing. As for the plot vs. character debate, I suspect that we fiction writers enjoy getting to know our characters and we focus on character development because of that interest. But I feel that both character and plot are absolutely essential to crime fiction. There is no story without a great plot and there is no plot without great characters. I don't enjoy the kind of story where wonderful characters hang out and do nothing. Worked well for Seinfeld, a self-described television comedy "about nothing." But this doesn't work for crime fiction. So for me, the characters do propel the plot, but the plot must be paramount. Now, maybe a particular plot only works because of the characters involved in it. And to be sure, the characters must be compelling. But without a great plot, or at least a good one, there is no crime story.

Have you ever started from an actual historic event or does nearly everything come from your imagination?

Where do good story ideas come from? For me, they come from everywhere—I see so many more stories than I can ever write. Sometimes, a story in the newspaper will intrigue me. Sometimes it's a conversation with friends or something overheard at a party. Once, I put together a story after three different but somewhat related incidents came to my attention. But like all writers, when the initial idea intrigues me and I figure out whether there's enough there to make a good story, almost everything will be fictionalized. The stuff I make up is so much more fun for me than the exacting details of, say, the technothriller or fictionalized historical events. I enjoy reading those books, but not writing them.

Have you worked in other genres?

I co-authored a nonfiction management book and [have] written countless nonfiction articles on a variety of subjects. But the only short story and book length fiction I've published is crime fiction. That might change some day. For now, I'm enjoying the genre too much to write something different.

How would you compare and contrast Wilhelmina with other women sleuths (Kinsey, Gail, Lupe)?

Wilhelmina Carson is different from all of them. Willa's life is much more structured and restrictive. Being a lawyer requires one to live by the rules and being a judge adds another whole layer of requirements. Willa has no children. I made this decision intentionally, and I get a lot of questions about it. But mostly, I didn't want Willa to have to deal with kids in the stories, too.

Willa isn't as free-wheeling or easygoing as some of the other popular female protagonists. This is partly because of her position and partly because of her personality. She's very hard-working, heroic and funny. Her sense of humor is much like mine: situational more than slapstick. Like many of the other female protagonists, Willa is principled and has a very strong view of the world and how it should work. This sense of justice and values is what propels her into trouble and why she's sometimes criticized for doing things no real judge would do. For instance, Willa investigates crime. Real judges don't do that.

And Willa has always been married in the books I've written so far. I wanted a stable relationship for her so that she could focus on other aspects of the situations she finds herself involved in, rather than issues with her husband. But, in *Marital Privilege*, Willa's husband does get himself into a bit of a bind. Which proves, I guess, that all husbands are uncontrollable, even the fictionalized variety—thank God.

What are you working on now?

I'm writing a new series. Karen Ann Brown is a young lawyer disillusioned with the law's compromises enough to leave her job as a prosecutor and strike out on her own. She now works as a self-styled, independent "retrieval specialist" with a cover identity as a travel writer. Karen is forced to make tough choices when her clients' needs are thwarted by gaping holes in the law. The underlying theme in the Karen books is trust, breach of trust, and betrayal.

Karen Brown is named after a real travel writer. While the fictional Karen's home base is Tampa, the books will feature locations contained in the seventeen *Karen Brown Guides*, which have sold more than 2.5 million copies worldwide. If all goes well, there will be at least fourteen novels featuring Karen. Karen was introduced in the short story "Surviving Toronto," inspired by the plight of a good friend who is embroiled in a futile ten-year custody battle. The only lawful solution is to run out the clock on the ex-husband's parental rights when his daughters reach majority. But Karen Brown seeks a better answer. When children are abducted and removed to foreign countries, international law attempts to solve human problems by treaties and diplomacy. The process is bureaucratic and tedious. Too often, it's also a complete failure.

What are some of the major subjects that you deal with directly or indirectly—social/ economic issues, the environment, family concerns, for example—that appear in your work?

While the stories I write deal with many of these issues, the themes are almost always personal responsibility and trust, two values I believe in strongly. Who and what we trust and why, along with the choices we make based on that trust, define us. I believe we can make better choices if we understand and accept that we have the power, ability and obligation to do so. In my work as a lawyer, I see many people who choose to become victims—often without realizing it. Of course, there are real victims of natural disasters and random violence and fate. But for most people, in many situations, feeling victimized is a choice and an enormous waste of life. My stories empower us by saying that you are never a victim unless you choose to be, regardless of what happens to you. That it's not so much what happens to you that matters, but how you handle it; if we view our setbacks as opportunities for growth, we can find meaning and direction in life.

Because this is my basic theme, I don't write about random violence or gang murder or any other types of crime that seem to be totally outside a victim's control. Like everyone else, I'm trying to make sense of a chaotic world and I don't understand random violence and don't want to dwell within it. Although it's sometimes fun to watch a scary movie or read a scary book, it's not something I want to create myself. Psychopathology of criminals is truly frightening and outside our personal control, but it is also much less prevalent in our society than the damage we do to ourselves and our loved ones through the choices we make. Self-determination is a more empowering world view.

I want to provide an exciting or challenging read, to entertain and bring the experience a reader seeks, but also to offer hope. I think life is full of hope and I want people to know that.

Bibliography

Vogt, M. Diane. "Death's Deceit."*North Florida Noir*. Panama City: Pottersville Press, 2006.
____. *Gasparilla Gold*. iUniverse, 2002.
____. *The Little Bathroom Book of Crime Puzzles*. Gloucester, MA: Fair Winds Press, 2006.
____. *Marital Privilege*. Los Angeles: New Millennium Press, 2004.
____. *Silicone Solution*. Pittsburgh: Sterling House, 1999.
____. *Six Bills*. Los Angeles: New Millennium Press, 2003.
____. "Surviving Toronto," *Thriller: Stories to Keep You Up All Night*. Mira, 2006.

Randy Wayne White, Naturalist and Crime Writer

by Bill Ott

Randy Wayne White's Doc Ford crime novels, starring the Sanibel Island marine biologist and reluctant operator for an under-the-radar offshoot of the CIA, have grown steadily in popularity and critical acclaim since the first of the series, Sanibel Flats, was published in 1990. The series, now in its thirteenth installment, can always be counted on for an engaging mix of character interplay and straight-ahead action-adventure. Fans have come to love not just Ford, a reluctant warrior who, once engaged, goes after bad guys with a lethal mix of tradecraft and righteous indignation, but also the whole crew at Dinkin's Bay Marina, where Ford lives and hangs out with the fishing guides and live-aboards, including the mercurial Tomlinson—latter-day hippie, Internet spiritual advisor, and the yin to Ford's yang.

White, who was a fishing guide at Tarpon Bay on Sanibel Island for 13 years, also writes nonfiction and is an editor-at-large for *Outside Magazine*. He has been awarded both the Conch Republic Prize for Literature, also given to John Cheever, Peter Matthiessen, Jim Harrison, and Thomas McGuane, and the John D. MacDonald Award for Literary Excellence, whose previous winners include Carl Hiaasen and James W. Hall. White's PBS documentary, *The Gift of the Game*, about taking baseball gear to kids in Cuba, won the 2002 Best of Show Award at the Woods Hole Film Festival.

White lives on Pine Island, Florida, in an old house on an Indian mound. He can sometimes be found hanging out at Doc Ford's Sanibel Grill and Rum Bar, a restaurant named after his main character.

BILL OTT: *How's the sunset tonight?*

RANDY WAYNE WHITE: Just gorgeous. My dock's 210 feet long, and right off the end of it, a couple of hundred yards out, some dolphins are sharkin,' and they're mullet everywhere. The sky's streaked orange and gold and purple... Beautiful.

Nothing like that here in Chicago. Tell me how a farm boy from Iowa and Ohio came to be on Sanibel Island watching the sunset and, beyond that, how you became a writer.

What it comes down to, I guess, is that I wasn't smart enough to get into college... Pretty much I had no alternative. I grew up in rural areas—and when I say rural, I mean rural. But I always loved books. My brother was five years older, and my sister was five years younger. I guess there's a lot to be said for boredom as a motivator, at least as long as there isn't crank or crystal meth around. So I turned to books, but for whatever reason, I was not a good student. School just never caught on with me, but I loved reading—novels in particular—and I thought if I could one day write a book, I could somehow become part of the magic I found in books. I never thought I was smart enough or qualified enough to do that, but I got a job on a newspaper for a few years—that was a huge break for me—and I worked very hard writing when I was a fishing guide.

Did you begin writing when you were a guide?

No, I started trying to write early on. I wrote journals, and I would rewrite sentences that I liked, just to get the feel of the language. So I got out of high school, and about four or five years later, I got the job on the *Fort Myers News Press*. I had no college, but the editor just sort of said, "Well, you seem like a nice guy, you're hired." I was very lucky. I did about four years there, and it was a wonderful learning experience and a great opportunity to meet people. I was a copy editor, but I did feature stories when I could for free, and I was very eager to learn, very motivated. I knew I didn't want to spend my life in newspapers, though, and I eventually became a fishing guide. I did that for nearly 13 years, almost 3,000 charters, but in 1987 my marina was closed to powerboat traffic, and I was out of a job. So I wrote a novel.

Had you been doing your outdoor writing while you were a fishing guide?

Yes, while I was still a guide, I was lucky enough to place a story with *Outside Magazine*, where there was this incredible lineup of writers: Tom McGuane, Jim Harrison, Peter Matthiessen, Jon Krakauer, David Quammen, and Edward Abbey. They liked my story, and after that—while I was still fishing—I was sent somewhere to write something every few months.

What did you like to do more back then, fish or write?

I still don't exactly like to write—it's very hard—but I would say I prefer to write. I was never a fisherman by nature. I like boats, and I like being on the water, but I was never a great fisherman. I never had great fishing instincts. My mother had great fishing instincts—my Deep South mom—and one or two of my uncles did, too. I never did, so fishing was always work for me. I did love watching the interaction of things on the water. When you're on the water for 300 days a year, as I was then, the repetition of things becomes so automatic that they tend to reassemble themselves in your mind, and you tend to see things that otherwise you wouldn't see.

Sometimes, in your novels, it almost seems as if water is the main character. How did you come to use the outdoors in general, and water in particular, in your work in the manner you do? Is it something you set out to do, or did it evolve naturally, given your interest?

I guess it's more like alchemy than chemistry. It just kind of happened. I didn't say this originally—maybe John D. MacDonald did—but if you're writing about two people in Florida, you're writing about three very powerful characters. The outdoors, and water especially, is always the fabric behind my books, for whatever reason. When I started the first one—and they've all gone this way—I tried to write a fun, fast, interesting story, and then, beneath that, there was an environmental backdrop, which I didn't want to be obvious, although it was slightly more obvious than the third element: all of the books have a very intricate religious subtheme, with private words and unexpected names. There's no reason why any reader in the world should care about that, and I didn't expect them to, but it's just been my deal. Water is a major part of that, in terms of chemistry—not versus spirituality but chemistry as compared to alchemy. I'm only just now comfortable talking about that, but in books like *Everglades*, there is a character I see as genuinely evil, and he meets his end in a volcano in Nicaragua—I've been there—that's called Messiah, but because of the spelling no one would get it.

That helps me understand your villains. A lot of people talk about Carl Hiaasen's psycho bad guys, but I'd put some of your evil characters up against anybody in the genre. You have that guy in Everglades; *you have the pyromaniac in* Tampa Burn *and the crazed ecoterrorist in* Dead of the Night. *It's almost like there's a horror novelist deep within you—Stephen King, maybe—trying to get out.*

I'll take any comparison I can get to Carl Hiaasen or Stephen King. I'd like to be as good-looking as Carl and as smart as either one of them. Not that Stephen King isn't a good-looking man because, damn it, he is.

Can we talk a little about plot and character? How do you manage to tell fast-moving, exciting tales and still get so much depth to your characters?

Well, let's start with characters. I feel like if I know the people I'm writing about well enough, they should be able to take over without behaving out of character. So that becomes a kind of scaffolding I depend on. When I start a new book, I write a lengthy bio of the characters, especially the villain. Before I started the first Ford novels, I wrote very long bios of Ford, Tomlinson, and Ford's crazed uncle. I've lost all those—they were typed manuscripts, probably 50 or 60 pages long for each person. I mean, I knew everything about these guys before I started writing the novels about them. And in every new book, I tell readers a little more about them, gradually revealing more of the iceberg. I think if you know your iceberg well, you can add depth to your story by revealing it bit by bit.

With plot, I start with one incident, and then it's one terrifying day after another trying to build on that. Fortunately, the characters tend to take over and drive me through the story. Sometimes I know the ending, and that's wonderful. Other times I don't, and holy shit, that's the terrifying part.

Which do you find harder to do, characters or plot?

I find the plotline more difficult because I think people are more interesting than events, frankly. Events are at least seemingly random, but people, their motivations and their flaws, I find fascinating. In one of the Ford books, there's a line, spoken by Ford, that goes, "We like small, brave people who find small, brave ways to endure and achieve." That's certainly the way I feel, and I think it's behind my interest in character. I've met quite a few writers—not the ones from Florida, who by and large are a fun-loving bunch—but quite a few writers who generally seem to dislike people. They seem kind of crabby, lacking in zest, and very much the type who want to inspect their bellybuttons over and over again. I don't find that very appealing. I like people, and I like to write about them.

Talk some more about how you work out your plots. I think you manage to blend character and plot superbly.

Well, thanks for that. I work at it, and my plots are certainly intricate. Whenever I start a new book, I think, "By golly, Randy, just keep it simple this time," and every time toward the end, I say, "Randy, you asshole, you've done it again."

It seems today like mystery readers and critics can't stop talking about character-

driven crime novels. It's almost as if plot has become a dirty word. And, yet, don't you think that a book needs a solid plot if readers are going to engage with the characters?

I do think so. Why go ahead and keep reading if the story isn't grabbing you? People have a lot of stuff to do, after all.

I wanted to follow up on your "small, brave people" quote by asking about the characters who make up the Dinkin's Bay family. I've read that most of them are clearly autobiographical. Do you want to talk about that some?

Sure. Dinkin's Bay Marina is actually Tarpon Bay Marina, on Sanibel Island. I was a guide there for almost 13 years. Mack ran the marina, and he was a character. If you were kind of a straight, hard-working lug, Mack probably wouldn't hire you, but if you had some quirks or oddities, he might. Mack collected clowns, literally; he loved those awful paintings of clowns. Mack hired a guy named Graeme from New Zealand. Graeme became one of my dearest friends and still is, though he's kind of disappeared. Graeme had been all over the world, worked on a kibbutz in Israel, lived in South Africa, and he probably had some connections best not investigated. So Graeme was here illegally, and Mack hired him to run the marina. Tarpon Bay is in a national preserve, which meant that an illegal was interacting all the time with federal officials, who never had a clue. And Mack liked that. He also hired a guy named Nick, who's a great big, muscular, good-looking guy with a cleft chin, but he had a terrible stutter. Mac put Nick (Jeth in my books) in charge of answering the phone in the fish market and gradually the stutter got better. All the fishing guides in the Doc Ford books are real people, as is Tomlinson, who's a mixture of two of my best friends.

Talk some more about Tomlinson. He's certainly one of the most dominant and interesting sidekicks in mystery fiction. Do you need to hold him in check a little, for fear he'll take over the series?

No, I don't really worry about that. Tomlinson's got his own deal, and I just let him have it. He's not an easy character to write—none of them are—but he's tough because I never really had a hippie period of my own to draw on. But a couple of my friends did, and I use them. One of them is Bill "Spaceman" Lee, who pitched for the Red Sox for years. He's an incredibly brilliant guy and one of my closest friends. Much of Tomlinson comes from Bill and from one other guy, whose name I'm not going to mention, but between those two, I get all the hippie background I need.

Speaking of Tomlinson, how long are we going to have to wait before the whole issue between Doc and Tomlinson—whether Doc will be able to save his friend from Doc's employers, who want him dead—comes to the fore?

A lot of that will be in the book I'm working on now. The series will go on after that, but I'm getting into what happened with Tomlinson in this book, and at least some of the questions will be answered.

That leads to an issue every series writer faces: the problem of heroes getting older. Some writers more or less freeze time, allowing them to keep reusing the basic dynamic that made the series work in the first place, and others very consciously allow the characters and the situations to change. You've allowed some change already, but how do you plan to deal with that problem in the future?

That's a great question. Yes, my characters have changed so far, and boy, it's pissed some people off. I get letters saying things like, "Don't ever hurt Tomlinson again," or, "What do you mean letting Doc Ford get beat up! What kind of bullshit is that!" But they care about my characters, and so do I. The thing is, the characters do have their own lives, and of course they're going to change, get older. It helps, though, that we really do live in the best time in history in the sense that a man 45 or 50 years can still be a kick-ass guy—or even 65. I mean, I know guys who are 65 and still swim 3 miles or ride bikes for 6 miles, so it's the best time in history for that.

You don't have a problem like you would have if you were writing, say, 40 years ago.

Yeah, when guys were smoking and drinking whiskey all day.

Those were the days. But emotionally and psychologically, there are still some change issues to deal with, even today.

That's true, and I've tried to be aware of that. Ford's changed, and Tomlinson has, too, to a degree, and they will continue to change somewhat, but we reach a certain age when we start to become simply more of who we are. We expand, expand, expand, and then we begin to condense.

Sometimes our worst characteristics take over as we get older.

Right. Take Ford. He's a very blunt guy, who's never had a full-time romantic relationship. There's always a reason for him to end those relationships, and, unlike Tomlinson, he's not inwardly obsessed, he's outwardly obsessed. But, again unlike Tomlinson, he's not a very nice guy—well, he is a nice guy, but there is a certain panel of chill there that never goes away.

That tension between whether Ford is a nice guy or not is at the heart of the novels. His attraction-repulsion to violence seems to come into play in almost every book, and in one place, you talk about his "lizard brain," the part that's all about survival. I admire the way Doc Ford struggles with that lizard brain, but we all like to root for him when it kicks in, and he lets go. I think we all wish we could let go like that.

Yes, there is that part of the brain—it's called the *amygdala*—and, yeah, Ford struggles with it. Extreme behavior is something we're all told is not appropriate, but sometimes we have the desire for it. But I don't think there is all that much violence in my books, and when there is, I hope it makes sense.

No, there's not that much violence, but when it explodes, it does explode.

It does, but I've seen violence, and if someone gets punched in the nose, or you punch someone in the nose, it hangs on in your mind for months. It's not something that, afterward, you just go on, chattering about it. Violence hangs on, sometimes a lifetime. People sometimes say there wasn't a big fight scene in the book, or there's not enough sex—which probably reflects my early life. But violence is a powerful thing, not to be taken lightly.

I also wanted to ask you about your last book, Dark Light, *because I know that living through a hurricane is a topic close to your heart. You've talked about this elsewhere, but could you say something about what happened to you in real life and how you went about translating that into fiction? You said in* Dark Light *that after you've been in the eye of a hurricane, you feel like you've been "shit on by God, by nature, by government, by insurance agencies." Maybe that sums it up.*

Yeah, if you've ever been in the eye of a hurricane—which is statistically very unlikely—it's a whole different deal. If a hurricane comes, and the eye misses you by 10 miles, it's just bad weather—really bad weather—but if you're in the eye, it's life-transforming. Despite what you may have read in magazines or seen on television, there have been far fewer category three and four hurricanes—in fact, hurricanes of any kind—in the last 20 years than in the previous decades. But, yeah, the eye of Hurricane Charlie went right over my house. The roof was taken off—the house is better than ever now—but I spent maybe three weeks without power and water. As my friends have pointed out more than once, "Who's better suited to live like that than Randy?" But, yeah, it was certainly life-changing in that many people who were in the eye—it was two years ago, August 13, 2004—their lives are still not back on track.

How did you manage to sit down and turn that into a novel when it was so close to you?

I write for a living so I had to do a book anyway. The curious thing is that in 2000, four years before the hurricane, I came out with a book called *Ten Thousand Islands*, which is about a category 4 hurricane that comes up the exact same path as Hurricane Charlie. Doc finally escapes it by climbing atop an Indian mound. Well, I live on an Indian mound. Charlie was a category 4 hurricane, and in my book, written years before Charlie, the name I gave my hurricane was ... Hurricane Charles. An even weirder connection is that the mounds built where I live were made by people, contemporaries of the Mayans, called the Calusas, articulate, brilliant people, very colorful. The Spaniards, at the time of the Spanish contact, named the king of the Calusas Carlos, which means Charles, or Charlie. That's why I named the hurricane Charles. Tomlinson would say that none of that is a coincidence.

Before we stop, I want to talk some baseball. I know you still play, and, of course, Ford and Tomlinson, so different in so many ways, both love baseball. Can you talk some about the game in your life and in your novels—and in the movie you made about baseball in Cuba, Gift of the Game?

Baseball. Yeah, Doc Ford still plays, and I play a little, though it's become kind of pathetic. I used to go down to Cuba with a team of guys, charter a bus, and drive around, playing anybody we found. All that is in the movie. "Spaceman" Lee is a big part of it, and he's terrific. I was a mediocre athlete, played ball in school and high school. I was the starting catcher on my team, a very big high school in Iowa. I continued to play later and have for many years. I love catching, and because of where I live in South Florida—pitchers come down early for spring training—I've had the opportunity to catch some amazing people (Bill "Spaceman" Lee, of course, and Tim Hudson).

I like the way you bring baseball into the books. It's such a shock for the reader to learn that Tomlinson is a great pitcher.

Well, that's Bill "Spaceman" Lee again. He's one of the purest people I've ever met, and Bill plays baseball, that's what he does. If you talk about money, his eyes kind of roll back in his head. He was with Boston, of course, and then Montreal, and when he was a free agent, he got offered a million-dollar-plus contract by another team, but he turned it down because, he said, "Well, I really like being in Canada." That's Bill.

Before we quit, let me ask you who you like to read. Not just crime writers, anybody. Who did you read early on, and who do you like to read now?

I can tell who I hate to read, and who I try not to read: the other Florida writers. For one simple reason: they're too good, and that's not being self-condemning or something. When I started writing, I would read magazines, and I would get pissed off for two reasons: one, I would think I could do so much better, or, on the other hand, I would think no way I could something as good as this. And the Florida writers, the few things I've read, I'd think, holy shit, I need to move to Nebraska. Because we write about the same canvas, I try not to read any of their stuff, but I have read them all enough to know they're all amazingly gifted: Carl Hiaasen is extraordinary, and Tim Dorsey—I should probably stop because I'll leave somebody out—but Tom Corcoran, James Hall—Hall is really an amazing writer—Les Standiford, Jeff Lindsay, Tom McGuane, and so many others.

Do you have a notion why Florida breeds crime writers?

Well, I live on the west coast, and most of them live on the east coast. I think it's probably because of the drug abuse there... I'm kidding. I don't know, it's a big state, and it's an interactive state. They're a number of people who come to this state, and they move from an air-conditioned condo to an air-conditioned car to an air-conditioned office. Those people aren't particularly interactive, but other people here are. And, Florida, because everyone here is from somewhere else, attracts predators. People can come here and say they're anything they want to say, reinvent themselves. Here on the west coast, you'll see people who run for office claiming they were colonels in the air force or ran IBM; then they get elected, and you find out they worked for a telephone company in Dubuque and had 7 DUIs. I don't know: I wish there were fewer Florida writers.

So who do you read then?

I read natural history and history all the time, and often the research I do for my books leads me to get interested in learning about something. Lately I've become fascinated with song lyrics. In *Dark Light*, I use the lyrics of a composer and lyricist named Wendy Webb, who's just extraordinary, as yet undiscovered but amazingly talented. So I've been spending a lot of time looking at music lyrics and trying to figure out how lyricists do what they do—Buffett, I've come to realize, is an incredible lyricist. But I rarely read fiction, partially because I'm afraid of stealing something accidentally.

Bibliography

Nonfiction

White, Randy Wayne. *An American Traveler: True Tales of Adventure, Travel, and Sport.* Guilford, Conn.: Lyons Press, 2003.
_____. *Batfishing in the Rainforest: Strange Tales of Travel & Fishing.* New York: Lyons Press, 1991.
_____. *Last Flight Out: True Tales of Adventure, Travel, and Fishing.* Guilford, Conn.: Lyons Press, 1992.
_____. *The Sharks of Nicaragua: True Tales of Adventure, Travel and Fishing.* New York: Lyons Press, 1999.

Fiction

White, Randy Wayne. *Captiva.* New York: G.P. Putnam's Sons, 1996.
_____. *Dark Light.* New York: G.P. Putnam's Sons, 2006.
_____. *Dead of Night.* New York: G.P. Putnam's Sons, 2005.
_____. *Everglades.* New York: G.P. Putnam's Sons, 2003.
_____. *The Heat Islands.* New York: St. Martin's Press, 1992.
_____. *The Man Who Invented Florida.* New York: St. Martin's Press, 1993.
_____. *The Mangrove Coast.* New York: G.P. Putnam's Sons, 1998.
_____. *North of Havana.* New York: G.P. Putnam's Sons, 1997.
_____. *Sanibel Flats.* New York: St. Martin's Press, 1990.
_____. *Shark River.* New York: G.P. Putnam's Sons, 2001.
_____. *Tampa Burn.* New York: G.P. Putnam's Sons, 2004.
_____. *Ten Thousand Islands.* New York: G.P. Putnam's Sons, 2000.
_____. *Twelve Mile Limit.* New York: G.P. Putnam's Sons, 2000.

Dirk Wyle, Author of Scientific Crime Novels

by Ellen Smith

Dirk Wyle is the pen name for Duncan H. Haynes, Ph.D., who conducted biomedical research at the University of Miami for nearly three decades. Commercialization of his inventions in drug microencapsulation and delivery enabled an early retirement, which has allowed him to devote full time to his storytelling. "A potent mix of science, business and crime," *Publishers Weekly* said of his Ben Candidi mystery-thriller series. Together with soul mate Rebecca Levis (M.D.), the youthful scientist takes on "straightforward" projects which quickly become perplexing, mysterious, sinister, and finally life-threatening. Wyle's mysteries play out in authentically rendered medical schools, pharmaceutical companies or exotic locations. When describing this author, words like "*Doppelgänger*" and "Jekyll and Hyde" come to mind. While Dr. Haynes delights in showing mainstream readers the fascinating world of drug discovery, Mr. Wyle enjoys feeding mystery lovers clues for a whodunit puzzle which gets "timed out" just before the bad guys (or gals) strike back. As noted by *Booklist*, his novels are "pleasing for their intellect as well as their intrigue."

ELLEN SMITH: *Why is Florida so popular with so many current writers?*

DIRK WYLE: It is semi-tropical, semi-exotic and half-crazy—especially South Florida. Elmore Leonard chose it as a stage for some of his low-life characters to strut and fret, and Carl Hiaasen provided surrealistic sketches. Then Michael Mann painted it in pastel on the TV screen. Thus, an arena was cleared for all kinds of *shtik* in the sand. Of course arena means *sand* in Spanish.

Why did you choose South Florida for your setting?

First off, I chose it as a place to live. I've been living in the Coconut Grove district of Miami since 1973. Like my protagonist, I visited Miami after completing my education and fell in love with it. Where else can you go out sailing on a Sunday in January and then go back to work at a decent job on Monday morning? Where else can you walk out to your backyard and pick a grapefruit for breakfast? In 1992 I got the itch to write. My take on Florida focuses on regular people with honest dreams who came here for quality of life. I find white-collar crime more interesting than lowlife and violent crime.

How close is your presentation of Miami to the geographical reality?

As close to reality as can be without getting in the way of the story. I try to stage every scene in a place of interest—like Ben and Rebecca's first date in Miami's Little Havana section, like Dr. Westley's debriefing of Ben on the balcony of his Biscayne Bay waterfront condominium, or like Ben's escape to the Bahamas in his sailboat. Examples from the second novel in the series include a corporate getting-acquainted session on a motor yacht and Ben's breathless footrace against that yacht as it travels through Coral Gables in the book's final pages. My favorite geographical scene in the third novel is Ben's meditation on the bank of Wagner Creek, which winds through the medical center. In the fourth novel it's the funky 1920-vintage house where Ben and Rebecca live on the north bank of the Miami River, less than a mile from downtown and half a mile south of the medical center. In the latest novel I sent Ben and Rebecca sailing to the Bahamas, which lies only 40 miles east of Miami. Like Ben, I ride through different sections of town on a bicycle, taking mental snapshots. Then I try to make these snapshots come alive for the reader.

Some of my landmarks have disappeared within a year of their description on the printed page. The *fruteria* that Ben and Rebecca visited on their first date is gone. A mural in Little Havana has been whitewashed. The Venetian Bridge was torn down and rebuilt. Central Coconut Grove has become a tourist drag. And developers now have their eye on the Miami riverfront neighborhood where Ben and Rebecca are renting a house in the fourth book.

Did any other Florida writers serve as inspiration or as mentors?

In the late 1980s I received, as a Christmas present, Edna Buchanan's *The Corpse Had a Familiar Face*. A couple of years later, I heard Les Standiford on public radio reading from the first of his John Deal novels. I liked both authors' approaches to crime fiction. I have been following their work ever since. They feel like kindred spirits. When my first Ben Candidi novel was published in 1998, Les gave me a generous quote and described the novel as "evocative." Edna read my second novel and described it as "nifty and light-hearted." Praise from these great Florida writers has helped a lot.

Is there anything distinctive about the state that impelled you to begin writing?

Yes, and there is much about the state that impels me to *continue* writing. In what other state can you be inspired to sub-poetic description just by walking around the neighborhood?

How did you get into the business of writing mysteries? Have you been a fan or frequent reader of the genre?

I was a frequent reader of *all* types of literature and a fan of none in particular. Reading has been a lifetime hobby. During some stages of my life it devoured evenings and whole weekends. Since completing my doctoral exam in molecular biology at the age of 25, I have always had a novel on my night stand and have devoted my last waking hour to it. Over the years, I read a lot more quality mainstream literature than anything else. I read my first Sherlock Holmes story in my mid-thirties. Read them all within a couple of weeks. Felt sorry that Doyle hadn't written any more. I loved his logic and his ruses. But my Anglophilia wasn't strong enough to attract me to country-house mysteries, and I didn't read many P.I. mysteries.

I can offer two reasons why I didn't read more mysteries before starting to write them. Firstly, I didn't crave intellectual stimulation by the challenge of puzzle solving. As a biomedical research scientist, I confronted puzzles every day as part of my work. After busting my brain all day, every day on Mother Nature's puzzles, I wasn't motivated to spend my evenings with puzzles contrived by human beings. The second reason had to do with my training as an educator. A good educator is trained to *de*mystify a subject, not to make a mystery out of it. A good educator uses the carrot and stick, the Socratic method, syllogistic reasoning and a trail of bread crumbs to coax the student into the subject matter to find answers to questions. On the other hand, the mystery writer works as "an educator in reverse," using misdirection, sleight of hand, and even weasel-wording that borders on lying to lead the reader down the wrong path. This delayed my interest in mysteries.

How did I get into the business of writing mysteries, then? First I got into writing. One fine evening in late August, 1992, Hurricane Andrew came through, and for the next several weeks our section of Coconut Grove was without electric power. On those evenings, rather than compete with my wife and two kids for reading space under the Coleman gasoline lantern, I went to a dark corner of the patio and started composing scenes and sketches on my cheap, battery-operated laptop. I had always thought I had within me the Great American Science Novel. Those interminable evenings were the time to prove it. After considering several mainstream fiction formats, I decided that the best fictional treatment of scientists and their quest would be framed as a mystery.

Ben Candidi quickly emerged as a gifted but underachieving 26-year-old who was proud of his B.A. in chemistry and humanistic education from Swarthmore College, but who was stuck in a dead-end job at the Miami-Dade Medical Examiner's laboratory. And Chief Medical Examiner Geoffrey A. Westley, M.D., quickly coalesced from the spirits of a half-dozen English biochemists that I had known. In my mind, Dr. Westley was quite competent in his job, had fox-like instincts for professional survival, strove to preserve British cultural hegemony, and always seemed to know better than Ben. He delivered Ben a much-needed kick in the pants when he "fired him for his own good" and persuaded him to go into a pharmacology Ph.D. program at a local medical school. And while you are there, Ben, would you be good enough to help me gather some information? Clandestinely, of course. It seems that one of the professors there poisoned his chairman. Which one? We don't know, actually. Could have been any one of them, it seems. And with all those exotic chemicals and toxins sequestered in their refrigerators, one would hardly know where to start looking. Thus spake Dr. Westley.

The assignment was bewildering for Ben, until he met a medical school sophomore named Rebecca Levis.

The first book was a product of enthusiasm and imagination, but it didn't write itself all at once. It took two years of weekends and evenings before I even called it a novel. And after that came the painful process of learning why it was *not* a novel and of discovering what sorts of adjustments I'd have to make in my thinking to even have the chance of making it into a novel. And there were some habits of thought that I had to first recognize as bad, and then unlearn. For example, a scientist delivering a scientific proof will expect and demand the reader's attention. A novelist can never make demands. A novelist must lure the reader.

Over the next two years, I must have rewritten that manuscript 15 times. I joined the South Florida Chapter of the National Writers Association and participated in a critique group. Before the novel was published in 1998, it had been read by three dozen people. I had read and considered every one of their margin comments. To some of the readers I had handed out pocket tape recorders to talk their comments into while they read. I played the tapes back, listening to every word. Other test readers were kind enough to sit with me for a full afternoon, answering my questions about how they felt about the characters and scenes. All of these people helped me "calibrate my gunsight," so to speak. At the end of the process, I had a pretty good idea of how intelligent people with vastly different personalities and tastes will react to different aspects of my work. Anyway, that was how I got started writing mysteries.

Did you have any previous preparation for writing?

When I was a child, my mother sparked my imagination by reading bedtime stories to my brother and me. My father was a newspaper reporter. I seemed to pick up the craft of writing news and feature stories from him, without any special help. For a year, I served as "Wednesday Editor" of the *Shortridge High School Daily Echo* in Indianapolis, Indiana. Unwittingly, I was following in the footsteps of Dan Wakefield, who had been an *Echo* editor a decade earlier, and of Kurt Vonnegut, who had been an *Echo* editor a decade earlier than that. Kurt Vonnegut is still singing the praises of that high school. Dan Wakefield is the author of *Going All the Way*, which was made into a movie. He is a writer in residence at Florida International University and has a lot of good books to his credit.

While in college, in the middle of a demanding chemistry/biology/physics curriculum, I selected creative writing as a three-credit elective. The prof. was bad. He wouldn't entertain a discussion of differences in style of the major authors. But the textbook he chose, *Techniques in Fiction*, was pretty good. It later inspired me to apply some of its principles—insights, actually—to the writing of my scientific research papers.

As a 30-year-old, I came across a book that turned out to be quite useful: *The Sense of Beauty* by George Santayana. He provided a treatment of aesthetics from many angles. His insights gave me some unifying principles with which to analyze, understand and judge diverse forms of artistic expression. Paintings, architecture, motion pictures, stage plays and novels have many aesthetic principles in common. Expressing the same idea negatively, they will not be works of art if their parts are allowed to fight each other.

Regarding formal training, the aspiring novelist has one distinct advantage over practitioners of other arts: No real live instructor is needed. Furthermore, there are no trade secrets or occult knowledge to deal with. It's all there on the printed page, transparent in the works of the great novelists. If he (or she) is inquiring and self-organizing, the aspiring novelist can learn what he needs from the master storytellers.

How do you go about planning your next novel? With elaborate outlines? By serendipity? Or by letting the characters dictate the events?

My process may be different from other novelists because I use biomedical science as a backdrop and starting point for the story. For example, the second Ben Candidi novel dealt with a biotech company that promised an effective treatment of cancer. The third novel took place in a medical school and at a national scientific convention. The fourth novel involves drug discovery and Amazon rain forest preservation. And the fifth novel involves Ben and Rebecca in surveying a medicinally important sponge species while they are on "vacation" in the Bahamas.

I am always collecting scientific backdrops for possible stories. I keep up my general scientific reading and sort general-interest articles into more than a dozen different files. As an example, while rewriting the first draft of the fifth Candidi novel, I selected the backdrop for the sixth Candidi novel. After getting "over the hump" on the fifth one—meaning that everything was properly "imagined in" and written in, and there were no big outstanding problems with it—I turned my creative energies to the sixth one and left the polishing of the fifth one as a "back burner project."

I love to talk about the process of writing. I look at process as a technique for getting the most out of myself, not as a "formula" for getting out 100,000 words, strung together acceptably. Books that are formula-written come out as predictable and uninspired.

Any chosen scientific backdrop will usually suggest a scientific *quest*. The next step is to identify the conflicts that would arise from it. If vivid characters do not step up to take part in the conflict, then I will do the work of "imagining them in," starting with a list of their necessary attributes. At this stage, I also do a lot of thinking about dramatic scenes. If four strong scenes do not come to mind right away, the whole project goes back in the file drawer and I start toying with something else. With strong scenes in mind, a story usually organizes around them. Then I give a lot of thought to story logic, making sure that all the characters are acting according to their own logic and feelings.

One technique that helps me visualize a story is to make a word-processing table labeled "Cause and Effect." Each character gets a column, and the left-most column is labeled "event." When an event occurs or a character performs a significant action, I add a row to the table and write down the reaction or probable thoughts of each character. These lead to new actions of one or more characters, which are then entered as new events. I use the process to work up what the bad guys did, where Ben comes into the story and what he sees initially, what the bad guys do to cover their tracks, what clues Ben comes across, how he acts on them and how the story will end. My cause-and-effect tables might grow to be 50 rows long. If the plot is perfectly conceived, then the charting process just serves as a double check on the story logic. If the plot is poorly conceived, the charting process will tell me so in a hurry. Usually, my initial story idea lies between the extremes of "excellent" and "poor."

I must emphasize that not everything that goes into the cause-and-effect table gets transferred to the pages of the novel. Most of it is for my benefit, only. I'm writing a mystery, after all.

With my plot-point milestones set up, I create a new text file in which I list—in capital letters—the major dramatic steps of the story. If any scenes have written themselves already, I paste them in under the appropriate heading. Then, I go back and look at those pages. If I feel uninspired at the time, I do the necessary work of filling in a list of things that have to happen or which must be described under each heading. But usually I feel quite inspired. Often, I sit down and write a whole chapter in a single sitting.

When the Muse is with me, I don't let anything interrupt us. I type on—grammar, spelling and good form be damned—capturing the essence of what I am visualizing and experiencing in my head. If I feel that a transition sentence I'm writing is going to be a bummer, I don't stop to improve it. I extend my right-hand pinky finger and click one of those curlicue parentheses to mark it as probable junk. I rush on, following the Muse. An inspired first draft will be full of incomplete sentences, maudlin adjectives and mixed metaphors. That's fine with me as long as the spirit of the scene shines through the clutter.

When the Muse is absent, I tidy up any story logic that has been deranged by my last session with the Muse. Then I go back to those lists of things that have to happen and start working on "imagining them in." Usually the Muse reappears right quick because she doesn't want me messing up what she has already given me.

After the story has been filled in as a first draft, bow to stern, I do more work to tune it up as a mystery. I print it out, put it in a three-ring binder, and sit down with it in a comfortable chair, far away from any computer. I read it, skim it and go back and forth in it. I ask myself questions. I make margin notes about things to do. And I ask more questions. Have Ben and the reader been fed clues at the right rate? And are the clues sufficient for the reader to solve the mystery before the killer strikes and Ben is fighting for his life? I hold to a rigorous version of the Doctrine of Fairness. The reader must be given a fair chance to solve the mystery before the solution is revealed. In the traditional mystery, the sleuth makes clever deductions, the villain self-incriminates and the constable is called to slap on the irons. That is too cozy for my taste. I find it more exciting to end the story with a life-or-death struggle.

I classify my Ben Candidi novels as "mystery-thrillers," starting as a mystery and ending as a thriller. This imposes an additional plot requirement: In the closing pages, Ben must be either too exhausted or unlucky to be able to insert the last piece into the puzzle before the villain strikes. This is not my story invention. It happened before, many times, to the best of them—to Travis McGee and to Alex Delaware. And it requires only a moment's reflection to appreciate that this sort of thing is trickier to do in first-person narration than in third.

An additional plot-related burden that I have taken on with Ben is to give him a stable, loving relationship with Rebecca. In the first two novels she was off-stage when push came to shove. In the third, she was tuned in to Ben's predicament but was tied down in Washington, D.C. But in the fourth novel, I sent Rebecca off on her own adventure on the Amazon, leaving our hero and storyteller at home to mind his consulting business. Then I escalated mystery and threat to the point where he had to go down there and "rescue" her. In the fifth novel, Ben and Rebecca have a very exciting time together "on vacation." Lots of excitement, but two protagonists are more difficult to choreograph than one.

What I have just discussed can be considered "operating constraints" for the novel, not a formula for writing it. I do not have a standard operating procedure for creating a novel. Each one is a child of different premises, and each one comes out with a somewhat different personality.

When reviewing a first draft, I give a lot of thought to the progression of attitude and mood from chapter to chapter. Ben's assignments usually seem straightforward at first. Then they turn perplexing and sinister. It is important to keep attitude and mood in mind while reshaping the raw material. It is very difficult to change these qualities once the material has been polished. The same is true for the insertion of needed facts or physical description. As you might imagine, the first draft becomes completely covered with blue ink, with stapled-on inserts, and with red-inked instructions on spin and mood. Often, my cause-and-effect table suffers the same fate, as I struggle to keep my mind around a story while revising it for maximal impact. A mathematician might say that I "go through many iterations."

Anyway, after I have done this through several drafts, I hope to have a compelling novel.

What encouraged you to use medicine, chemistry and biological science as a subject in the genre?

Having lived the life of a bench scientist for 30 years, I was unhappy with how we were depicted in fiction. Also, it seems that there were only two kinds of stories about scientists. They were either scientist-glorification stories like *October Sky* or *Good Will Hunting*. Or they were "Frankenstein monster" stories—defined by the movie, not the book. For a long time, I thought myself capable of writing a novel that could bring the reader into the world of the scientist. Going back to your question about my literary influences, Stephen Coonts' *Flight of the Intruder* made me feel what it is like to take off and land on the deck of an aircraft carrier. Now why couldn't someone breathe as much excitement into the search for an unknown poison using a high-pressure liquid chromatograph coupled to a mass spectrometer? Imagine being able to buy a DVD version of the *CSI* television series in which you could slow down those lab images and click a button to bring on a friendly voice that tells you what those machines are actually doing to prove the crime. Well, that's what I try to do in my novels.

As children, we are naturally curious. But by the time we reach adulthood, poor teaching, tough exams and competing inducements have killed our interest in natural science. But Ben is a survivor. He is a guy who can still feel the magic of Nature. Rebecca, too.

How do you go about making scientific material understandable for your "common reader"?

By presenting it viscerally, in ways that the lay reader can feel. By presenting it intuitively and trying not to make a project out of it. By spending hours of spare moments searching for the best analogy to make the point. Here is how Ben described his research at the beginning of *Biotechnology Is Murder*: "Those molecules live in a state of submicroscopic innocence. They spend half their time drifting around, waiting to bump into a properly built partner. And they spend the other half of their time in writhing copulation. I caught them in the act and handcuffed them.... I threw them on the gel electrophoresis slab, turned on the electricity and marched they down the lane."

Another method that I sometimes use is to have significant interpersonal action running in parallel to the necessary scientific dialogue. It guides the general reader through the scene almost as effectively as those shapely legs and designer dresses guided the viewers through legal dialogue in L.A. Law.

Have you had any reactions from scientists to your choice of subjects?

First off, I am gratified with the reception of my books by mystery readers and by readers of literary fiction. Secondly, I do have an enthusiastic following among biomedical scientists. My readership among them is still growing. As an outreach to them, we exhibit and sell my books on "Publisher's Row" at several major scientific conventions, including the Federation of Societies for Experimental Biology and the Neuroscience Society. The initial response of scientists visiting my booth is surprise that this type of book exists. Some of the older scientists are put off by the murder-mystery angle, for reasons mentioned earlier. But most of them are glad to see their professional lives portrayed realistically.

My books have been used as teaching and motivational tools in college classes. *Pharmacology Is Murder* provides a good picture of Ph.D. programs in biomedical science. It has been fun to participate in faculty-organized teleconferences and to answer questions from students.

While we are on the subject of scientists' reactions, *Pharmacology Is Murder* received a giddy review from the Executive Director of the American Society for Pharmacology and Experimental Therapeutics in a semi-professional journal published by them—*Molecular In(ter)ventions*. However, that Executive Director turned very unhappy when *Medical School Is Murder* came out and laid open the possibility that multi-million-dollar corruption could exist within a medical school administration.

The most gratifying response that I have received from a scientist was from one who pulled an all-nighter with *Medical School Is Murder*. "I just couldn't put it down," she said. "I was reading my life."

Have your plots been developed from your actual experiences?

Yes, my actual experiences have provided the foundation for the plots of all my books to date. Of course, my plots are fictional constructions and are not meant to depict any person, living or dead. But 30 years of experience with medical schools provided a wealth of material for *Pharmacology Is Murder*. As for the premise that a professor would get mad enough to poison his chairman—fact followed fiction, it seems. A year after the novel was published,

I clipped from the paper a news article about a medical faculty member who was arrested by security guards in a medical center parking garage, disguised and lurking in wait for his chief of service who had refused to write him a letter of recommendation. In his hand was a large syringe, filled with boric acid. That happened in Tennessee, not Florida, incidentally.

And what about corruption in medical school administrations? Evidence for that could be found in one-third of the lawsuits filed by professors around the country against their medical schools. However, the messy details are seldom aired in public because the cases are settled out of court, with air-tight non-disclosure agreements as part of the settlement.

On the positive side, my experience with inventing, patenting and commercializing an injectable delivery system for water-insoluble drugs gave me a solid basis for *Biotechnology Is Murder*. The question there was, Why should the inventor be unhappy after investors have put big money behind his three anti-cancer compounds and things look rosy for a big NASDAQ stock offering? Besides offering readers what I think is a good story, the novel informs them why drugs are so expensive and why it costs over $20 million to commercialize a new drug, even if it works all right and you know what you're doing. Interestingly, scientists seemed less able than mystery fans to deduce the method by which the inventor was murdered.

I should add that success with my medical inventions has enabled me to retire and devote my full time to writing.

I still do a lot of scientific reading. *Amazon Gold* was inspired by my reading on Yanomama Indian anthropology and on drug discovery instrumentation. I followed that up with ten days in the rain forest, on the Amazon and Rio Negro, and around Manaus. The idea for *Bahamas West End Is Murder* came to me when we cruised the Bahamas in 1997. Ben and Rebecca are supposed to on vacation. But that ends when they save a $200,000 cabin cruiser from sinking and find a dead man on board. It would have been easier if they hadn't filed a $100,000 salvage claim. While working on the book, I sailed back there for research purposes, staying a week to verify details of land geography and to tool around in our hard-bottomed inflatable, exploring the Little Bahama Bank, the ledges and the shoreline.

Is Ben Candidi at all autobiographical?

I gave him my basic philosophy and values. His I.Q. is much higher than mine but he has less self-motivation. Of course, one must keep in mind that Ben is about 30 years old and that I'm 60. His life experience is little more than one-half of mine. But he's a quick study. I am fluent in German and have a little bit of Spanish. Ben is fluent in Spanish and has a little bit of German. Writing Ben into existence and seeing the world through his eyes has been something of a Faustian rebirth for me. And now it feels like Ben is rewriting my biography.

How did you create Dr. Geoffrey A. Westley?

Like I said, he sort of condensed from the spirits of all the elderly English biochemists I have known. Those old boys made a strong impression on me when I was Ben's age and younger. Culturally, they were always *so* much better informed. And they always found some way to let one know it. When I was between the ages of 21 and 30, contact with those guys could be exasperating. But as I grew older, I had to fight the same pedantic tendencies developing in myself. Thus, I do not have much trouble popping into Dr. Westley's skin—for a few hours at a time, anyway. Actually, Dr. Westley and I share some most delightful commonalities, not the least of which is that we were both cathedral choirboys—Anglican, of course—he at Exeter and I in Indianapolis. And although our respective chorister careers were separated by decades and oceans... There I go again, sounding like Dr. Westley.

What will happen to Dr. Westley?

Oh, he will lapse into agelessness, I presume. The process seems to have started already with Ben, although I should hope that Mr. Wyle will not be so heartless as to—

Perhaps cryopreservation will be an option for Dr. Westley. Have you ever thought of going from hard science to science fiction?

That's a good question. I am interested in how technology is affecting the way we live and think. Witness how cell phones and e-mail have changed how we talk to each other. Think of how using the computer as a tool has affected the way we think. So many things have changed so fast. Yet, many things seem resistant to change, even over the last 40,000 years. Can we make sci-fi predictions for the near future? What will personal relationships be like in 2103? What about love? Maybe a sci-fi novel *is* floating around somewhere inside me.

Returning to the present, do you see any Florida crime writers as having any effect on the state beyond the pleasure they give their readers? John D. MacDonald and Carl Hiaasen on overdevelopment, for example.

Well, Carl Hiaasen deserves a lot of credit for hammering away in his newspaper column against overdevelopment and official corruption. I would guess that he has helped to put some bad guys in jail. I think that John D. MacDonald had a more positive message, with stories that captured Florida's beauty as well. I became acquainted with Travis McGee around 1999, and have read every one of those novels, many times since. They have created an indelible image of Florida. It is the place where, if you want to, you can live on a boat and motor or sail away to a sandy key where the beer tastes stronger, where romance is more delightful, and where time seems to slow like a Salvador Dalí limp watch.

Yes, Travis McGee is a legend. So is Edna Buchanan's gal newspaper reporter, Britt Montero. So will be Les Standiford's stalwart contractor, John Deal. And to these will be added Barbara Parker's lawyer couple, Gail Conner and Anthony Quintana. And what about the rest of us? We're doing our best, in proportion to the size of our audiences and the strength of our voices, to add to America's collective image of Florida. Many see it as banging-off-the-wall hilarity, others see it as a script for a future Coen Brothers movie, and others see real-life people here. But Kurt Vonnegut had it right with the quote that he furnished for the Travis McGee book covers: "To diggers a thousand years from now ... the works of John D. MacDonald would be a treasure on the order of the tomb of Tutankhamen." And in that respect, the *Orange Pulp* anthology [edited by Maurice O'Sullivan and Steve Glassman] of pre–MacDonald crime fiction is already serving that purpose.

Bibliography

Wyle, Dirk. *Amazon Gold*. Highland City, FL: Rainbow Books, Inc., 2003.
_____. *Bahamas West End Is Murder*. Highland City, FL: Rainbow Books, 2005.
_____. *Biotechnology Is Murder*. Highland City, FL: Rainbow Books, 1999.
_____. *Medical School Is Murder*. Highland City, FL: Rainbow Books, Inc., 2001.
_____. *Pharmacology Is Murder*. Highland City, FL: Rainbow Books, Inc., 1998

About the Contributors

Cal Branche is a retired English teacher with degrees in philosophy, English and education. He has been a book reviewer and a lecturer on Florida mystery writers as part of the Florida Humanities Council Speakers List, and has also presented several programs on John D. MacDonald. He served as chair of the 1996 John D. MacDonald Conference and as chair of the 2002 Mystery: The Florida Connection.

Melanie Brown was born in Ft. Lauderdale and raised in Central Florida. She lives in St. Augustine, where she is Dean of Distance Learning at Saint Johns River Community College. She earned an M.A and a B.A. in English from Stetson University, and a Ph.D. in texts and technology at the University of Central Florida. Her publication and research areas include popular culture, theories of the posthuman, distance learning and alternative teacher certification programs.

Cynthia Davis is a professor of English at Barry University in Miami. She received her Ph.D. at the University of Maryland. Her research interests include Hispanic and African American women writers. Her most recent book, co-authored with Dr.Verner Mitchell, is *Anita Scott Coleman: Western Echoes of the Harlem Renaissance* (University of Oklahoma Press, 2007).

Mary Beth Ellis is a lecturer at Embry-Riddle University. She was granted a MFA and has published creative fiction and nonfiction.

Steve Glassman is a professor of humanities at Embry-Riddle University in Daytona Beach. He has authored, edited or co-edited ten books, most about Florida and many about crime writing.

Amy Gottfried is an associate professor at Hood College in Maryland. She attained a Ph.D. from Syracuse University.

Roderick Hofer is a professor of English at Indian River Community College in Fort Pierce, Florida. He holds a doctorate in English from Kansas State University, where he developed a scholarly interest in modern poetry, drama, and criticism through courses in Eliot and Yeats, among others, and through his dissertation on W.H. Auden. He has published poetry of his own, and has recently written and lectured on Aeschylus, Frost and Herbert. His interest in crime fiction remains avid some fifty years after having first met Frank and Joe in *The Sinister Sign Post*.

Anna Lillios is an associate professor of English at the University of Central Florida, where she teaches courses on the modern American and British novel, Florida writers, and European fiction. She is past president of the Florida College English Association and the International Lawrence Durrell Society and current executive director of the Marjorie Kinnan Rawlings Society. She edited *Lawrence Durrell and the Greek World* and is the editor of the *Marjorie Kinnan Rawlings Journal of Florida Literature* and *Deus Loci: The Lawrence Durrell Journal*.

Matthew McLendon is a native of Palatka, Florida. He graduated from Florida State University with undergraduate degrees in music and art history. He then went on to study with Professor Christopher Green at the Courtauld Institute of Art, London, where he received his M.A. and Ph.D. in art history. He currently teaches art history and interdisciplinary arts courses at St. Johns River Community College.

Dan McGavin teaches at Palm Beach Community College. He holds a Ph.D.

Richard McKee is a freelance writer living in Venice, Florida. Creator of the gonzo critic B.M.W. Schrapnel, Ph.D., McKee has published over seventy pieces of satire and creative nonfiction, and one book, *The Clan of the Flapdragon and Other Adventures in Etymology* (University of Alabama Press, 1997).

Bill Ott is editor and publisher of the American Library Association's *Booklist*.

Hank Raulerson is an assistant professor of English at Indian River Community College. Hank earned a B.A. in English from Auburn University and an M.A. in English from Florida State. A fifth-generation native Floridian, Hank resides with his wife and children in Okeechobee, a town his ancestors helped to settle.

Nancy M. Shelton teaches humanities at Valencia Community College in Orlando, Florida. She earned a master of liberal studies degree from the Hamilton Holt School at Rollins College and an MBA from the Roy E. Crummer Graduate School of Business. Her work has appeared in the *Journal of Graduate Liberal Studies* and the anthology *Shifting Gears*. An essay, "The Nature of Honesty," is scheduled for publication in early 2008.

Claudia Slate, Ph.D., is a professor of English at Florida Southern College in Lakeland. She is co-chair of the college's African American Studies program and editor of the *Florida Studies Proceedings of the Florida College English Association's*. She is also the author of articles focusing on the South from slavery through the civil rights movement.

Ellen Smith is professor emeritus of English at Stetson University. She holds a Ph.D. in English from the University of Oklahoma and is widely published in the field of crime fiction.

April Van Camp is associate professor and chair of the English/Modern Languages department at Indian River Community College in Ft. Pierce, Florida. She holds an M.A. in English from the University of Central Florida and is an ABD student in an English doctoral program at the same institution. She was the 2006-2007 vice president and program chair of the Florida College English Association.

Index

Fictional characters are listed by first name.

Abbey, Edward 191
Abraham Lieberman 74
Air Dance Iguana 39
Alex Rutledge 32, 34, 39
Always Say Goodbye 87
Amazon Gold 236

Backstab 202
Bahamarama 149
Bahamas West End Is Murder 236
Barth, John 140
Bartholomew, Nancy 7–14
Ben Candidi 223, 225, 226, 228, 230, 233
Bermuda Schwartz 149
The Bible 122, 165
The Big Bamboo 49
Biotechnology Is Murder 236
Bitter End 112
Bitter Sugar 57
Black Mountain 191
Blackwater Sound 62
Blood of the Lamb: A John Jordan Mystery 127
The Blood-Red Rec Yard Ruse 127
Blood Relations 159
Bloody Secrets 57
Bloody Shame 57
Bloody Waters 57
The Blue Corn Murders 169
The Blue Edge of Midnight 101
Body Language 62
Body Wave 31

Bone Island Mambo 39
Bone Key 191
Bones of Coral 62
Born, James O. 16–23, 114
Branche, Cal 5, 74–87, 88–100, 113–118, 192–194, 235
Braudel, Fernand 2
Brown, Melanie 195–202, 235
Buchanan, Edna 114, 152
Bum Steer: A Jenny Cain Mystery 168
Burke, James Lee 82, 84, 88, 122
But I Wouldn't Want to Die There: A Jenny Cain Mystery 168
Buzz Cut 62

Cadillac Beach 49
Cain, James M. 68, 72, 167
Captiva 222
Chandler, Raymond 68, 132
Christie, Agatha 201, 206
Cohen, Nancy 24–31
Confession: A Jenny Cain Mystery 168
Connelly, Michael 32, 82
Coral Gables 191
Corcoran, Tom 32–39, 66, 221
Crew Cut 31
Criminal Justice 159
Cross Current 112
Cruel Poetry 72

Dark Light 222
Davis, Cynthia 50–57
Dead Crazy 168

Dead of Night 222
Dead Roots 31
Deal on Ice 191
Deal to Die For 191
Deal with the Dead 191
The Deep Blue Alibi 118
Denial 87
Died Blonde 31
Doc in the Box 202
Done Deal 191
Dorsey, Tim 40–49, 66, 114, 220
Drag Strip 14
Dying in Style 202
Dying to Call You 201

Ellis, Mary Beth 32–39, 235
Escape Clause 23
Everglades 222
Eye of Vengeance 101

False Dawn 118
Faulkner, William 86, 130, 188, 192
Field of Fire 23
Film Strip 14
Flagler, Henry 100, 183, 190, 191
Flesh and Blood: John Jordan Stories 127
Flesh & Bones 118
Florida Keys 151
Florida Roadkill 49
Fool Me Twice 118
Forests of the Night 62
Fort Lauderdale 92, 109
Fowler, Connie Mae 3, 181
Fred Carver 128

Garcia-Aguilera, Carolina 50–57, 66, 68
Gardner, Earle Stanley 204
Gasparilla Gold 211
Generous Death: A Jenny Cain Mystery 168
Glassman, Steve 16–23, 24–31, 181–191, 236
Gone Wild 62
Gonzales, Elian 52, 104
Gottfried, Amy 170=180, 235
Gumbo Limbo 39

Hair Raiser 31
Hall, James W. 3, 58–53, 66, 88, 89, 106, 114, 125, 152, 185, 213
Hammerhead Ranch Motel 49

Hammett, Dashiell 53, 68, 122
Hard Aground 62
Harrison, Jim 213, 214
Havana Heat 57
Havana Run 191
The Heat Islands 222
Hemingway, Ernest 2, 62, 183, 190, 193, 198
Hendricks, Vicki 64–73, 114
High Heels Are Murder 202
Highlights to Heaven 31
Hofer, Rick 58–63, 236
Huck Finn 45, 206
Hurricane Punch 49
Hurston, Zora 2, 183

Iguana Love 72
Inspector Rostnikov 74
I.O.U. 168

Jake Lassiter 115
Jamaica Me Dead 149
Jenny Cain 162
John Jordan 119
Josie Marcus 197
Just Murdered 201

Kaminsky, Stuart 74–87, 195
Kellerman, Faye 82
Kellerman, Jonathan 82, 84
Key West 36, 190
Kill All the Lawyers 118
A Killing Night 101
King, Jonathan 88–101, 114, 206, 215
Kling, Christine 102–112, 114
Krakauer, Jon 214

A Land Remembered 59
Last Train to Paradise 191
Le Carré, John 33
Lehane, Dennis 66, 185
Leonard, Elmore 22, 40
Lethally Blond 14
Levine, Paul 113–118
Lew Fonesca 74
Lillios, Anna 128, 238
Lindsay, Jeff 221
Lister, Michael 119–127
Luck of the Draw 57
Lutz, John 128–136

MacDonald, John D. 3, 89, 114, 139
MacDonald, Ross 33, 68, 90
The Man Who Invented Florida 222
The Mango Opera 39
The Mangrove Coast 222
Marital Privilege 211
Marriage Is Murder: A Jenny Cain Mystery 168
Matthiessen, Peter 89, 213, 214
McGavin, Dan 102–112, 237
McGuane, Thomas 213, 214, 221
McKee, Rich 40–49, 236
McLendon 119, 238
Mean High Tide 63
Medical School Is Murder 236
Meet You in Hell 191
Miami 20, 35, 51, 52, 133, 150, 151, 152, 181
Miami Blues 44
Miami Purity 72
Miami Vice 3
Midnight Pass 87
A Miracle in Paradise 57
The Miracle Strip 14
Morris, Bob 114, 137–149
Mortal Sin 118
Mosquito Lagoon 137
Murder Between the Covers 201
Murder by Manicure 31
Murder Unleashed 202

Naked Came the Manatee 73
Night Vision 118
9 Scorpion 118
No Body: A Jenny Cain Mystery 168
North Florida Noir 127
North of Havana 222

Octopus Alibi 39
Off the Chart 63
One Hot Summer 57
Opening Day, or The Ghost of Satchel Paige 191
Orange Crush 49
Ott, Bill 5, 212–221, 237

Panhandle 9
Paper Products 63
Parker, Barbara 42, 54, 66, 106, 150–160, 185

Parker, Robert B. 88, 90, 122, 167
Paterniti, Michael 134
The Perfect Fake 159
Perish by Pedicure 31
Permed to Death 31
Pharmacology Is Murder 236
Pickard, Nancy 161–169
The Pink Flamingo Murders 202
Power in the Blood: A John Jordan Mystery 127
Presidential Deal 191
Putt at the End of the World 191
Pynchon, Thomas 33, 40

Raulerson, Hank 137–149, 237
Raw Deal 191
Rawlins, Marjorie K. 2
Red Sky at Night 63
Retribution 87
Ring of Truth 169
Rosewood Massacre 3, 180
Rough Draft. Tropical Freeze 63
Rubout 202
Rule, Ann 82

Sam Spade 53, 78
Sanibel Flats 222
Sarasota 74, 78, 133
Say No to Murder: A Jenny Cain Mystery 168
Sayers, Dorothy 68
Schumacher, Aileen 170–180
The Secret Ingredient Murders 169
Serge Storms 40
Shadow Men 101
Shakespeare, William 98, 122
Shark River 222
Shelton, Nancy 161–169, 237
Shock Wave 23
Shop Till You Drop 202
Silicone Solution 211
Six Bills 211
Sky Blues 73
Slashback 118
Slate, Claudia 150–160, 237
Smith, Ellen 5, 13, 64–73, 203–211, 222–234, 237
Smith, Patrick 59
Solomon Vs. Lord 118
Sophie's Last Stand 15

Spill 191
Stand By Your Man 15
Standiford, Les 59, 66, 69, 111, 114, 125, 170, 181–191, 223, 234
Stella Get Your Gun 15
Stella Get Your Man 15
The Stingray Shuffle 49
Stone, Robert 36
Storm Warnings 169
Surface Tension 112
Surviving Toronto 211
Suspicion of Betrayal 159
Suspicion of Deceit 160
Suspicion of Guilt 160
Suspicion of Innocence 160
Suspicion of Madness 160
Suspicion of Malice 160
Suspicion of Rage 160
Suspicion of Vengeance 160
Swain, James 192–194

Tampa 34, 35, 66, 208, 210
Tampa Burn 222
tart noir 70, 73
Ten Thousand Islands 222
Thorn 58, 61
Three Men and a Body 31
To Speak for the Dead 118
Toby Peters 74
Torpedo Juice 49
Travis McGee 97, 207
Triggerfish Twist 49
The Truth Hurts 169
Twain, Mark 45, 201

Twelve Mile Limit 222
The 27-Ingredient Chili Con Carne Murders 169
Twilight: A Jenny Cain Mystery 168

Under Cover of Daylight 63
Updike, John 96

Van Camp, April 7–15, 237
Vengeance 87
Viets, Elaine 195–202
The Virgin of Small Plains: A Novel of Suspense 168
Visible Darkness 101
Vogt, Diane M. 203–211
Voluntary Madness 73
Vonnegut, Kurt 43, 140, 188, 227

Walking Money 23
West Palm Beach 18
Westlake, Donald 82, 84
What Stella Wants 15
White, Randy Wayne 3, 6, 106, 114, 152, 212–221, 222
The Whole Truth 169
Willeford, Charles 3, 4, 5, 33
Wreckers' Key 112
Wyle, Dirk 222–234, 236

The Yearling 2
Your Cheatin' Heart 15

Zack Chasteen 137, 139, 142, 144, 146, 147

www.ingramcontent.com/pod-product-compliance
Ingram Content Group UK Ltd.
Pitfield, Milton Keynes, MK11 3LW, UK
UKHW041939140426
5217IPUK00014B/555